B
V
PRAY FOR...
You Just Might Get It

ALSO BY LARRY DOSSEY, M.D.

Prayer Is Good Medicine
Healing Words: The Power of Prayer and the Practice of Medicine
Meaning & Medicine
Recovering the Soul
Beyond Illness
Space, Time & Medicine

BE CAREFUL WHAT YOU PRAY FOR...
You Just Might Get It

What We Can Do About
the Unintentional Effects of
Our Thoughts, Prayers, and Wishes

LARRY DOSSEY, M.D.

HarperSanFrancisco
A Division of HarperCollins*Publishers*

Grateful acknowledgment is made to Henry Holt and Company, Inc., for permission to quote from *The Logic of Failure* by Dietrich Dörner, © 1989 by Rowholt Verlag GmbH, English translation © 1996 by Rita and Robert Kimber.

HarperCollins books may be purchased for educational, business, or sales promotional use. For information please write: Special Markets Department, HarperCollins Publishers, 10 East 53rd Street, New York, NY 10022.

HarperCollins Web Site: http://www.harpercollins.com

HarperCollins®, ☷®, and HarperSanFrancisco™ are trademarks of HarperCollins Publishers Inc.

FIRST HARPERCOLLINS PAPERBACK EDITION PUBLISHED IN 1998

Designed by Laura Lindgren

Library of Congress Cataloging-in-Publication Data
Dossey, Larry, 1940–
    Be careful what you pray for . . . you just might get it : what we can do about the unintentional effects of our thoughts, prayers, and wishes / Larry Dossey. — 1st ed.
       p.   cm.
    Includes bibliographical references and index.
    ISBN 0-06-251433-4 (cloth)
    ISBN 0-06-251434-2 (pbk.)
    1. Prayer—Controversial literature. 2. Blessing and cursing—Controversial literature. 3. Religious addiction—Controversial literature. I. Title.
BL560.D67   1997
291.4'3—dc21   97-15085

    03 04 05 ❖ RRD(H) 10 9 8 7 6

for Barbara

The statement to which I am prepared to attach my name is this: that, conjoined with the rubbish of much ignorance and some deplorable folly and fraud, there is a body of well-established facts, beyond denial and outside any philosophical explanation; which facts promise to open a new world of human enquiry and experience, are in the highest degree interesting, and tend to elevate ideas of the continuity of life and to reconcile, perhaps, the materialist and metaphysician.

—Sir Edwin Arnold (1832–1904)

Contents

Author's Note

This book deals with a controversial subject that traditionally has been ignored by both science and religion—the power of prayer, and of thought in general, to cause harm. To those brave souls who have come forward to share their personal experiences with me: you took a risk, and I am grateful.

I am thankful also to that courageous cadre of researchers who are investigating negative mental intentions. Many of them have risked professional and public derision in pursuing this field because they believe *all* the truth is worth the telling. Without exception, they have freely shared their data and their views with me when I requested them.

Without the genius of my editor, Caroline Pincus, this manuscript might itself have proved toxic. She is a healer—of unruly writing— who has understood my work from the start.

Thanks also to Tom Grady, who provided a home at Harper San Francisco for my writings on the role of prayer in medicine; to my literary agent, Muriel Nellis, who has rallied around my work in invaluable ways; and to Kitty Farmer, who helps make my work public.

To the shamans and healers of northern New Mexico who offered prayers of strength and protection to me during the writing of this book, I bow deeply in honor and gratitude. If you choose to continue them, I would not be disappointed.

Introduction

THERE ARE SORCERERS AMONG US. They are mothers and fathers, businesspeople and physicians, our friends and neighbors next-door. They are people who go to church on Sundays—and who pray.

If *sorcerer* sounds like too strong a term, consider a 1994 Gallup poll which found that 5 percent of Americans have prayed for harm to come to others.[1] They are just the one-in-twenty who will *admit* it; the actual prevalence of using prayer to hurt others is undoubtedly much greater. What is the difference between a prayer to harm others and the curse of a sorcerer?

I began seriously to explore prayer's potential for harm shortly after the publication of my book *Healing Words* in 1993, in which I discussed a variety of scientific experiments that strongly suggest that the effects of prayer are real. Most readers responded warmly to this information, grateful to discover that their belief in prayer could be grounded in science. A small minority, however, wrote vehement letters to me condemning the prayer experiments as heresy, blasphemy, and sin. The researchers, they said, were trying to "test God" and attempting to "set a trap" for the Almighty.

A few angry believers vowed to pray that I would see things the right way—*their* way. At first I was happy for all the attention—the book became a best-seller. I was grateful that others would be willing actually to pray for me, and I responded with letters of my own, in which I thanked them for their concern and for their prayers. Then I began to think more deeply about the prayers they were offering. To me, many of them felt like attempts to turn my life upside down, to force me to become someone I was not. The pray-ers, I felt, wanted radically to rearrange my thinking, change my behaviors, and install their views in place of my own. Some of these prayers appeared indistinguishable from curses and hexes—attempts to control the thought and behavior of a victim against his or her will.

Paradoxically, the pray-ers claimed to be acting solely out of love and concern. Perhaps they were, but their prayers didn't *feel* compassionate, and their words didn't *sound* loving, and eventually I found myself shrinking from this brand of prayer.

As a result of *Healing Words*, opportunities arose to discuss prayer with audiences around the country. Almost invariably someone would ask, "If there is evidence that prayer can help, is there proof that it can harm?" The response of audiences to this question was fascinating. The questioner usually drew disapproving looks, as if he or she had entered forbidden territory.

We don't fully trust prayer, perhaps because it invokes powers that we feel cannot be understood and controlled. Our ambivalence toward prayer is embedded in our language. For instance, our word *deprecate,* meaning to belittle someone, is related to the Latin root of prayer, *precarius.* Mythologist Karl Kerényi points out in his book, *The Gods of the Greeks,* that the name of the Greek god of war, Ares, "sounded like 'ara'—'curse'—although, indeed this word also means 'prayer'—and was almost another name for war."[2] Prayer, therefore, has long seemed connected with violence and harm.

The fear of prayer often erupts even when prayer is used benevolently, as was the case at an upscale mental health facility in New England. A psychotherapist was summoned by the clinic director to explain why her patients were recovering and being discharged earlier than the patients of other therapists. "Why are your patients getting well faster? What are you doing that's different?" he inquired. When she revealed that she prayed for her patients and that she felt this might account for the differences in clinical outcome, an urgent meeting of the clinic staff was called to discuss the situation. Everyone was extremely nervous about this highly controversial therapy. As a result, she was commanded to discontinue praying, because it gave her patients "an unfair advantage."[3]

Florence Nightingale, the founder of modern nursing, was a deeply spiritual woman who was concerned about the potential of prayer to manipulate others. The excellence of God, she said, is that he is inexorable. If he could be changed by people's praying, we should be at the mercy of those who attempt to change his mind through their prayers. She spoke of "old James Martin," who preferred having all prayers set down and arranged, because he worried that some people, for all he knew, might be praying that "the money might be taken out of *his* pocket and put into *theirs.*"[4]

Recipients of prayer can also be ambivalent. In his book, *Surviving AIDS*, singer and activist Michael Callen wrote, "I recently discovered that my Methodist mother has organized a prayer group that regularly prays for my healing. I was simultaneously deeply moved and horrified."[5]

Some people say they resent prayer because it is an uninvited invasion of their "psychological space." I would propose that deep down, however, there lurks a primordial fear of being controlled or harmed by the thoughts and wishes of others—and a revulsion at the possibility that they, too, might possess the power to harm others with *their* minds.

The Greeks were not as squeamish as we are in confronting the potential to harm others with the mind. In his *Laws*, Plato met the issue head-on. He recommended the death sentence for anybody using "spells, charms, incantations or other such sorceries" for purposes of mischief. . . ."[6] What if we took seriously the evidence favoring the negative effects of the mind, which we shall soon examine? Would we, as Plato advised, prosecute negative pray-ers? What if we actually convicted the 5 percent of our population who have "committed" negative prayer? Would we imprison them? Not likely. Prayer cannot be blocked by bars.

As of this writing, eleven medical schools in the United States offer courses dealing with spirituality in clinical practice, and sixty of them—roughly half of the medical schools in this country—have expressed interest in developing such programs.[7] This trend reflects a growing recognition of the role of religious practice and prayer in health. But as the evidence for the *positive* effects of prayer becomes more widely known, medicine will have to begin grappling with the potential *harm* associated with these practices as well.

Dr. Marilyn J. Schlitz, director of research at the Institute of Noetic Sciences in Sausalito, California, has helped draw attention to these concerns. Her background in anthropology enables her to take a broad view of the powers of consciousness. "If a person can influence the physiology of another person at a distance, it is clearly possible that that influence may not always be positive," she states.

Along the Sepic River in Papua, New Guinea, for example, one person is both the healer and the sorcerer. He is both the solution to your malaise and the cause. Is this the kind of person you really want to have as your healer? Clearly, as we move forward, we must think about the moral and ethical implications of [these issues].[8]

In conventional medicine, however, we have not considered the ability of individuals to harm others with their thoughts at a distance, mainly because we've been reluctant to acknowledge the existence of distant mental phenomena in general. But denying the dark side of prayer is like ignoring the harmful side effects of a drug. It is completely unjustified, no matter how great the drug's benefits may be.

Schlitz explains why these issues are important to everyone.

The most profound implications ... are at the societal level. . . . We . . . assume that we are isolated beings and that "my thoughts are my thoughts and yours are yours, and ne'er the twain shall meet." In fact, I think [the] data support the idea that we are interconnected at a level that has yet to be fully recognized by Western science and that is very far from being integrated into our worldview. If my intentions can influence the physiology of a distant person, if your thoughts can be incorporated into mine, not just in clinical settings but everywhere, it requires that we be more thoughtful and responsible not only for our actions but for the ways in which we think about and interact with other people.[9]

If we accept that human thought has distant effects, it is irrational to think that individuals throughout history would not have tried using this power for harm. This is the domain of curses, hexing, the casting of spells, and the use of prayer to harm others. However, for every negative prayer or curse that is employed deliberately, there are a thousand "little curses" that are launched unintentionally. As we shall see, these are offered unthinkingly by perfectly nice individuals who would not willfully harm anyone. The goal of this book is to explore how these practices manifest in everyday life.

Are prayers and curses related? Dion Fortune (1890–1946), who was trained in Freudian psychology and who was one of the best-known spiritualists of her day in England, believed the connections are profound. She observed, "There is no essential difference between sticking pins into a wax image of an enemy and burning candles in front of a wax image of the Virgin."[10]

Michael Murphy, cofounder of California's Esalen Institute and author of *The Future of the Body*, is also convinced that there is a thin line between curses, hexes, and religious practices. He observes,

> It is held in most sacred traditions that virtually any capacity can be communicated without sensory cues. Such capacities . . . can be used destructively. The same religious traditions that celebrate metanormal transmission of illumined states also bear witness to communication abilities employed for egocentric, bullying, even monstrous purposes. There is a lore in virtually every religious culture about adepts who use their special powers . . . for selfish ends.[11]

Including the Jewish and Christian traditions. In spite of the fact that many believers insist that curses are employed only by diabolical individuals, they are right at home in the Bible and have often been employed by the spiritual elite. The prophet Elisha, for example, caused forty-two children to be devoured by bears for making fun of his baldness (2 Kings 2:23–24). The apostle Paul struck a sorcerer blind (Acts 13:11). And even Jesus blasted an apparently innocent fig tree for not bearing fruit (Matthew 21:9, Mark 11:13–14, 20–22). These instances challenge our tendency to make firm distinctions between curses and prayer. From the standpoint of the children devoured by bears, the blinded sorcerer, and the withered fig tree, is there any essential difference whether they were done in by a negative prayer or a curse? The most important consideration is the *outcome* associated with these events, not what they are called—a point made in the following joke:

A preacher and a New York City taxi driver die and suddenly find themselves facing St. Peter in heaven, who declares that they both deserve admission. St. Peter provides the preacher a modest home for his heavenly dwelling but awards the taxi driver a fabulous palace with fountains, vast lawns, and an army of servants.

"Unfair!" complains the preacher. "I spent all my life ministering to people. If this guy deserves a palace, so do I."

St. Peter explains, "When you preached, people slept. When he drove his taxi, people prayed. We're into outcomes up here. The decision stands."

We reject negative prayers, curses, and hexes because we want to "keep God's skirts clean," as philosopher Alan Watts once put it. As one woman insisted, "My God is good. There is no room in him for negative prayer." But denying the dark side of the Almighty is inconsistent with biblical teachings. Consider Isaiah 45:7: "I form the light, and create darkness: I make peace, and create evil; I the Lord do all these things." And Amos 3:6: "Shall there be evil in a city, and the Lord hath not done it?" And Ecclesiastes 11:14: "Good things and bad, life and death, poverty and wealth, come from the Lord."

One of the major obstacles in confronting the issue of negative prayer, thus, is the desire always to put a good face on prayer. "If prayer appears to harm someone," a devout physician told me, "it really wasn't prayer that was responsible, but something else." "Like what?" I asked. "I'm not sure," he responded, "perhaps 'mind over matter,' but certainly not prayer." Others don't agree—such as the 5 percent of our population who *say* they have used prayer to harm others, mentioned above.

Like my physician friend who rejected out of hand the idea of harmful prayer, we never pause to ask *why* prayer might be capable of causing harm. Could a death-dealing form of prayer serve a valuable purpose? Might it come in handy?

The slightest examination of prayer reveals reasons why it *can* and *should* have negative consequences. When we pray for the recovery of someone who is sick with pneumonia, AIDS, or any other infection, we are praying for the death of millions of microorganisms that are causing the illness, whether we realize it or not. When we pray for cancer to disappear, we are asking for the wholesale destruction of the malignant cells. When we ask for heart disease to resolve, we want the obstructing lesions in the coronary arteries to be utterly obliterated. Even when we pray for our daily bread, we are requesting the death of wheat plants and the grain they bear. We ought to stop being so squeamish about prayer. We'd better *hope* our prayers can have lethal effects—because if they can't, we are left holding the bag with a watered-down ritual that cannot deliver what we often ask of it.

Why are we so reluctant to acknowledge that prayer has a dark side? Why are we so intent on preserving prayer's reputation? Many people associate prayer so intimately with God that they fear they are debasing the Almighty if they grant an untidy side to prayer. But prayer is what it is, warts and all, and I believe we should come clean with prayer and honor the evidence for its positive *and* negative sides. Acknowledging prayer's potential for harm does not annul its power for good, which remains immense.

We should not fret that we will debase the Almighty by recognizing that prayer has a dark side. True, honoring the Absolute through prayer is a time-honored function of prayer, but one that is hardly needed by the Almighty. And prayer, like the Almighty, is majestic enough to survive the negative elements it contains. In any case, any "honor" we might bestow on the Absolute through prayer is rather like shining a flashlight into the sun; it adds little to the sun's brilliance and just runs down the batteries. One might even say that *our* efforts to keep prayer clean are disrespectful of the power of the Almighty and therefore rather blasphemous. We don't need to help out the Almighty; she is fully capable of handling the challenges posed by prayer's complexities with no help from us.

Still, acknowledging that we can cause harm through prayer creates immense uneasiness; it is never comfortable to face one's demons. But the greater risk is to deny our capacity to harm others with our thoughts and prayers. Not only will the mischief we cause continue unabated, we will remain potential victims ourselves by ignoring prayer's possibility for harm.

Refusing to contemplate the negative side of life constitutes what depth psychologists call repressing the shadow—banishing our nasty, undesirable qualities to the unconscious corners of the mind. To grow psychologically and spiritually, we must engage the dark side of the self. As C. G. Jung put it, a whole person is one who has both walked with God and wrestled with the devil.

But lots of people fear a wrestling match with the devil. For example, in the course of writing this book I received numerous cautions from friends who felt it unwise to discuss negative prayer publicly. To do so might actually encourage the destructive use of prayer, they worried, and might trigger an epidemic of harm.

In spite of these concerns, I am convinced that our least attractive option is to deny prayer's dark side. We are not "introducing" negative prayers and curses. Surely these phenomena have been around since time immemorial. If so, we almost certainly have evolved forms of protection against the negative thoughts of others—a kind of "spiritual immune system" that is analogous to our immune system against infections. These protective mechanisms are likely built into our biology, are operating outside our conscious awareness, and are there when we need them.

In extreme situations, however, these protective mechanisms, like our immune system against infections, can be overwhelmed and may need to be strengthened. Thus throughout history methods have been developed to accomplish this protection—a rich variety of rituals, counterprayers, affirmations, and so on, some of which we will soon examine. There is another natural safeguard against negative prayers and intentions. Most people who use prayer to harm others are doomed to failure by their own ineptitude. In fact, they often pose a greater risk to themselves than to others; it is common lore that these malevolent efforts often backfire and harm the perpetrator instead of the prey.

I do not believe that a frank discussion of negative prayer will popularize its use and spawn an epidemic of harm. Negative prayer is *already* prevalent. It exists in the background of daily life, like an unnoticed hum. The noise is probably no louder today than ever before. Our goal is to become aware of it, and that is why I have written this book.

Like a magnet, prayer has both positive and negative poles. Like fire, it can be used for either good or harm. For two thousand years we have emphasized the "light" side of prayer. Now we shall explore its neglected shadow side.

—LARRY DOSSEY, M.D.

PART I

CAN PRAYER HARM?

It's a lot easier to hurt somebody through prayer than to help them.

—Bill Sweet, former president, Spindrift, Inc., a prayer research organization

CURSES AND CHURCHES

MY EARLIEST MEMORY of the dark side of prayer dates back to childhood, when I was five years old.

I grew up in a farm family in the bastion of Christian fundamentalism, the cotton-growing farm belt of central Texas. Community life in those days oriented around the one-room, country Baptist church, which sat at a dusty crossroads. The preacher was a ministerial student from Baylor University in Waco, forty miles away. One miserably cold Sunday night in December, the young preacher warmed things up with a fiery sermon on hell. Only a dozen or so stalwarts had braved the weather, including my grandfather, a deacon in the church, with whom I had tagged along that night. The young evangelist had a dramatic flair. After a horrifyingly vivid description of the eternal agonies of hell awaiting the unsaved, he began to pound with his fist on the pulpit to simulate what he called "the drums of hell." Although I was already sufficiently terrified, the steady BOOM! BOOM! BOOM! of the drumbeat plunged me even further into the depths of fear. Then the preacher gave a signal to someone at the back of the church, who pulled a lever and plunged the church into total darkness. As the drumbeat and graphic exhortations continued, now in pitch-black surroundings, I descended further into paralytic terror. When the lights were turned on again, the preacher began to pray—earnest, desperate pleadings watered with a river of tears—for lost souls. Then the invitational hymn was sung, and I found myself moving, like a stupefied zombie, down the aisle to give my life to Christ and escape the horrors of hell. Everyone was overjoyed that I had decided to accept Jesus' love and forgiveness, but I realized later that no choice was involved. I was functioning as an automaton, literally out of my mind with fear, having been tortured psychologically in the name of Jesus, just as the heretics of earlier days were tortured physically.

The justification for this strategy has always been that the welfare of a soul is at stake and any means are permissible to rescue it. The practices that are employed, which I experienced as a small child, are not too different from those used by sorcerers worldwide. In both cases the victim is cursed (in sorcery, by the sorcerer's ritual; in the church, by original sin and the fall). In both situations the victim is prompted to imagine all sorts of horrific outcomes that will prevail unless certain conditions are met. I am assured by many churchgoers that this type of mind manipulation is less common these days, although I know of no data supporting this claim. These customs are not limited to Christianity, of course; I mention them in a Christian context because that is the tradition I know best.

It is ironic that we are so repelled by curses when they so thoroughly permeate our religious life. I'd say we have become blind to the elephant in our living room. In truth, virulent condemnations are right at home in Christianity and often rival the darkest curses of sorcerers and magicians. Perhaps the most obvious example is the condemnation of the unsaved to eternal, unimaginable suffering in a burning hell.

As an example of an official curse that is still on the books, consider the commination ritual in the Book of Common Prayer, the official prayer book of the Church of England. *Commination* comes from Latin words meaning "to threaten" or "to menace." Although the ritual is considered a relic by many Anglicans and does not appear in the Episcopal Book of Common Prayer, it is intended to be enacted on Ash Wednesday, the first day of Lent, the season of fasting and penitence. It includes nine specific curses based on the twenty-seventh chapter of the Book of Deuteronomy, among which are the following:

> Cursed is he that curseth his father and mother. Cursed is he that maketh the blind to go out of his way. Cursed is he that perverteth the judgment of the stranger, the fatherless, and widow. Cursed are the unmerciful, fornicators, and adulterers, covetous persons, idolaters, slanderers, drunkards, and extortioners. . . .

At the end of each of these curses, the congregation replies, "Amen."

The minister then reminds the congregation of "the dreadful judgment hanging over our heads, and always ready to fall upon us," and "that it is a dreadful thing to fall into the hands of the living God," who shall "pour down rain upon the sinners . . . fire and brimstone, storm and tempest. . . ." The ultimate result of the curse is eternal agony and punishment—"Go ye cursed, into the fire everlasting, which is prepared for the devil and his angels"—unless one opts for repentance through Jesus Christ. The Reverend Ted Karpf, of the Episcopal Church of the United States of America, states, "This is an example of ritual cursing to remind the faithful of the tenuous nature of their condition . . . a psychodrama of our fallen state that we might prepare for the season of penitence and fasting called Lent."[1]

CHRISTIAN MAGIC?

As we venture into the domain of negative prayer, let us bear in mind that religion has always kept close company with the sinister side of things. The briefest glance at the history of any religious tradition shows that the divisions separating spirituality and magic, light and shadow, have always been permeable. Paying attention to history is one of the best safeguards I know of resisting the temptation to reject the evidence for negative prayer without a hearing.

In his critically acclaimed biography of the apostle Paul, A. N. Wilson states that what made Judaism so attractive in the eyes of many Gentiles was the "superior potency, when compared with the other spiritual systems, of its magic powers."[2] Powerful words and symbols were at home in the Jewish tradition. Alexander the Great worshiped the tetragrammaton—the four consonants of the ancient Hebrew name for God, considered too sacred and powerful to be spoken—carved on the mitre of the high priest at Jerusalem. The name of the Jewish god was so powerful it could make people drop dead if they even whispered it. Moreover, the names of the angels of the God of Israel had great power, and people were able to attend the synagogues and pick up an oral knowledge or actual copies of the Hebrew Scriptures for magical use. Incantations employing God's name and the names of his angels could be used to drive away devils, heal the sick, and generally add to the reputation of the magician using them. It was considered essential for astrologers to master the

Scriptures, since the Hebrew Deity claimed to be the architect and mover of the planets. Indeed, "all the Jews at this date, ranging from the Jewish Platonists of Alexandria to the Essenes of Qumran, would appear to have been obsessed by astrology," Wilson states.[3]

Historically, when unbelievers looked on Christianity from the outside, they often suspected that it embodied magical and possibly malevolent elements. "Jesus himself was clearly in some senses of the word a magician," Wilson observes, "since he called upon powers outside himself to heal and to destroy. He was, according to his followers, able to control the weather, to wither fig-trees with a word and to drive out evil spirits."[4]

According to Richard Cavendish in his well-documented work, *A History of Magic,* Jesus was accused early on of being a magician.[5]* Celsus, in a polemic against Christianity written about 180 C.E., suggested that Jesus learned his magic in Egypt. Descriptions of his life by early Christian writers lent fuel to the fire.

> The miraculous birth of Jesus, accompanied by the portent of the star and the homage of the Magi; the portent at his baptism in the Jordan; the miracles of healing, calming the wind and sea, walking on water and providing supernatural quantities of food and drink; the ability to restore the dead to life; the portents at the Crucifixion, his mysterious disappearance from the tomb and his reappearances after death; the story of his descent into the underworld; these marvels, which helped to persuade Christians that Jesus was divine, could be represented as the achievements of a magician. His power to cast out evil spirits had caused his enemies among the Jews to accuse him of black magic.[6]

---

* *Magic* is an imprecise term. As Richard Cavendish notes, it is useful to make a rough distinction between high magic and low magic. High magic is an attempt to gain a mastery and understanding of oneself and the environment, so as to transcend all human limitations and become superhuman or divine. This was the magic Pythagoras and other philosophers were reputed to have learned in the East, which allegedly made possible superhuman powers such as the ability to control the weather or to be in two places at once. Low magic, in contrast, Cavendish states, is comparatively minor and mechanical, engaged in for immediate worldly advantage, to acquire wealth, take revenge, or attain success in love. In practice these distinctions blur, and many magicians have engaged in both. See Richard Cavendish, *A History of Magic* (New York: Penguin, 1987), 12.

The accusations were not limited to Jesus. For centuries, Christians were believed responsible for plagues and all sorts of catastrophes.

> Tertullian said that whenever anything unusual and alarming happened, the Christians were blamed. If the Tiber flooded or the Nile did not, if the earth moved or the sky stayed still, if there was famine or pestilence, the cry went up: "the Christians to the lion." Ironically, in course of time the same instinct drove Christians to tar heretics, Jews and witches with the same brush.[7]

Christian holy symbols and rituals have often given the impression of being magically effective in controlling the unruly side of nature. In the fifth century in France, many pagans were converted during an outbreak of cattle disease when they saw that the cattle of the Christians either did not get sick or they recovered, both of which were attributed to the use of the sign of the cross. Medieval Christians crossed not just their cattle but their crops, houses, children, and themselves to stave off misfortune, of which there was plenty. They wore amulets inscribed with holy verses, were baptized and rebaptized, and took holy water from church and sprinkled it on their beds each evening to repel nocturnal devils and ghouls. Their cures were laden with "Christian magic." For snakebite, an Anglo-Saxon medical book recommended drinking holy water in which a snail had been washed. Hildegard of Bingen recommended that bewitchment be treated by cutting a cross into the top of a loaf and nibbling away the loaf around the cross. John of Salisbury recommended repeating the Lord's Prayer and the names of the four evangelists when gathering and using medicinal herbs. Childbirth could be eased by the Agnus Dei, a wax figure of a lamb that had been blessed by the pope and immersed in holy water. The specialist in these measures was the priest, who manned the Church's front lines against paganism and evil—forces people saw everywhere. As a specialist in the sacred, the priest acquired a magical mystique.[8]

So did the mass, which is perhaps the most magical of all Christian rituals. "A rite in which bread and wine were transformed into the flesh and blood of God ... were bound to give the impression of being a magical ritual of awe-inspiring force," Cavendish observes. It is not surprising that the mass gained a formidable reputation over the centuries. "The impression [that the mass was magical] was driven home by the Church's doctrine that a priest could say Mass effectively even if he was in a state of sin, had evil intentions or was a heretic. The Mass seemed to have . . . power of its own, regardless of the spiritual condition and motives of those who used it."[9]

Such a powerful ceremony would naturally be employed for all sorts of purposes. The Galasian Sacramentary of about the sixth century includes masses for rain, good weather, the sick, preventing disease in cattle, conceiving children, safety during travels, and for the souls of the dead. Masses for cattle, farm implements, and fishing boats and nets were common during the Middle Ages and remain so today.[10]

As a result of its magical aura, the mass, perhaps inevitably, was employed also for sinister purposes, such as the use of the black mass in honor of the devil. In 694 the Council of Toledo condemned priests who said mass in which they named a living man with the intention of killing him. In the 1200s there were reports of priests saying mass over a wax image of the victim placed on the altar, cursing him. The use of the mass in magic was condemned in 1398 by the University of Paris. "The authorities were constantly instructing priests to keep the hosts and the holy oil under lock and key, to prevent people from stealing them for use in sorcery, love charms, medicines and poisons."[11]

Throughout the history of Christianity, the diabolic and the divine are inextricably intertwined—for example, in the Eden story, the archetypal account of the contamination of paradise with evil, and in the transformation of the heavenly angel Lucifer into the devil. These connections suggest an underlying fascination with the dark side, which often erupts, as we shall see, as the attempt to manipulate, control, or harm others through prayer.

UNINTENTIONAL CURSES AND PRAYER

Although as we've noted, one in twenty Americans say they have deliberately prayed for harm for others, most negative prayers are unintentional. They can be offered so casually we're not even aware we're engaging in them. As Rupert Sheldrake, the British biologist and author of *Seven Experiments That Could Change the World,*[12] puts it, "When people in irritation shout 'damn you' this is, of course, a curse."

Sheldrake believes that people often pray with reckless abandon, without giving sufficient thought to the nature of their prayers, and that when they do so their prayers may take the form of a curse. He relates the following example:

> There was an international plan during the last phase of the Cold War for praying for peace in particular places. People adopted a nuclear base in say Britain and one in say Czechoslovakia. They then prayed for these bases to be dismantled and the weapons removed. This was to try and give nuclear disarmament a more concrete set of images, rather than the nebulous notion of peace. . . . When this was going on, there was some discussion as to the way in which people should pray. Some individuals, particularly within the New Age world, thought the best way to pray was to hold the nuclear base in mind and see it bathed in an incredibly bright light which would purify and transform it. However, since all these bases were nuclear targets, the most obvious way in which this prayer could come true would be to have a nuclear war, in which an incredibly bright light would indeed have descended on every one of these bases and purified and transformed them. I myself preferred to envisage sites being cleared by bulldozers, remnants of rusty barbed wire being cleared away and the land liberated for ordinary people to walk on again, and for children to play on.[13]

When we stop to think about it, it is surprising how often we may be engaging in reckless prayer. A woman from Chicago wrote,

> If I am driving and start honking my horn and thinking to myself that another driver is a jerk because he's blocking the intersection, I could, in a sense, be sending a negative prayer to that driver. I have been the driver stuck in the middle of an intersection, and have felt some pretty negative stuff. I believe most of our daily thoughts may be "unconscious prayer," and that all my little "damn yous" may get around.[14]

This comment suggests that negative prayers are woven into the fabric of everyday life. We launch them not as formal curses, but simply through the process of thinking negatively of another person.

Consider the experiences of Katherine, a woman who was involved in corporate management. She was deeply interested in the nature of human consciousness and considered herself a serious student of this area. At one point in her career, Katherine was in charge of a project involving several companies. Two women, representing the companies involved, were opposed to the organizational changes she knew were necessary. The project was bogging down, and Katherine became increasingly annoyed at what she considered petty politics.

A crucial meeting was coming up. In the days prior to it, Katherine decided to use the skills she had learned in her study of consciousness to "intend" and "manifest" events. She "wished" that the women who opposed the changes would somehow "go away" so she could get on with the job at hand. One week before the meeting, both the troublesome women, in unrelated accidents in different parts of the country, fell and broke their right wrists.

Katherine was horrified by the thought that she may have been responsible. While she didn't physically push the women down a flight of stairs, she believed her "mental push" had had physical consequences. She commented,

> Someone would have to be killing my child before I would bring those forces to bear again. Coincidence or not, I was suddenly confronted with the ethics of power. I believe people use "spells" all the time. If we want someone to like us, then we put that desire out. And have you noticed how, in the presence of someone who believes you are a certain way, that you sometimes tend to act that way? These are what I call "little spells," which arise in the continual flow of intentions going on between all of us. Then there are the "big spells," which have the power to change reality in a major way. If you play in this arena, you better be very clear about the ethics of your actions. Our thoughts are a loaded gun.[15]

Katherine's experience is a reminder that we're all a little scared of the power of our minds. As anthropologist Francis Huxley observes,

"Even the most blasé of us will experience a twinge of guilt if we lose our temper with someone and damn him, and he then goes off and breaks his neck. We try to take the sting out of this coincidence by various forms of rationalization, such as the use of statistics, but even so the fit between a wish and an event may well bring on an apprehensive shudder."[16]

An unintentional "little spell" was related to me by a well-known physician and author who writes about the role of the mind in health and healing. He frequently includes the stories of his patients in his books and is extremely careful to disguise their identities. On one occasion he asked permission to publish the experience of a man who was well known in the community, and he showed the man the new identity he had crafted for him. Although the man's name, occupation, and other features had been changed, the patient was not satisfied. He felt he could still be recognized by the kind of cancer from which he had recovered. So the author rewrote the account and gave him a different kind of cancer—a sarcoma, a rare tumor—in the muscle of his right thigh. The man was totally in the dark about the rewrite. The next week, however, he called the physician complaining of a new problem—pain in his right thigh, which he had never experienced before. The physician was alarmed, wondering if he had somehow "given" the man cancer. An evaluation showed no problem, however, and the pain gradually diminished and eventually went away.[17]

PRAYER MUGGINGS AND DRIVE-BY PRAYER

Another common form of unintentional, reckless prayer is praying for something that belongs to another. Like most types of negative prayer, this is usually done casually, without considering the potential harm it may cause. Consider a mother's request for her child: "Dear God, let my daughter be elected head cheerleader this year instead of Mary's kid, who has held the position long enough." Or the prayer of a sales representative: "Dear Lord, you let Jim win the sales contest last year. Reward me this time, as I, too, am your faithful and equally deserving servant." If this type of prayer is answered, someone else loses—someone who, for all we know, may be more deserving than oneself.

I call incidents like these "prayer muggings" because of their resemblance to street muggings. In both street and prayer muggings, the mugger tries to take something that belongs to another. Both prayer and street muggers operate through stealth and surprise; the victim never sees it coming and usually does not respond until it is too late.

In the United States, mugging is the commonest crime involving physical force: one in every three hundred of us has been mugged.[18]

But this statistic is probably minuscule compared to those of us who have been mugged by prayer.

In general, prayer that is offered without regard for its consequences can also be called "drive-by prayer"—a random, reckless, thoughtless act, perpetrated from a distance.

SPORTS AND PRAYER: MY GOD VS. YOURS

I attended a large university in the Midwest that was football crazy. On the campus there was a four-story mosaic, clearly visible from the stadium, of Jesus with his arms raised over his head, looking just like an official signaling a touchdown. Our team rarely lost.[19]

Looking back over my childhood, I can recall many other ways in which prayer was used as a quasi-curse. One such use was connected with high school football. I remember being confused by the pregame prayer, in which both teams gathered in their respective locker rooms and prayed to the Almighty for success in beating the daylights out of their rivals. Since both teams were praying essentially the same prayer, I wondered how such a prayer could possibly be answered.

Professional sports contests often bear a strong resemblance to religious struggles, and sports fans can certainly resemble religious fanatics. So perhaps it isn't surprising that prayer is at home in both religion and sports. Almost one-quarter of the American population admits to praying for their sports team to win and thus praying for the defeat of another team.[20]

I was reminded of how we often unintentionally use prayer to harm others when my favorite professional football team was competing in the 1996 NFL Superbowl. During the first half of the game I was comfortable with how things were going, and I found myself merely wishing and hoping my team would win. During the third quarter, however, the game evened out and I began to feel genuinely concerned about the outcome. At this point I began seriously to pull for my team with a forceful kind of willing. Then, as the situation degenerated into white-knuckled desperation in the final quarter, I found myself actually *praying* for victory.

Sports contests are one of the greatest incentives for prayer in our culture. During the NFL playoffs in January 1997, the Jacksonville Jaguars were in Denver to play the Broncos. *Sports Illustrated*'s Rick Reilly described what happened on Friday night prior to the Sunday game:

> The Jaguars' 6'7", 325-pound left tackle, Tony Boselli, the rock of the team, was sprawled out on his bed, sick to his stomach, horrible headache, throwing up. At about 9:30, a handful of his teammates came into his room, surrounded his bed, knelt and prayed for his recovery. Fourteen hours later, bingo! "God actually healed me," said Boselli, who held one of the [Bronco's] leading sack men, Alfred Williams, to no sacks and one tackle while serving him about a dozen mouthfuls of turf.[21]

In November 1996 the sports world was shocked when the aging Evander Holyfield defeated the heavyweight boxing champion, "Iron Mike" Tyson. I am a talk radio fan, and about a month following Holyfield's victory I tuned in to my favorite program. The topic under discussion was sports heroes. An enthusiastic male caller announced, "My hero is Evander Holyfield. He prayed to God that he beat Mike Tyson, who was a Muslim. Now, I'm not putting down Allah, but Holyfield's victory proves the biblical teaching that 'I can do all things through God, who strengtheneth me.'"

But of course the caller was putting down Allah as well as the religion of Islam. Praying for victory, however, is not something that only Christians do. The urge toward religious triumphalism is universal, and "My god can beat up your god!" has been the refrain of the combatants in holy wars for the past two thousand years.

The Tyson-Holyfield contest is a reminder that our peacetime battlefields are the boxing arena, the basketball court, the baseball diamond, the hockey rink, and the football field.

In his landmark book, *The Future of the Body*, Michael Murphy, the founder of California's Esalen Institute, suggests that the emotions we experience during sporting contests often shade into cursing and hexing.

"Many sports fans consciously or half-consciously feel that rooting has an effect that goes beyond mere encouragement to a contest's participants; witness the many hexes aimed at games via radios and television sets." Do these efforts work? "If rooting channels or triggers powers of mind over matter," Murphy states, "it is no wonder that during certain contests balls take funny bounces and athletes jump higher than ever or stumble inexplicably. Many of us have sensed the uncanny at sports events, when an innocent game suddenly becomes a theater of the occult." Hexing has been used even in chess competitions: "witness the Korchnoi-Karpov world championship in Manila during which Karpov was assisted by a parapsychologist while Korchnoi hired meditation students to influence Karpov at a distance."[22]

Most of the contests in life, of course, take place beyond the playing field. In many of them, the sports-and-prayer scenario, in which there is a winner and a loser, is duplicated in precise detail. Consider international relations. Most of the bloodbaths between nations are saturated with prayers for victory by the competing "teams." In Northern Ireland, for example, or in Bosnia, with its recent orgies of "ethnic cleansing," opposing factions pray essentially the same prayer to the same god: Let us be victorious over our enemies. From the perspective of the enemy, these are negative prayers because they require death and destruction for their fulfillment.

The irony of competing prayers between warring factions has been recognized since antiquity—surfacing, even, in a Zen parable:

> A monk said to Kegon, "The loyal army builds an altar to the Heavenly Kings, and seeks for victory; the rebel army also builds an altar to the Heavenly Kings and seeks for victory; which prayer do they answer?" Kegon replied, "Heaven's rain drops its dews, and does not choose the flourishing or the declining."[23]

PRAYER AS MANIPULATION AND CONTROL

Being manipulated by another can be hazardous to our health.

Stanford University psychiatrist George F. Solomon, M.D., is widely considered the father of psychoneuroimmunology, the field of medicine that explores the connections between our minds and our neurological and immune systems. With Lydia Temoshok, Ph.D., of the University of California at San Francisco, Solomon undertook a study of long-term survivors of AIDS. What psychological and behavioral traits helped the survivors beat the odds? They discovered a consistent personality pattern, described by Henry Dreher in his admirable book, *The Immune Power Personality:*

> The most striking finding in the formal study was a correlation between an affirmative answer to one specific question and stronger immune functions: "Would you refuse to do a favor requested by a friend if you did not wish to?" The subtext was, "Can you say 'no'?"
>
> The long survivors answered "yes"—they would absolutely refuse the favor. *That single trait was powerfully correlated with stronger, more active immune cells.*[24]

What does the ability to say no mean? Says Solomon:

> It reflects assertiveness, and the ability to resist becoming a self-sacrificing martyr. It also demonstrates the capacity to monitor and take care of your own needs, psychologically and physically. For example, a person with AIDS may not feel well. Is he going to go out and help move furniture because a friend asked him to do it? Or will he be able to say "No, I don't feel up to it."[25]

What about the ability to say no to someone else's prayer, if we know it is being offered, if it conflicts with our needs? What if a friend is praying, wishing, or hoping we'll help him move his furniture or go out with her to a movie or dinner, and we don't feel up to it or simply don't want to? If we allow ourselves to be continually manipulated by the wishes, desires, or prayers of others, Solomon's and Temoshok's findings suggest that we may be putting our health at risk.

These findings have profound ethical implications. If we try to bully others with prayer, disregarding their needs and desires, we run the risk of actually increasing sickness and ill health in those we pray for. This may be one reason why prayer so often seems ineffective and why prayer sometimes harms.

This is a plea, not to abandon prayer for others, but to pray empathically. *Empathy,* derived from Greek words meaning "in" and "feeling," involves the ability to share another person's emotions or feelings, to know what something is like *for the other*. If we pray for others without empathy, we run the risk of imposing our agenda and creating real mischief in the life of someone else. I have often thought that a handy definition of negative prayer is "prayer without empathy."

The problem is, we usually *think* we know what's best for others, and we waste no time telling God how to fix the person we're praying for. But anytime we're tempted to pray for the destiny of someone else, we ought to examine our motives. We may discover that we have our own wishes uppermost, not theirs.

A mother of three wrote to me:

> The past year was extremely difficult. My youngest child left for college, and my husband and I felt intensely alone. I prayed that our children pay more attention to us and that they visit us more often. The more I prayed, however, the more they stayed away. When I discussed this with my kids, they turned their backs. They told me to keep my prayers to myself, because they needed a life of their own.[26]

This woman decided that, since her prayer strategy was not working, she must be doing something to keep her children away. She and her husband entered a midlife transitions program at their church, made up of people with similar concerns. They gained insight into the subtle ways they had been trying to control their children for many years. In time, their kids came back. Today, the woman no longer uses prayer to make them love her; now "it just happens naturally," she says.

If our prayers restrict the freedom and choices of others, they can be a curse, a way of manipulating others and enslaving them to our point of view. A reader's letter makes the point:

> During the early seventies I was deeply involved in my personal development, practicing meditation and yoga, reading extensively in areas of metaphysics and world religions. At that time a relative, an aunt by marriage, came to visit for a few days. As we visited, we seemed to share some common interests and ideas about faith, healing, prayer, and meditation.

Several weeks later, after she had returned to her home on the East Coast, I received a vitriolic letter from her. She condemned books she had seen on my shelves, saying I must burn all books on yoga, Eastern and Western religions other than traditional Christianity, all the books of a metaphysical nature. She labeled them "satanic" and "of the devil," saying they must be destroyed so that they wouldn't get into the hands of others who might read them. This was the first indication to me of our different basic perspectives on the topics we'd talked about. Instead of destroying the books, I destroyed the letter.

A few days passed, and I thought no more of the matter. Then I began to have strange "headaches" each morning right at 9:00 A.M. For a few minutes I would feel as if my brain resembled a mass of cooked spaghetti on a plate. I couldn't think straight. The feeling and image would soon pass and I'd be fine until the next day. For help in understanding what this might indicate, I turned to a friend who was a psychiatrist.

He had previously worked with me on some intensive psychotherapy followed by classes on meditation and healing. After questioning me awhile, he suggested that the next time I began to feel that way, I was to imagine a telegraph wire leading out from me to see where it went. Then to imagine that wire being flooded with love, pouring out universal love to whomever was at the other end of the wire.

I followed his instructions, and to my surprise the wire went immediately to the East Coast community where my relative lived. That really was a surprise! As I flooded that wire with universal love, the feeling of the scrambled mass of spaghetti dissipated. After doing that imagery for two or three days, the problem went away completely and has never returned.

After the arrival of this relative's letter, I learned that she had become deeply involved in [a particular religious movement] that was beginning to gain national attention. She had told me that daily at noon she spent a few minutes in prayer. Noon her time on the East Coast was 9:00 A.M. my time on the West Coast.

This was a strong lesson for me in the power of prayer. If her thoughts three thousand miles away could affect me that way, what other greater powers could thoughts and words have?

Distance was no object. I gained an even greater respect for the power of prayer. I became even more careful about the content of my own prayers . . . and thoughts. . . . [27]

Some of the clearest warnings about the use of prayer to manipulate and control others can be found in the writings of Mary Baker Eddy (1821–1910), the founder of Christian Science. In "Obtrusive Mental Healing" she wrote, "Who of us would have our houses broken open or our locks picked? and much less would have our minds tampered with?" She believed that praying for others without their knowledge and consent was immoral. "Our Master said, 'When ye enter a house, salute it.' . . . I say, When you enter mentally the personal precincts of human thought, you should know that the person with whom you hold communion desires it."[28]

Mary Baker Eddy saw two exceptions to this general guideline. If the friends of a patient desired prayer for him or her without the person's knowing it, if other means had failed, and if they genuinely believed in the efficacy of the mental treatment, she recommended proceeding without consent because the end—recovery from illness—justified the means. The additional extenuating circumstance justifying prayer without consent, she said, is desperate situations or emergencies "when there is no time for ceremony and no other aid is near." As she put it, "It would be right to break into a burning building and rouse the slumbering inmates, but wrong to burst open doors and break through windows if no emergency demanded this."

Aside from these two situations, she advised people to keep their prayers to themselves and to mind their own business. To do otherwise "is a breach of good manners and morals; it is nothing less than a mistaken kindness, a culpable ignorance, or a conscious trespass on the rights of mortals."[29]

CONTROLLING OTHERS IN THE NAME OF LOVE

Dr. Loudell F. Snow, of Michigan State University's Department of Community Medicine, studies folk medical beliefs and their implications for health. She is an expert on curses, hexes, and spells. Writing in the prestigious *Annals of Internal Medicine*, she reports, "In virtually every case [of hexing] reported in the literature and in my own data as well, the evildoer is specifically identified and is usually a girlfriend or lover, husband or wife, a parent, a sibling, or an in-law."[30]

As in formal curses, when people use prayer to manipulate and control others, the object of the manipulation is frequently a family member or loved one. Moreover, the pray-er usually claims to be acting from compassion, for the person's own good.

An example is the experience of Richard, who had wanted passionately to be a novelist since his early teens. It seemed a realistic ambition; every teacher he encountered commented on his exceptional talent. When he eventually obtained his Ph.D. in English literature, Richard felt poised for a bright future as a writer. Ten years later, however, none of his work had been accepted for publication and he felt a failure. The rejection slips contained the usual comments about "streaks of brilliance" and "great promise," but something was not clicking, something he could not put his finger on. Richard did not give up. He began to attend writers' conferences and seminars, hoping to remedy flaws in his technique that he could not see. Still nothing worked. Nearing forty, he began to console himself by recalling that many great writers had late beginnings.

Following his latest rejection slip from a major publisher, he decided to set his work aside and visit his mother for Christmas.

"You look depressed, darling. What's going on?" his mother asked shortly after he arrived.

Richard had never revealed to his mother his increasing sense of failure, but now he decided to share his disappointments. His mother listened patiently, then said, "Richard, I know why you haven't become a writer. Since you were a teenager I've prayed to God every night that he give you something else to do."

Richard was stunned. "You mean that for twenty-five years you've prayed that I would *fail* as a writer?" he stammered.

"Yes, because I've always known God has something better for you. And he has answered my prayers!" she said sweetly.

"*Why have you done this?*" Richard demanded angrily through tears.

His mother, too, began to cry. "Richard, I *love* you. I want only the best for you." Then she said, almost coldly, "Writers reveal things that should not be told—about themselves, about their families. Writers tell secrets that are nobody's business!"

Richard saw in his mother's face a lifetime of pain, sadness, and fear. Buried in the family's past were shameful events his mother could not face—infidelity and divorce, alcoholism, and feelings of failure as a wife and mother. For over two decades she had nurtured a personal horror—that if Richard became a successful novelist the family skeletons would surface in his writings, and the family would be disgraced.

Richard saw his mother's prayers as a curse offered in the name of love and God's will. He did not stay for Christmas dinner. After ruminating for a month, he decided to enter psychotherapy, an idea he had considered for many years, wanting to sort out his confused feelings about his mother and the stormy relationship they had always endured.

Richard knew his mother would continue to pray "for" him, and he was determined not to be sabotaged by her prayers. For the first time in years he began to pray, asking for strength and guidance for his life's work and for protection from his mother's prayers. Richard's writing took on a maturity and depth it had not contained before. Three years after his confrontation with his mother, his first novel was accepted by a major publisher.

AGENTS FOR THE ALMIGHTY

As in Richard's case, the excuse that one is praying for someone else's "own good" keeps company with the justification that one is following "God's will" in doing so. In this situation, intercessory prayer often shades into concrete action. One of the most grisly episodes in human history, the Inquisition, which began in the thirteenth century, was one of the most prayerful. The goal of the inquisitors was to discover and punish heretics, with the added hope of saving their souls. As the torturers twisted the thumbscrews and tightened the racks, they prayed piously, and their tears mingled with the blood of their victims on the floors of torture chambers throughout Europe. The pattern endures; piety and prayer remain mingled with killing in the name of God. When Yigal Amir confessed to assassinating Israeli prime minister Yitzhak Rabin, he claimed he had acted on "God's orders."

We may insist that we don't use prayer to manipulate and control others and that we would never deliberately cause physical harm in God's name. Yet all of us find ourselves in situations where we believe, at the end of the day, that we are right and "they" are wrong. And in our culture, where 80 to 90 percent of people pray regularly, the stage is always set for in-your-face prayers, in which we ask the Almighty to defeat, in one way or the other, those who do not share our views.

Consider, for example, how spirituality can become contaminated with revenge without being noticed by those involved. A woman wrote to me,

[There has been] a grisly affair here in Oregon. A man murdered a family of five by cutting their throats (father, mother, two children, and the father's brother). He was quickly apprehended because both men identified him before they died. . . . Several "godfearing Christians" of my acquaintance oozed with hate and vengeance—"that man ought to be taken out and shot!"[31]

When we find ourselves slipping into self-righteousness, which often leads to manipulative prayer, we might recall an incident in the life of Abraham Lincoln:

At a White House dinner, a churchman offered a benediction and closed with the pious affirmation: "The Lord is on our side."

When President Lincoln did not respond to this sentiment, someone asked him, "Don't you believe, Mr. President, that the Lord is always on the side of the right?"

"I am not concerned about that," was Lincoln's answer, "for we know that the Lord is always on the side of the right. My concern is that I and this nation should be on the Lord's side."[32]

NONBELIEVERS AND NEGATIVE PRAYER

Some people consider *all* prayer negative. In fact, some actually despise it—such as a professor of biology who said, "If my doctor prayed for my recovery, I'd consider a malpractice lawsuit."[33]

In 1994, when the Office of Alternative Medicine at the National Institutes of Health funded a study on intercessory, distant prayer, the attention of the national media was drawn to psychiatrist Scott Walker, M.D., the experiment's principal investigator at the University of New Mexico School of Medicine at Albuquerque, where the study was conducted. The purpose of this controlled experiment was to examine the effects of prayer in patients undergoing rehabilitation from substance abuse. When the news got around, criticism erupted. One of the most vocal objections came from the Freedom From Religion Foundation in Madison, Wisconsin. This organization wrote a letter to Secretary Donna Shalala of the Department of Health and Human Services, decrying the use of federal tax dollars to evaluate prayer. They condemned this practice and demanded that it never happen again. This was a violation, they believed, of the constitutional separation of church and state. Annie L. Gaylor, spokesperson for the Freedom From Religion Foundation, said, "If I knew my doctor was praying for me, I'd get another doctor. I'd rather they believe in medicine," suggesting that physicians can't believe in both and that agnostics and atheists make the best doctors. Gaylor denied that any evidence supporting prayer's efficacy exists, apparently unaware of the experimental findings.[34]

These objections should be taken seriously by those of us who believe in the power of prayer. It is undeniable that some people feel manipulated when prayed for and regard intercessory prayer as condescending, arrogant, interfering, and controlling. I confess that I have not always been sensitive to this position. When I became convinced of the positive aspects of prayer, after spending years exploring the data in this field, I felt initially that its use was justified for practically anyone in need. I no longer feel that way, for several reasons.

For one thing, I underestimated the often unpredictable consequences of prayer, as described throughout this book. Moreover, I focused almost exclusively on the evidence favoring the positive effects of prayer, and I paid too little attention to the evidence of prayer's potential for harm.[35] In addition, I underestimated the importance of what people *believe* about prayer and what prayer *means* to them.

TOXIC REACTIONS TO PRAYER?

There is an immense body of evidence showing that our beliefs and meanings are not just "thoughts in the brain." We channel them into our bodies, where they can make the difference in life and death. It really doesn't matter what our beliefs and meanings may be or whether they are based in truth.[36]

Much of this evidence comes from the study of placebos, which are fake medications with no physiological effects of their own. In one placebo-controlled study of the treatment of stomach cancer, one-third of the patients who received placebos developed nausea, one-fifth developed vomiting, and almost one-third lost their hair.[37] In another experiment, a patient who received a placebo suddenly fainted fifteen minutes later in an anaphylactic shock reaction with nausea, lowering of the blood pressure, and clammy pale skin.[38] Cases have been reported in which patients have become addicted to placebos when they believed they were the real thing. During a single year, one such patient took approximately ten thousand placebo tablets.[39] In another study, two-thirds of patients receiving a placebo developed evidence of streptomycin toxicity—streptomycin being the antibiotic they believed they were taking—including high- and low-tone hearing loss, a known side effect of this particular antibiotic.[40]

The power of belief raises questions about the effect of prayer. If people object to prayer and believe it causes harm, are they at risk of developing "prayer toxicity," just as the above individuals developed toxic reactions to a placebo they thought was the real thing? I feel the answer is yes. I have known a few individuals who oppose prayer so vehemently that it is quite likely that they would be seriously stressed, physically as well as psychologically, to discover that someone was praying for them and that the discovery might result in serious harm.

PRAYER ON THE SLY

This possibility raises ethical issues for those of us who believe in prayer. If we know that someone opposes prayer, should we pray for them? Some pray-ers feel this problem can be averted by praying for others secretly. If the recipient is unaware of the prayer, he or she won't object and the problem is avoided. Yet praying secretly for someone whom we know objects to prayer has a sinister ring and smacks of dishonesty. Prayer on the sly violates the spirit of prayer. Should we therefore always seek informed consent before praying for another? If we did so, this would give the recipient the opportunity to say no to prayer and might avert a toxic reaction. And if the recipient said yes, he or she would *know* prayer was being engaged in, and this might add to the power of prayer.

On balance, it is wise to consider praying with the consent of another. There are instances, however, when this is impossible—in an emergency, for example, when the recipient may be unconscious; or when an infant, who cannot give informed consent, is involved. In these instances we should follow our best judgment. If we are guided by love, compassion, and good intent, and if we set our personal agendas aside to the greatest extent possible, it is unlikely that we will take a wrong step.

WHY PRAYER BACKFIRES

No wonder Jung was later to tell me with a laugh that he could not imagine a fate more awful, a fate worse than death, than a life lived in perfect balance and harmony.

—*Sir Laurens van der Post*

ROGER'S WIFE WAS DYING from cancer. He believed that a loving God would not want a beloved wife and mother to die, leaving him and their young children alone. Convinced that his prayers and those of others would surely result in a cure, he recruited groups of believers in his church to pray for the miracle. Roger's belief amounted to a certainty. When the cure didn't happen, he suffered a mental collapse from which he never fully recovered. The children were taken in by loving friends who supported them through school and college, and they did well in life. Roger, however, remained a broken man.

Why did Roger's prayer strategy devastate him? Beryl Statham, the British writer who relates this story, says, "There is an important difference in demanding a specific answer and the open-ended prayer for help; a specific demand may or may not be the best answer to the need and it may or may not be granted. Making specific demands can have tragic results."[41]

When we pray for a specific outcome in a particular situation, we are presuming to know how the world should proceed. But our wisdom can be limited, and the best answer to our prayer may not be what we want at the time.

PRAYERS FOR HAPPINESS

> . . . enormous prayers which heaven in vengeance grants.
> —Juvenal (c. 60–c. 140 C.E.)

Consider the prayer for happiness, which is one of our most common requests. The quest for ultimate happiness—whether called the quest for God, bliss, satori, or enlightenment—is universal. Books instructing people on how to find happiness dominate the best-seller lists. Most ads, whether for automobiles, clothes, household products, vacations, or alcohol, try to convince us that the product in question will make us happier. Even drug ads in medical journals commonly imply that a particular medication not only will cure illness but also will make a patient happy and fulfilled in the process.

If the drive for happiness is innate, as it appears to be, what could be more natural and justified than a prayer to be happy?

RELIGIOUS PRACTICE, PRAYER, AND HAPPINESS

In general, religious commitment and prayer are good for people. Those who are religiously active and who pray are twice as likely to report that they are "very happy" than those lowest in spiritual commitment.[42] Research studies consistently show a positive correlation between mental and physical health and religious commitment, which usually involves prayer.[43] Why are those who pray generally happier than those who don't? In study after study, researchers have found four traits that characterize happy people. First, they like themselves; they have high self-esteem. Second, happy people generally feel a sense of self-control—over their lives, their situations, their health, and so on. Third, they are optimistic. Fourth, they are generally outgoing, not focused on themselves.[44] Because prayer fosters all these traits, it makes happiness more likely. But this doesn't mean we can "get" happiness by praying for it.

Many spiritual traditions, in fact, deemphasize the importance of being happy, as in the following account from the Zen tradition:

One day it was announced by Master Joshu that the young monk Kyogen had reached an enlightened state. Much impressed by this news, several of his peers went to speak with him.

"We have heard that you are enlightened. Is this true?" his fellow students inquired.

"It is," Kyogen answered.

"Tell us," said a friend, "how do you feel?"

"As miserable as ever," replied the enlightened Kyogen.[45]

OUR PREDILECTION FOR UNHAPPINESS

Why do spiritual masters caution against a fanatical desire to be happy? Why do we often become melancholy at moments when we least expect it, even when things are going well? Why do unhappy thoughts seem so easily to get the upper hand? These questions have been asked by every major religion, and answers have never been in short supply. Our responses to these conundrums influence how we pray—and, as we shall see, whether our prayers produce harmful results.

One might wonder whether we have some sort of biological predilection for negativity. Mihaly Csikszentmihalyi, professor and former chairman of the University of Chicago's Department of Psychology, explains in his admirable book, *The Evolving Self,* why the mind seems to drift inevitably toward unhappiness. He suggests that we may be hardwired for negativity. A pessimistic bias may have been ingrained in our thinking through the long course of evolution. According to evolutionary theory, those traits and behaviors that help an organism survive and reproduce become built in biologically and are perpetuated in subsequent generations. Unhappiness, not happiness, Csikszentmihalyi proposes, is more likely to help an organism survive in a hostile environment. If we dwell on negative possibilities, we will be more alert and poised to respond to dangerous events that could happen at any time. "By dwelling on unpleasant possibilities," Csikszentmihalyi states, "we will be better prepared for the unexpected." If this hypothesis is correct, the mind has become trained across our species' long history to turn toward negative thoughts, like a compass needle points northward.[46]

The possible link between our biology and our fascination with the negative side of life raises interesting questions about religion.

One of the distinguishing characteristics of many Western religious views is their focus on the innate depravity of human beings and their need to be redeemed or saved. Could our collective religious fascination with the dark side of human nature be a hangover from our remote biological past? Do we find the image of intrinsic depravity more alluring than inner divinity because we have a built-in bias toward unhappiness? Are we destined by our DNA to be more enchanted by our weaknesses than our glory?

Not only do we focus naturally on the unhappy, negative side of life, sometimes negative events seem uncannily to seek *us* out. As Csikszentmihalyi relates,

> A few years ago a Canadian professor . . . was planning retirement with his wife. Being sensitive and rational people, they decided to retire to the safest spot on earth they could find. They spent years poring over almanacs and encyclopedias to check out rates of homicide and health statistics, inquire about the directions of prevailing winds (so as not to be downwind of probable nuclear targets), and finally found a perfect haven. They bought a house on an island early in 1982. Two months later their house was destroyed: Their choice had been the Falkland Islands.[47]

If our capacity to focus on negative possibilities and to be unhappy has given us a survival advantage in our long evolutionary history, then unhappiness is a friend and ally deserving our respect and gratitude. Were it not for our intrinsic capacity to feel sad, we might not be around to lament the fact that we are not always ecstatic. Instead of trying to pray away our melancholy, we might consider giving thanks the next time we feel down in the dumps, recalling that unhappiness has paved the way for happiness across the eons. From this perspective we might see that gloominess and joy, like light and shadow, are really in cahoots. This perspective might actually help us endure sadness and might prevent us from becoming trapped in that pathetic, negative feedback loop of becoming unhappier about not feeling happy. If we realized the value of unhappiness in life—not just in our individual life but in the history of our species—we might be more balanced, more stable, and tougher. We might need less Valium.

A CHALLENGE FOR PRAYER

If unhappiness plays a positive role in life, this does not mean that more is always better. Excessive melancholy can shade into depression, which can overwhelm and destroy. But it is also possible for us to have too little unhappiness. Life needs to push back; we need resistance if we are to build strength and stamina on the mental as well as the physical plane.

Although it is never easy, we need to look suffering and unhappiness in the eye and resist the reflex tendency to pray away every hint of discomfort. We need to reflect on the value of unhappiness and how it has enriched our lives. We should ponder those times we have suffered and allow the meaning of these experiences to unfold at its own pace. When we find ourselves using prayer to try to "be happy," we should declare time out and evaluate the potential consequences of this type of prayer. Above all, we should resist equating psychological and spiritual progress with always feeling good, and we should be careful not to blame ourselves as spiritual failures because we are not ecstatic 100 percent of the time.

THE PROBLEM OF TIGHTLY COUPLED SYSTEMS

> Good intentions pursued in the name of goodness ... are no guarantee. It is far from clear whether "good intentions plus stupidity" or "evil intentions plus intelligence" have wrought more harm in the world.[48]
>
> —Dietrich Dörner, *The Logic of Failure*

+ + +

> But evil is wrought by want of thought,
> As well as want of heart
> —Thomas Hood (1799–1845),
> *The Lady's Dream*

Why does prayer so often lead to outcomes we did not ask for and could not predict?

One of the most helpful frameworks for thinking about how prayer backfires has been developed by sociologist Charles Perrow.

Unintended consequences occur, he states, when we intervene in complex technological systems whose components are so intimately connected that changes in one part of the system results in unforeseen changes in others. In such a system, Perrow states, "operator error" is inevitable.[49]

All systems, says Perrow, are either tightly or loosely coupled. An example of a loosely coupled system is the relatively simple gasoline engine of a lawnmower. Its carburetor, spark plug, gas tank, cylinder, piston, and fuel line function as reasonably autonomous parts. If one of them malfunctions, you can replace it and restore function. Breakdown in one part does not usually destroy another component. The parts are not very complex and they are loosely coupled, to use Perrow's terminology. But when machines become extremely complex, their parts can become so tightly coupled that the breakdown of one of them results in the malfunction of others. Sometimes a chain reaction is set off, one malfunction leading to others. This cascade can be entirely unpredictable, even by experts.

In his brilliant book *Why Things Bite Back: Technology and the Revenge of Unintended Consequences,* historian Edward Tenner says,

> [M]any late-twentieth-century systems are not only tightly coupled but complex. Components have links that can affect each other unexpectedly, as when an airline coffeemaker heats concealed wires and turns a routine short circuit into a forced landing and near-crash. Complexity makes it impossible for anyone to understand how the system might act; tight coupling spreads problems once they begin.[50]

It is impossible to anticipate all the things that can go wrong in extremely complex, tightly coupled systems. This can be embarrassing to experts, as in December 1995 when a ringtail, a small desert cousin of the raccoon that is about three times the size of a domestic cat, jumped over a ten-foot-high barbed wire fence, slipped past guards, and short-circuited an outdoor transformer, briefly knocking out a reactor at the Palo Verde nuclear plant in Wintersberg, Arizona, one of the nation's largest.[51]

TIGHTLY COUPLED SYSTEMS AND PRAYER

Why should anyone interested in prayer be concerned with tightly coupled, complex systems?

A human life is one of the most tightly coupled systems in the universe, which means that there are many unpredictable ways it can malfunction. Although fail-safe mechanisms are built into both our bodies and our lives, which provide us with immense flexibility and hardiness, these backup systems are imperfect and do not always work.

When they don't, prayer is one of the perennial ways we try to fix things. Prayer becomes our ultimate backup, the device to which we resort when nothing else works. This is not a criticism; why *shouldn't* we use a device whose effectiveness has been affirmed in human experience throughout millennia? But instead of fixing things, prayer can make matters worse, because it is yet another interference in a system that *remains* tightly coupled and highly complex, meaning that we can cause *additional* problems after beginning to pray.

The issue is not *that* we pray, but *how* we pray. When something goes wrong in our life, we tend to invoke prayers involving highly specific, designated outcomes. We're certain we have the knowledge to set things right, and we waste no time telling the Absolute what to do. We do not realize we are interfering in a highly complex, tightly coupled system that, when tweaked, often responds in unpredictable ways. Giving orders with prayer invites disaster. It is rather like hitting a card table from below, hoping that the pieces of the jigsaw puzzle on top will fall into greater order than before. This may happen, but usually the result is more disorganization.

To get a feel for how human interference and prayer, even if well intended, can make matters worse, let's look at an example from the field of urban planning. In one city, described by German psychologist Dietrich Dörner in his provocative book, *The Logic of Failure*,[52] the city council approved two measures designed to limit noise and air pollution—limiting the speed limit to twenty miles per hour and installing speed bumps. The results were not what anyone expected. The lower speeds forced cars to travel in a lower gear, producing more noise and exhaust than before. Shopping trips that formerly required twenty minutes now took a half hour, resulting in increased congestion. Shopping downtown became increasingly burdensome, which meant that fewer people went there. Even though this meant a decrease in traffic, noise and air pollution didn't change because of the effects of the speed bumps and lower speed limits. To make matters worse, the downtown area began to suffer economically as shoppers discovered it was less hassle to shop in outlying malls. To the dismay of the mayor and the city council, downtown businesses began to drift to the verge of bankruptcy. Tax revenues plummeted. "The master plan turned out to be a major blunder," relates Dörner, "the consequences of which will burden this community for a long time to come."

Most of the situations we pray for are infinitely more complex than the design of downtown city areas. Our lives are exquisitely linked with the members of our family, community, nation, and world. Our tight coupling with others and our world sets the stage for a negative outcome when we employ specific interventions, as it did for the well-intended urban planners. When the results are worse than before, prayer is often blamed for "not working." But the real problem may not be prayer, but an operator error—how prayer is used and what is asked for.

Can we avoid the unintended consequences of prayer by praying not for something specific but for something general, such as abundance, prosperity, or a better life for those in need? Even with this strategy it is difficult to escape operator errors.

Dörner and his colleagues at the University of Bamberg devised a computer game in which the task was to improve the living conditions for the Moros, a seminomadic tribe who wandered with their herds from one watering hole to another in the Sahel region of West Africa, and who also raised a little millet. Life was hard for the Moro people. Infant mortality was high and life expectancy low, their economy was decimated by recurrent famines, and tsetse flies ravaged their cattle, preventing an increase in their herds. But now—in the computer game—money was available and changes could be made. The tsetse fly could be combated and deeper wells drilled. Pastureland and the millet crop could be expanded through irrigation and the application of fertilizers. New strains of millet could be introduced. A health service could be installed. In the computer-simulated Sahel, there was no limit to the prosperity that could be extended to the Moros.

One day an economist and a physicist from a large, well-known company came to visit Dörner and his colleagues. They wanted to participate in the game simulation to see if it might be of use in their employee training program. Dörner discussed with them the purpose behind the game, which was to illustrate the failings of human thought and action and the inevitability of the arrogant belief that such failings were always somebody else's fault and that "we" could do better. The economist and physicist went to work at the computer game to improve the life of the Moros. They gathered information, scrutinized the map of the Moro region, formulated strategies, rejected one program and chose another, and finally reached a decision, which was fed into the computer to calculate the effects of their choices.

When the computer finished its analysis, it revealed that the fate of the Moros was worse. The participants were shocked. The physicist began to blame the economist for the blunder. The economist denied the charge and began to blame the physicist.

What had happened? Initially their joint decisions had paid off; the Moros became better off. But across the simulated two decades of the computer game, decline had set in quite rapidly. As a result of an excellent health care system, infant mortality had plummeted. Initially there had also been a great increase in the size of the Moro herds, due to control of the tsetse fly infestations. Moreover, successful drilling of deep wells led to a large increase in available groundwater, leading to enlarged pasturelands. Shortly thereafter, however, disaster struck. The ravenous cattle tore up the grass roots, and the vegetated land area actually shrank. By the twentieth year there were hardly any cattle remaining because the pastures by then were almost totally barren. More wells were drilled to remedy the problem, but although this helped in the short term, the water supply was exhausted all the more rapidly.

"How could this have happened?" Dörner asks. Although the academicians were not specialists in the development of third world countries, they considered themselves capable of dealing with complex problems and reaching rational solutions.

Nevertheless, they made terrible decisions. They drilled wells without considering that groundwater is a resource that cannot easily be replaced. They set up an effective health-care system, reducing infant mortality and increasing lifespan, but did not institute birth-control measures. In short, they solved some immediate problems but did not think about the new problems that solving the old ones would create. They now had to feed a significantly larger population with significantly reduced resources. Everything was much more complicated than before.[53]

There were no tricks in the simulated Moro computer game. No particular expertise was required to play it, and everything that happened was really quite obvious. It is precisely because the cause-and-effect relationships are *so* obvious, Dörner believes, that the participants are so dismayed and irritated when they fail. "The outcome of the Moro planning game illustrates the difficulties even intelligent people have in dealing with complex systems," Dörner states. "The economist and the physicist were by no means worse planners than other people. Their actions were no different from those of 'experts' in real situations."

The simulated Moro situation actually came to life for Africans in the Okavango delta region in the mideighties. Scientists developed a simple plan: eradication of the tsetse fly and replacement of wild animals in the region with herds of cattle. Everything went well at first. Then hundreds of additional cattle herders migrated into the area. Overgrazing and drought followed, and the originally habitable land became a desert.[54]

As with the world, so with the human body, which, as we've mentioned, is one of the most complex systems known. Our cells and tissues are so intimately related that a change in one can create immediate changes in others. These interconnections are controlled by a marvelous balancing process called homeostasis, in which self-correcting changes are automatically brought into play when any particular function goes awry.

Our body's tight coupling can present special problems when we try deliberately to change any particular bodily function through prayer or any other strategy. For example, if we pray for an increased level of immunity and we overshoot, are we setting the stage for allergies, fatal anaphylaxis, or autoimmune diseases, which are diseases of too much immunity? I have known allergy sufferers who do not understand that their problems are due to an overactive immune response. Some of them have actually prayed for an "increase in the immune system" in the mistaken belief that they need more, not less, immune activity. This is self-inflicted negative prayer.

If we pray for greater willpower to follow a vigorous exercise program, might we be making excessive demands on our cardiovascular system? What if we pray for the discipline to follow a strict vegetarian diet in an attempt to lower our cholesterol level? Experts now know that some men who drastically lower their cholesterol level experience depression, suicidal tendencies, and a higher rate of accidents. Or, suppose we experience a kidney stone and pray for the discipline to follow a low-calcium diet. In some people such a diet actually *increases* the rate of subsequent kidney stone formation, for reasons that are not clear.[55]

We should not blame ourselves for causing operator errors with prayer; when tightly coupled systems are involved, as they always are with prayer, even the experts get tripped up. We should, however, continually evaluate how we pray. Instead of telling our body specifically how to behave, we might pray for our bodily function to "return to a normal state" or "achieve balance and harmony." Experiments with cancer cells suggest that this nondirected, nonspecific form of prayer can be highly effective (p. 173) and can avoid the "operator errors" often associated with prayer.

CONSULTING WITH THE EXPERT

In view of the potential of our prayers to make matters worse, it is easy to drift into a sense of futility and to abandon prayer altogether. But we should not give up on prayer. There *is* an expert who knows the specific interventions needed in any complex situation—the Absolute—God, Goddess, Allah, the Tao, Brahman, Universe, however named. Scientists have recently discovered new evidence of this wisdom and have been inventing new terms for it. Experts in chaos theory, for example, have stumbled onto a force called a "strange attractor," an invisible ordering principle or "tug from in front" that guides current situations toward more highly ordered, future states. Some scientists believe that this apparent goal directedness is evidence of a Universal Intelligence, or God, working behind the scenes. The details of these developments need not concern us here. The point is that an innate, invisible wisdom does seem to be present in the universe. We are not required to understand this ordering force. Our task instead may be to cooperate and not interfere with it and to facilitate it where we can—perhaps by setting our personal agendas aside and praying "*Thy* will be done" instead of "*My* will be done."

LIVING IN THE GRAY ZONE

But it is not easy to set aside our personal agendas, because often we are certain we have the answers. Throughout history, humans have often believed—mistakenly—that they possessed insider knowledge about how to solve problems. In his book *Reclaiming our Health,* John Robbins describes how this certainty is often nothing more than a mixture of intolerance, ignorance, and religious zeal.[56] After the plague killed half the population of China in the thirteenth century, it was carried by rats on board ships to Europe and North Africa, where it acquired the name of Black Death. The city of Strasbourg decided the epidemic was caused by Jews and proceeded to murder sixteen thousand of them. The folks of Basel took up the orgy and voted to "kill all the Jews, destroy their homes and ban Jews from entering the city for another two centuries." Physicians didn't help. They preached against the evils of bathing, which created ideal conditions for the proliferation of plague-carrying fleas. Between 1346 and 1350, more than a third of Europe's population perished from the pestilence. Another epidemic decimated Europe in the seventeenth century, wiping out half of London's population. Again, people responded with fear, bigotry, and venom, this time burning not only Jews but also homosexuals, witches, and *cats,* which were then considered diabolical. Assaulting the cat population gave plague-infected fleas a free ride on rats and mice and compounded an already tragic situation.

We pride ourselves in being more enlightened than our predecessors, but we are capable of equally colossal blunders. For example, we never consider the consequences of praying for perfect health for our children. If these prayers were answered—if our children literally never got sick—they would eventually die. Why? During the first few months of life, while our immune systems are developing, we depend on the antibodies contributed to us by our mother before birth. These antibodies do not last, however, and if we are to survive we must develop antibodies of our own. This process requires being exposed to viruses, bacteria, and fungi of every conceivable type. These exposures are really small illnesses, minidiseases without which we would have no immunity and no life. We *require* disease in order to develop our immune system; without illness we could not live. To pray away all disease is to pray away life.

"One thing I have noticed," says His Holiness the Dalai Lama, "is an inclination for people to think in terms of 'black' and 'white' and 'either/or,' which ignores the facts of interdependency and relativity. They have a tendency to lose sight of the gray areas which inevitably exist between two points of view."[57] If we were more mindful of the gray areas and saw the interplay between disease and health, we might *bless* the contributions of illness instead of cursing it or trying to abolish it through prayer and good intentions.

EMBRACING THE WORLD LIKE A LOVER

"It takes so much to be a full human being," writes Morris L. West.

> One has to abandon altogether the search for security and reach out to the risk of living with both arms. One has to embrace the world like a lover. One has to accept pain as a condition of existence. One has to count doubt and darkness as the cost of knowing. One needs a will stubborn in conflict but apt always to total acceptance of every consequence of living and dying.[58]

Easy to say; but the unity of good and bad, light and shadow, is infuriatingly elusive, and our wisest teachers never fail to remind us of these connections. Rumi, the great mystic of thirteenth-century Persia, remarked, "A difficult life is better for someone who truly wants to learn. Comfortable lives always end in bitterness." This is not just an Eastern point of view. George Bernard Shaw stated, "A lifetime of happiness! No man alive could bear it. It would be hell on earth." And Dostoyevsky observed, "This is my last message to you: in sorrow, seek happiness." Keats: "Do you not see how necessary a world of pains and troubles is to school an intelligence and make it a soul?" William Blake: "Without contraries is no progression." Nietzsche: "Thus the supreme evil is part of the supreme good, but this is the creative." His Holiness the Dalai Lama: "If I am to eliminate my own sufferings, I must act in the knowledge that I exist in dependent relationships with other human beings and the whole of nature."[59] The God of Judaism and Christianity sanctions this point of view. In scripture quoted earlier, we find, "I am the Lord, and there is none else. I form the light, and create darkness: I make peace, and create evil: I the Lord do all these things" (Isaiah 45:6–7, KJV).

Most of us, however, do not like our good seasoned with evil. But the effort that is required to keep them separate can be exhausting and sets the stage for the unending worry, *What if evil should win?* We need only to *imagine* what may go wrong to be filled with dread. We live our lives poised for disaster. Said Zen scholar R. H. Blyth,

> Just as the Kingdom of Heaven is among us and in us, so is the Kingdom of Hell. . . . An earthquake, a toothache, a mad dog, a telephone message—and all our house of peace falls like a pack of cards. We may go through life with not a single physical pain or loss, but the possibility of them, all the troubles that never happen, are ever-present. Their baleful eyes are fixed upon us, and when will they bite? This is our constant dread.[60]

The solution? Not to beat the world into submission through prayer—this is impossible in principle—but to honor the complexity of life and the mutual interdependence of *all* values. "Heaven means a state in which every possibility has been met, every bridge crossed," Blyth continues. "It is independent of tomorrow's newspaper or typhoid germs in the water."[61]

Our prayers for happiness and the security it entails are reflected in the hymns we sing: "Rock of ages . . ."; "How firm a foundation . . ."; "A mighty fortress is our God." But this kind of rock-solid security does not exist. We can blast away with prayer and good intentions in our attempts to clean up the world, but we shall invariably fail because there is no clear separation between good and bad. How would we know what to demolish and what to preserve?

Prior to his fall, the angel Lucifer, whose name is related to *light,* once resided in heaven. Does this invite us to "lighten up" in our attitude toward the things that so often repel us? If we did, we might avoid prayers of meddlesomeness, which, unfortunately, account for many of our prayers.

THE LEGION PRINCIPLE

One man's fortune is another man's curse.

—Folk saying

Among the foundations of physics are the so-called laws of conservation—the conservation of mass and the conservation of energy. These principles tell us that energy is never consumed but only changes form and that the total energy in a physical system cannot be increased or diminished. Similarly, matter can neither be created nor destroyed during any physical or chemical change.

I have often wondered whether there is a conservation law of evil, whereby it, like energy and matter, is neither created or destroyed but merely displaced or changed in form. This consideration may seem frivolous, but it makes a major difference in the consequences of our prayers.

Why suggest that evil may be conserved? One of the unintended consequences of prayer is that the problem that is solved does not disappear but becomes someone else's. An incident in the life of Jesus illustrates the point, recorded in the Gospel of Mark, chapter 5. When Jesus and his disciples entered the country of the Gadarenes, he was met by a man named Legion, whose name was derived from the multitude of demons who possessed him. Legion was an outcast who was so wild he could not be bound with chains. He lived in the graveyards and mountains and often cut himself with stones. When he saw Jesus come from across the sea and alight on his shore, he ran to him and worshiped him, begging him not to torment him. Jesus recognized he was possessed and replied, "Come out of the man, thou unclean spirit" (Mark 5:8, KJV). The devils did as told; but what was to become of them? They began to bargain with Jesus, pleading to be cast into a herd of about two thousand swine feeding nearby. Jesus obliged them. "And the unclean spirits went out, and entered into the swine: and the herd ran violently down a steep place into the sea . . . and were choked in the sea." When word spread to the city, the locals came to see what had happened. They saw Legion, calm as could be, "clothed, and in his right mind: and they were afraid"— and were upset with Jesus as well. On seeing what had happened to their swine herd, "they began to pray him to depart out of their coasts."

This event illustrates what we might call the Legion Principle— the displacement of one person's problem onto another. The Legion Principle suggests that evil is conserved like energy and matter; it can never be created or destroyed, only displaced, moved about, and given another form.

There are many examples in which problems are displaced but not eradicated by prayer. When a vast army of grasshoppers invaded the crops of the Mormons in the Great Salt Lake Valley of Utah in June 1848, church leaders called for prayer. Seagulls arrived in flocks and ate the grasshoppers, and the crops were saved.[62] From the Mormon standpoint, disaster had been averted through God's goodwill, and the effects of prayer were positive. But what was once a problem for the Mormons became a dilemma for the grasshoppers—misfortune shifted, not erased.

In World War II, the famous pilot Eddie Rickenbacker made a forced landing in the Pacific with seven companions. They were adrift in a life raft for twenty-four days until rescued by a navy plane. On the verge of perishing for lack of water and food, they prayed for help. Out of nowhere a bird landed on Rickenbacker, who captured and killed it, gaining life-saving nourishment for the men until they were rescued. From the human standpoint, the prayer was positive. But what if you were the bird, onto which the problem was displaced?[63]

Less than two weeks after nationwide prayers were offered for rain in Saudi Arabia in 1996, the desert kingdom was lashed with heavy rains and two people perished when their car was washed away. Most people may have been grateful for the rain, but what about those who perished?[64]

Is the Legion Principle inevitable? Are misfortunes always conserved? Must there always be a receptacle available to serve the function of the swine herd, to take on the things we "pray away"? When prayers for erasing poverty or illness are answered, do the poverty and illness settle onto somebody else, like the demons deserting Legion for the swine?

Christian theology implies that evil must go *somewhere*. Although the most common receptacle may be human hearts, the ultimate repository is hell itself. Hell in Christian theology seems to confirm the Legion Principle. It is the place where the devil will someday be confined forever, with no possibility of escape, as we are told in the book of Revelation. This suggests that evil is never really destroyed, merely relocated.

The story of Legion seems to contain an element of unfairness. What about the swine? Did they deserve the evil spirits that drove them to mass suicide? The Legion Principle suggests that what is good for one person may be bad for another. Is prayer a blessing or curse? It often depends on which end of the stick you're holding.

Our ancestors felt intuitively that evil needs a recipient. This was the origin of the scapegoat—an animal or a person onto whom the sins of the community were displaced. Christianity rests on the Legion Principle: human sins did not evaporate as a result of God's love; Jesus bore them on behalf of humankind.

Displacing our problems can be a perfect solution if done with skill; the swine don't *have* to commit suicide. An example took place in the Findhorn community in Scotland years ago. When the kitchen became overrun with cockroaches, the staff did not resort to insecticides, prayers, or curses. They made a deal with the cockroaches. They created a habitat for them that was better than the kitchen—a veritable cockroach heaven far removed from the house, made of food scraps and containers in which to breed. Then they invited them to migrate to their new home and threatened them with stronger measures if they did not. Almost overnight the cockroaches bailed out— no curse, no scapegoat, nobody hurt.

PART 2

NEGATIVE PRAYER IN EVERYDAY LIFE

If a way to the better there be, it lies in taking a full look at the worst.

—Thomas Hood (1799–1845)

MEDICAL HEXING

> In my practice, when I'm working with the patient, I
> am very careful of what I say, because any negative
> words could hurt the patient. So, with Western medi-
> cine, a doctor could be treating a patient, and he can
> mention death, and that is sharper than any needle.
> Therefore, with the tongue that we have, we have to
> be very careful of what we say at the time and point
> we're treating the patient.
>
> —*Navajo Medicine Man*

"IS IT THAT BAD?"

I WAS ONCE SUMMONED to the intensive care unit to see one of my
patients who was recuperating from multiple fractures sustained in a
near-fatal auto accident. The man had been doing well, but when I
arrived he was in a panic. His anxiety was triggered when a nurse
asked him if he believed in prayer. "Why are you asking?" he
demanded. "Do I *need* prayer? Are things that bad? What's going on
that I haven't been told about?" Although the nurse did her best to
console him, she was unsuccessful. He was convinced she was con-
cealing the seriousness of his situation, and he became severely agitated. I asked the nurse to accompany me once again to his bedside.
An hour later, with further explanations from both of us, he let go of
his fear, and the issue of prayer was not brought up again.

A physician related to me a similar encounter with a twenty-four-
year-old patient of his that took him off guard. The young man was
undergoing an evaluation for chronic abdominal pain. He was seriously
worried he had cancer because his family was riddled with the problem.
When all the tests were completed, the doctor was summarizing the
findings and making final recommendations in his office. When the
consultation concluded, the patient rose to leave. He was relieved the

doctor had found nothing wrong and that a simple change in his diet and attention to the stress in his life were all that was called for. Then the physician commented, "Good luck. I'll be praying for you." The young man stopped dead in his tracks, became expressionless, and appeared terrified. Finally he responded, "Doctor, is it that bad? Is there something you haven't told me?" Maybe cancer was there after all, lurking and smoldering, hiding from all the scans, X rays, and blood tests, he thought. Wasn't prayer something you used when the chips were down and all else had failed? The physician realized he had upset the man by implying that, in spite of the normal evaluation, he had a condition serious enough to merit prayer. The doctor spent an additional half hour assuring his patient that he was indeed healthy and that his prayers were for his general well-being and not for any sort of hidden ill-ness. "This experience taught me that my patients perceive prayer differently," he wrote. "I resolved to be more sensitive in mentioning prayer."[1]

This man's experience shows that the *meaning* of prayer to a patient is crucial. If prayer represents or symbolizes something negative, it is likely to have toxic effects.

At a conference on the role of spirituality in medicine, one of my fellow speakers was battling the flu. She was an internationally known scholar and held a high appointment at a prestigious medical school. She was feverish, hoarse, and looked altogether miserable. "What a marvelous place to be sick," I said, hoping to cheer her up. "You're surrounded by healers. Want me to recruit some of them to pray for you to get well before your talk tomorrow?" The woman turned to me with a horrified, ashen look. "Oh, God, no!" she exclaimed. "Don't do that! I'd rather suffer!" Which she did.

A recent survey showed that 75 percent of hospitalized patients believe that their physician should be concerned about their spiritual welfare, and 50 percent believe their doctors should pray not just *for* them but *with* them.[2] Against this background of enthusiasm, it is easy to forget that not everyone responds warmly to prayer. Prayer has the potential to harm, terrify, and offend. It should be extended not just with compassion but with delicacy as well.

Let's look further at curses and "medical hexes" and how they can be a matter of life and death. Even though some of the events that follow may not appear to be specifically related to prayer, it is impossible to understand them outside of the religious context from which they originate. Curses almost always are tinged with religious beliefs and assumptions about the nature of evil, the role of the devil, and the relationship of sin and punishment. Because these issues are invariably connected with religion, they are inextricably interwoven with prayer.

Medicine and curses often intersect, even in our enlightened age. For example, sixteen patients who believed themselves to be possessed were admitted to a psychiatric hospital in England from 1973 to 1977.[3] Or consider Thomas Passmore of Norfolk, Virginia, who recently cut off his hand because he thought it was possessed by the devil, then refused to let surgeons at Sentara Norfolk General Hospital reattach it. (His next step was to sue them for three million dollars, saying they should have known he was crazy.)[4] Criminal activities are also occasionally attributed to evil spirits, and when defendants claim that "the devil made me do it," medicine almost always becomes involved. In a 1994 case reported in the *British Journal of Psychology*, an Indian man who believed he was possessed by a ghost said the invisible entity impelled him to commit various thefts that led to his arrest. Two efforts at exorcism failed before he was successfully treated with an antipsychotic medication.[5] Medicine and the law also come together when people practice medicine without a license. For example, in December 1962 a woman was arrested in a suburb of San Francisco and accused of charging seventy dollars to cure stomach pains by rolling an egg back and forth on the patient's stomach, then smashing it to the floor. The egg, an object widely used in magical cures, was supposed to absorb evil influences from the sufferer.[6]

HEX DEATH AT BALTIMORE CITY HOSPITAL

Physicians at Baltimore City Hospital ran headlong into the power of a curse on July 29, 1966, when a twenty-two-year-old African American woman was admitted because of shortness of breath and episodes of chest pain and loss of consciousness. These symptoms had begun a month earlier. After she had been hospitalized for fourteen days, she revealed to her doctors that she had only three days remaining to solve a serious problem.

She revealed that she had been born on Friday the thirteenth in the Okefenokee Swamp and was delivered by a midwife who delivered three children that day. The midwife told the mothers of all three children that they were hexed. She proclaimed that the first would die before her sixteenth birthday, the second before her twenty-first birthday, and the third (the patient) before her twenty-third birthday.

The patient told her physicians that the first girl was killed in an auto accident the day before her sixteenth birthday. The second girl was fearful of the hex, and on her twenty-first birthday called a friend and insisted on going out to celebrate the end of the hex. She walked into a bar, and a stray bullet killed her.

The hospitalized patient was certain that she, like the other two girls, was doomed. She was terrified. On August 12 she died—one day before her twenty-third birthday.

The Johns Hopkins pathologists performed an autopsy. Although they found that a medical problem existed, a condition called primary pulmonary hypertension, they concluded that this was not severe enough to explain the woman's death, particularly its timing. Dr. Freisinger, assistant professor of medicine at Johns Hopkins Medical School, made these revealing statements in his discussion of this case:

> I am certain the he [the pathologist] will not be able to rule out the hex as the real cause of her death. It seems very clear that she was hexed at the time of her birth and she died precisely at the time predicted. . . . It is not a part of our society and hence we know little about it; I suspect many of us would prefer to think it did not exist. Special circumstances and beliefs in a community must exist before an individual can die by hex, but once the proper background and individual conditioning exist, there is no reason why [it] . . . cannot occur and lead to death, at the proper time.[7]

"LIKE A DEATH SENTENCE": THE POWER OF WORDS AMONG THE NAVAJO

In the United States, when a patient undergoes a medical test or surgical procedure, physicians are compelled by law and ethics to discuss the hazards that could occur. Many Navajo, however, believe that a frank discussion of the possible side effects of medical interventions is a curse.

A Navajo woman who is a nurse described what happened when a cardiac surgeon explained to her father the risks of coronary artery bypass surgery.[8]

The surgeon told him that he may not wake up, that this is the risk of every surgery. For the surgeon it was very routine, but the way that my Dad received it, it was almost like a death sentence, and he never consented to the surgery.

A Navajo woman who was pregnant was urged by public health nurses to attend a prenatal clinic, but she resisted doing so because of the way the clinic personnel emphasized the potential complications of pregnancy. She said,

I've always thought in a positive way, ever since I was young. And even when the doctors talked to me like that, I always thought way in the back of my mind: I'm not going to have a breech baby. I'm going to have a healthy baby and a real fast delivery with no complications, and that's what has happened.

These responses reflect the Navajo belief that it is important to think and speak in a positive way. This attitude is encompassed by the Navajo phrases *hózhoojí nitsíhakees* and *hózhoojí saad*. These words translate literally as "think in the Beauty Way" and "talk in the Beauty Way." In traditional Navajo culture, thought and language have the power to shape reality and control events. As a result, discussing the potential complications of surgery and pregnancy may actually cause these events to come to pass. Anthropologist Gary Witherspoon says, "In the Navajo view of the world, language is not a mirror of reality, reality is a mirror of language."[9]

Should physicians discuss potential side effects of medications and complications of surgical procedures with their patients? Not if you're a traditional Navajo medicine man. In the Navajo tradition, great value is placed on positive thinking rather than on disclosure. As a traditional Navajo diagnostician said,

In order to think positive there are plants up in the mountains that can help you. Also there are prayers that can be done. You think in these good ways, and that will make you feel better and whatever has stricken you in the deadly manner will kind of fall apart with all these good things that you put in place of it. . . . The doctor may say, "You're not going to live," but I say, "*Hózhoojí nitsihakees*"; that means "think in the Beauty Way."

A related Navajo ideal is "Don't talk that way!"—"*Doo ájíniidah*." But if one doesn't talk about the things that could go wrong, how can one plan ahead? If one does not contemplate death, how can one prepare a living will, for example, and give advance directives to the health care team about the use of cardiopulmonary resuscitation (CPR) and artificial life support? For traditional Navajos, talking about such things in advance may set them in motion—the equivalent of a hex or curse. When asked about advance care planning, a seventy-six-year-old man with chronic pain said,

That's *doo ájíniidah*, you don't say those things. And you don't try to bestow that upon yourself, the reason being that there are prayers for every part of life that you can put your trust on. The object is to live as long as possible here on earth. Why try to shorten it by bestowing things upon yourself?

I am not suggesting that we become Navajos in the way we use language in medicine or that we give up frank discussions of the potential hazards of medical interventions. But we can become more respectful of language and thought, as the Navajos have learned to be, and we can pay closer attention to how our own words, including our prayers, sometimes cause harm.

FOLK MEDICINE AND PRAYER

"The physician is unable to help the patient afflicted by evil because you cannot fight the Devil with drugs," observes Dr. Loudell F. Snow, of Michigan State University's Department of Community Medicine and an authority on folk medicine. She described a diabetic woman in Grand Rapids, Michigan, who consistently refused to inject herself with insulin because she believed her illness was "put on" her by the devil because of the sins of her youth. Eighteen months following her diagnosis, she was still being visited daily by a visiting nurse who performed the injection for her. Perhaps she believed, Snow suggests, that the insulin would do no good because of her previous wrongdoing. As a Baptist minister Snow interviewed admonished his congregation, "Medicine cannot reach the mind nor a heart diseased by sin."[10]

Snow found that when people believe they deserve their sickness because of their sins, they are likely to believe the disease will be chronic, which is just what they deserve. This explains why, in their view, "The more you go to the doctor, the sicker you get."[11] When the problem does not yield to treatment, their suspicions are confirmed: the divine curse is justified, and they deserve to suffer.

The belief in witchcraft, like the belief in the devil, is exceedingly widespread and is not confined to people of low socioeconomic status, as is often thought. A freshman coed told Snow, "I'm a little skeptical of letting just anybody use my comb or borrow too many of my personal possessions." Her fears reflected the notion that personal objects—a lock of hair, nail clippings, worn clothing, a used menstrual pad—can be used to inflict "contagious" magic. This is the premise that once things are connected physically to a person, they are always in some sense connected with him or her, and that what is done to the part is done to the whole.[12]

ANIMAL INTRUSIONS

In addition to personal items, animals can also be used as carriers of evil by being introduced into the body. "Animal intrusion" has long been considered a cause of illness in European and American folklore. This is often accidental, such as the ingestion of fresh water that might contain a "spring lizard," river water containing eggs that are fortuitously swallowed while swimming, a snake or lizard crawling into the mouth while one sleeps in the grass, and so on. In witchcraft, however, the animal intrusion is more sinister and magical: the animal is often dried, pulverized, and sprinkled on food. When eaten by the victim, it is reconstituted whole in the body. A sorcerer skilled in animal intrusion can turn the body into a veritable herpetarium. Lizards, snakes, spiders, toads, "satanic worms," and the victim's hair turning into snakes, just like Medusa's in Greek mythology, have all been reported.

We smile sanctimoniously at folk beliefs about being invaded by animals and attribute such beliefs to people less enlightened than ourselves. Yet, as with many folk ideas, there is often a grain of truth behind them. Doctors, for example, know that animal intrusion is real. We occasionally see tapeworms, several feet long, expelled from the bowel. We treat hookworms and pinworms, which represent animal intrusions. Some worms cause blindness; some burrow under the skin and can be seen to creep across the body. In the hidden recesses of our minds, these images tantalize us. Our fascination with them has permitted Hollywood to make millions by churning out a series of blockbusters such as the *Alien* series, whose main theme is animal intrusion.

I have often admired the resourcefulness of physicians on the American frontier in dealing with curses and spells. Although their tools were meager, their ingenuity often rose to monumental heights. In frontier Arkansas, for example, a woman who was a patient of young Dr. Charles Martin became convinced she was a victim of the evil eye, which resulted from a dispute with a neighbor. She knew she had a frog in her stomach as a result of the neighbor's curse and that she would die. All of Dr. Martin's logical arguments could not dissuade her, and the woman appeared to be nearing death. When he next visited her, Martin carried a toad in his pocket. First he administered a dose of ipecac, and when she began to vomit he surreptitiously transferred the toad from his pocket to the jar containing her stomach contents. When she saw the toad she knew she was healed. She was up in no time, fully recovered, singing the doctor's praises.[13]

A similar case took place about a century later, when Dr. Drayton Daugherty in 1938 admitted a sixty-year-old black man to a Tennessee hospital. The man had been sick for many weeks, had lost an immense amount of weight, and was emaciated and near death. Cancer or a widespread infection such as tuberculosis was considered the likeliest diagnosis. He refused to eat, and although a feeding tube was inserted he continued to deteriorate. He insisted he was going to die. He eventually became almost stuporous, barely able to talk, coming in and out of consciousness. At this stage of his illness his wife, extremely anxious and nervous, asked to speak privately with Dr. Daugherty. She swore the doctor to secrecy, a request he honored until after her death many years later.

She revealed that about four months prior to her husband's hospitalization, he had had an argument with a local voodoo priest, several of whom were believed to operate in the area. The priest summoned the man to a cemetery one night. An argument ensued, and the priest waved a bottle of foul-smelling liquid in the man's face and announced that he had "voodooed" him, that he was going to die, and that no one—not even medical doctors—could save him. The man felt doomed. He staggered home that evening and did not eat again. He and his wife had not revealed the story because the priest vowed to voodoo all their children and other people as well in order to keep them silent. Because the man was dying, which indicated the obvious power of the voodoo priest, they had not revealed any of this information to the physician. Now desperate, the wife had defied the priest and told Dr. Daugherty the tale.

Daugherty knew he must do something or the man would die. The next morning he summoned ten of his kin to the man's bedside. They were trembling with fear, not wishing to be associated any longer with the doomed man. In his most authoritative voice, Dr. Daugherty announced to everyone that he knew exactly what was wrong. He told them that the night before he had had a harrowing experience at the local cemetery with the voodoo priest, whom he had lured there under false pretenses. Daugherty told him he had uncovered the priest's curse of the dying man. The priest laughed at him, Daugherty stated, but he pinned him against a tree and choked him nearly to death in order to force him to reveal exactly how he had done it. The family, gathered at the bedside, was speechless. Then Daugherty announced to the dying patient, "That voodoo priest made you breathe in some lizard eggs and they climbed down into your stomach and hatched out some small lizards. All but one of them died leaving one large one which is eating up all your food and the lining of your body. I will now get that lizard out of your system and cure you of this horrible curse." He summoned the nurse who, prearranged, brought out a large syringe filled with apomorphine, a medication that causes profound nausea and vomiting. With great ceremony, Daugherty raised it in the air for all to see, inspected it slowly, and squirted a bit of the clear liquid into the air. By now the patient was sitting up, wide eyed, withdrawing from the shot he knew was to come. Daugherty injected half the dose into the man's frail arm, wheeled about, and stalked silently from the room.

Within minutes the man was vomiting violently. When the retching subsided, Daugherty entered the room once again. Standing by the metal basin containing the emesis, he secretively pulled from his black bag a live green lizard. At the height of the next wave of vomiting, he artfully slid the lizard into the basin. Then, in a loud voice, he cried, "Look what has come out of you! You are now cured. The voodoo curse is lifted."

Several relatives fell to the floor and began to moan. The stunned patient saw the lizard, then jumped back to the head of the bed, wide eyed and open mouthed. Saying nothing, he drifted off into a deep sleep within a minute or two. His pulse diminished, and his breathing deepened and slowed. He remained asleep until the following morning. Waking, he was ravenous and gulped large quantities of milk, bread, meat, and eggs before the medical personnel stopped him for fear he was overdoing it.

The spell was broken. Within a week he was home, and soon regained his weight and vitality. Ten years later he died of a heart attack. He had no further encounters with the voodoo priest, nor did any members of his family.[14]

This case was reported in 1992 by Dr. Clifton K. Meador of the Department of Medicine at Vanderbilt Medical School. He had known about the case for thirty years and had often reflected on it. He could make no sense of it until he read a classic paper entitled "'Voodoo' Death" by the eminent physiologist Walter Cannon, the Harvard researcher who elucidated the "fight-or-flight" mechanism.[15] Reading this landmark paper, Meador realized that all three essential elements that Cannon proposed for "hex death" to occur were present in the "lizard" case:

1. The victim, family members, and all acquaintances must accept the ability and power of the hexer to induce death. This belief must be commonly held with no exceptions.
2. All previously known victims of the hexing must have died, unless the hex had been removed by the same, or another, witch doctor.
3. Every person known to the victim, including family and friends, must behave toward him as if he will die. This involves leaving him alone and isolated, even by his closest relatives.

If all these elements exist, Cannon concludes, death usually occurs within a few days.

Meador published this strange case along with another, of an elderly white man who was dying from what he and his surgeon believed was esophageal cancer. Meador, an internist, had been asked to consult on the case. On entering the man's room, he saw a lump under a mound of covers. Pulling them back, Meador saw a small, unshaven man who looked nearly dead. The nurses revealed that he had been in this condition since admission. The man's evaluation revealed modestly elevated blood sugar (he had diabetes), but this did not account for his near-terminal state. His liver enzymes were also moderately high, which suggested that the cancer had spread from the esophagus to the liver. After ten minutes, the sheets stirred and the man peered cautiously out of the covers. The man saw Meador and said weakly, "Go away. Leave me alone." Meador complied.

The man's wife revealed a bizarre story. They had married a few months earlier. The man's problems began with severe difficulty swallowing. He was found on various tests to have an extensive carcinoma of the esophagus, and he underwent a major surgical procedure in which much of the esophagus and the stomach was removed. A pouch of colon was used to recreate a stomach. He was told he had only several months to live. The wife had married him thereafter, in full knowledge of his condition and what lay ahead. Her only request was that Meador make him comfortable. She said everyone knew he was dying, including the surgeon, who had told them his liver scan showed extensive spread of the cancer. Meador reviewed the tissue report and the surgical report from the original surgeon and concurred: the cancer had spread to the liver; the man's situation was hopeless.

In spite of this, the medical team rallied around the man. The nurses and physical therapists got the patient out of bed several times a day and made him walk, whether he wanted to or not. The more they attended him, the madder he got. He denounced everyone for harassing him. Yet he began to appear transformed—gaining a few pounds and developing a stronger voice and healthier demeanor. Meador used this opportunity to deepen his communication with him.

The man revealed that his first wife had been his soul mate. They had never been able to have children; they had worked hard all their lives to save and plan for retirement. After many years of struggle they achieved their goal and bought a retirement home. They loved water and boating and bought a house near an artificially created lake. One night the nearby earthen dam burst. The wall of water crushed their house; everything, including his wife, was swept away. Her body was never found. "Everything I ever loved or wanted in my whole life vanished," he lamented. "Gone forever. I never saw my wife again. Everything I worked for, . . . saved for, . . . went down the river that night. . . . My heart and soul were lost in the flood. . . ." He sobbed in sorrow for several minutes. Within six months following this terrible event, he developed his first symptoms of cancer of the esophagus and underwent his extensive operation about a year later.

"What do you want me to do?" Meador asked.

"I'd like to live through Christmas, so I can be with my wife and her family," he replied. "They've been good to me. I only met them a few months ago. Just help me make it through Christmas. That's all I want."

Meador reported, "He knew he was going to die; his wife knew it; his current surgeon knew it, as did the original surgeon. I also was certain that he had widespread cancer and that in a very short time he would die."

The man made immense progress, however, which Meador attributed to his superb nursing care and physical therapy. He left the hospital a changed man in October. Meador saw him frequently and believed he was doing quite well—until January, when he returned to the hospital just after New Year's, appearing near death. He had told his wife he was ready to die and had come to the hospital to do it. Meador was astounded at his rapid deterioration. He was dead within twenty-four hours.

Nothing about the man's final evaluation explained his death. Autopsy revealed a small patch of pneumonia, insufficient to cause death. The only cancer was a small nodule, less than an inch in diameter, in the liver, which was causing no apparent problem. The previously abnormal liver scan had been a false-positive result. No further cancer could be found around the area of the esophagus. Meador said, "I do not know the pathologic cause of his death. What is certain is that he died thinking he was dying of cancer, a belief shared by his wife, her family, his surgeons, and me, his internist."

Meador reasoned that neither of these patients—the man who had been hexed by the voodoo priest, and the man with the esophageal cancer—had sufficient organic disease to account for his moribund state. The major difference was that the hexed victim had been fortunate enough to have a physician, Dr. Daugherty, who was imaginative enough to break the spell of belief by employing a live, green lizard. Believing he was cured, the patient got well. "The second patient," Meador states, "believed that he was consumed with widespread cancer. Every living person he knew believed that, and unlike the first patient, he did not have a doctor who believed he could get well or who could pull the right kind of lizard out of a black bag."

Meador concludes,

> Are we so different from our ancient and primitive witch doctor colleagues? Is death from hexing . . . basic to many forms of human communication? . . . Hex death would represent a considerable anomaly in our dominant view of humans and disease. We tend to reject such anomalies as unfit for scientific inquiry, relegate them to the superstitions of ignorant and primitive people, and thereby avoid having to deal with them.
>
> If indeed we can cause something as drastic as death by what we say or how we act, then what lesser patterns of behavior do we induce in our patients? How effectively do we persuade patients to get well or sick? Is this phenomenon operating whenever we talk to our patients? Is the ubiquitous placebo effect not just a strange trait of the patient, but inducible by how the physician speaks and acts? Are some of us negative placebo inducers and some positive?

DEHEXING IN A MODERN HOSPITAL

It is sometimes possible to reverse curses, even in the context of a modern hospital. The main challenge is discovering they exist.

During my internship, my first year as a physician after completing medical school, I was caring for an elderly man who had been admitted to the hospital for massive weight loss. He was obviously dying. Suspecting cancer, I performed a great many tests, all of which proved normal.

Unable to pinpoint the problem, I discussed the dilemma with Dr. William Hensley, a fellow intern whose clinical judgment I admired immensely. Bill had grown up in South Texas in the Rio Grande

Valley bordering Mexico, where hexing and spells were a part of the culture. Acting on some sixth sense, within a few moments Bill discovered the cause of the old man's impending death. The patient revealed to him that he had recently visited a local fortune teller, who used his nail clippings to divine his future. When he refused to pay, the diviner then used the clippings to cast a spell on him in revenge and let it be known that she had done so. The victim, knowing he had been hexed and certain he would die, began to cooperate with the curse. He became melancholic, resigned himself to his fate, stopped eating, and soon resembled a skeleton.

Bill, relying on his past experiences with spells and hexes, suggested that we set modern medicine aside in favor of reversing the curse. We concocted an elaborate ritual in an attempt to save the man's life. Late one night, when the moon was full and the hospital wards were deserted, we rolled the victim in a wheelchair into a darkened examination room. Dressed in white coats in the near darkness, we stood silently for a long while, letting the tension build. Then Bill explained to the man what we were about to do, assuring him that our magic was more powerful than that of the fortune teller who had cursed him. He then clipped a lock of the man's hair and stated that the hex would be reversed as he burned the hair in the small eerie flame we had made in an ash tray. He added, to my immense relief, that if the victim told anyone we had done this, the curse would return stronger than before. The man was terrified but visibly impressed. When the zany ritual was finished we whisked him, trembling and speechless, to his bed. (There was at least one element of prayer in our ritual—my own, that we would not be discovered.)

The dehexing worked like a charm. The old man awoke the next morning feeling energetic, hungry, and happy, a victim no longer. He was eventually discharged from the hospital in perfect health.[16]

This case illustrated the ancient practice of using body parts to perpetrate curses—in this instance, nail clippings. The most famous magician of the modern era, Aleister Crowley, was hated by certain rival magicians and had much to fear. He was always careful that no one would get hold of his hair, nail clippings, or bodily excreta. As recently as 1929, in a famous case in York, Pennsylvania, John H. Blymyer was sentenced to life imprisonment for the murder of Nelson Rehmyer, who was notorious in the area as a black magician. Blymyer killed Rehmyer in a struggle to obtain a lock of his hair, which was to be used in a ritual against him.[17]

THE COMMON BELIEFS THAT UNITE HEXING, RELIGION, AND PRAYER

In her survey of folk medical systems in the United States, Dr. Loudell F. Snow found three core beliefs that set the stage for being hexed:

1. the world is a hostile and dangerous place;
2. the individual is liable to attack from external sources;
3. the individual is helpless and has no internal resources to combat such attack but must depend on outside aid.

Snow found that these beliefs were widespread among groups as diverse as African Americans, the Pennsylvania Dutch, the Hutterites, the Amish, Appalachian whites, the Cajuns of Louisiana, Kansas farmers, Puerto Ricans in New York and the Midwest, and Mexican Americans. These beliefs were found from rural Florida through the Ozarks and from California to the Upper Peninsula of Michigan.[18]

If we look closely at these three beliefs, we can see why curses, hexes, and spells are inextricably linked with religions and, therefore, with prayer.

The first core belief—that the world is hostile and dangerous— lies at the heart of many branches of Christianity. According to orthodox Christian doctrine, all of humanity is inherently blighted because of original sin and the fall, which pose the greatest danger of all. The second core belief—that we are liable to outside attack—is manifested in Christianity by the devil, in the constant lure of sin, and by the "principalities and powers" that lurk everywhere. The third core belief—that we are utterly helpless and dependent on outside aid—is expressed in the idea that we must be redeemed by Christ to escape the problems posed by the core beliefs one and two.

We can see, then, that hexing shares a common ontology with major features of the Christian faith. It is no wonder that hexing and religions keep such close company in our society and that both often involve prayer.

Sometimes these connections are so stark that it is impossible to fail to recognize them. One of the most dramatic examples, as we've seen, was the black mass. This ritual, which was practiced by priests for centuries, involved cursing someone by saying mass over a wax image of the victim, placed on the altar, while praying to the devil.

MEDICAL HEXING, MODERN STYLE

"They said there was nothing more they could do for me."

"They told me it would only get worse."

"They told me I would just have to live with it."

"They said I'd be dead in six months."

These are some of the most common complaints from patients reported by Andrew Weil, M.D., in his best-selling book *Spontaneous Healing*.[19] Dr. Weil practices natural and preventive medicine in Tucson and is one of the leading architects of curriculum design in American medical schools. He is associate director of the Division of Social Perspectives in Medicine and director of the Program in Integrative Medicine at the University of Arizona in Tucson. In *Spontaneous Healing* Weil writes candidly about how physicians often convey immense pessimism about the human potential for healing and how, in its extreme form, this practice constitutes a kind of medical hexing. Weil, who spent much time in shamanistic cultures as an ethnopharmacologist with the Harvard Botanical Museum, sees strong parallels between the practices of physicians and the curses employed by shamans and witch doctors. In the latter instance, the victim of the curse, after learning of it, withdraws from society, friends, and family, stops eating, weakens, and sometimes dies. "Although it is easy to identify this hexing phenomenon in exotic cultures," he states, "we rarely perceive that something very similar goes on every day in our own culture, in hospitals, clinics, and doctors' offices."

There are many theories about how hex death takes place. A leading idea is that the parasympathetic branch of the autonomic nervous system becomes overactive, causing an exaggerated slowing of the heartbeat and a fall in blood pressure, which may have happened in an apparent medical hex that took place at Harvard Medical School.

It involved Dr. S. A. Levine, a well-known cardiologist noted for his devotion and compassion toward patients. One day Mrs. S., a middle-aged librarian, came for a routine visit to the cardiac clinic, where she had been followed for years. She had a stenosis or narrowing of the tricuspid valve on the right side of the heart, but was capable of working and doing household chores. After examining her, Dr. Levine, in a hurry, turned to the entourage of trainees and said, "This woman has TS" and abruptly left. Mrs. S.'s demeanor changed immediately, she became pale and sweaty, and her lungs filled with fluid. The physician in charge asked why she was so upset. She replied that Dr. Levine had said she had TS, which she said meant "terminal situation." Although the doctor assured her TS meant "triscuspid stenosis," she was not reassured and her condition deteriorated. She lost consciousness, unable to breathe. Attempts to reach Dr. Levine to see if his presence or words might make a difference were unsuccessful. In spite of heroic measures, she died later that day from intractable heart failure.[20]

Medical hexing can be so outrageous it is almost funny. Weil relates an encounter with a patient who traveled all the way from Helsinki to Tucson to see him. "You wouldn't believe what those doctors did to me in Finland," she said.

> The head neurologist took me into his office and told me I had multiple sclerosis. He let that sink in; then he went out of the room and returned with a wheelchair. This he told me to sit in. I said, "Why should I sit in your wheelchair?" He said I was to buy a wheelchair and sit in it for an hour a day to "practice" for when I would be totally disabled. Can you imagine?[21]

Bernard Lown, the famous Harvard cardiologist, like Weil has written wisely about "words that maim" in his inspiring book, *The Lost Art of Healing*. Over the years he jotted down several hundred frightening remarks that patients recalled from their interactions with physicians. The following are the most common:

"You are living on borrowed time."

"You are going downhill fast."

"The next heartbeat may be your last."

"You can have a heart attack or worse any minute."

"The *Malach amoveth* (angel of death) is shadowing you."

Lown accumulated numerous variations of "You have a time bomb in your chest" and "You are a walking time bomb." For example, a cardiology consultant once pointed to an obstruction in a coronary artery on an angiogram and said to the patient's wife, "This narrowed blood vessel is a widow maker." Another patient remembered his doctor exclaiming, "I'm frightened just thinking about your anatomy." When another patient resisted having coronary artery bypass surgery, his physician said, "I can't guarantee that the next heart attack won't be your last." Another physician commented, "Surgery should be done immediately, preferably yesterday."[22]

SERIAL HEXING

If we've once had chicken pox, we won't get it again; not so with hexes. Having been medically cursed once does little to immunize us against the next episode, as the following case shows.

In 1957 Dr. Bruno Klopfer was treating a man with advanced lymphoma, a cancer of the lymph glands. The man had large tumors throughout the body and fluid in the chest, and his medical condition was considered terminal. All medical treatment had been stopped except oxygen to help him breathe. Klopfer expected him to die within two weeks. However, an experimental drug, Krebiozen, was injected in a last-ditch effort. Although it was later found to be an ineffective treatment for cancer, the results in this instance were amazing. Klopfer states:

> What a surprise was in store for me! I had left him febrile, gasping for air, completely bedridden. Now, here he was, walking around the ward, chatting happily with the nurses, and spreading his message of good cheer to anyone who would listen. . . . The tumor masses had melted like snow balls on a hot stove, and in only these few days they were half their original size! This is, of course, far more rapid regression than the most radiosensitive tumor could display under heavy x-ray given every day. . . . And he had no other treatment outside of the single useless "shot."[23]

After ten days the patient was practically disease free. He began again to fly his private plane without difficulty. His improvement continued for two months, until reports began to crop up denouncing

Krebiozen as worthless. After reading them, the man appeared as if he had been cursed. His attitude and medical condition deteriorated to their original terminal state.

Klopfer's actions at this point resembled those of a shaman intent on reversing the spell. He urged his patient to ignore the negative news reports about Krebiozen and informed him that "a new super-refined, double-strength product" was now available. He proceeded to give him an injection of sterile water. The dehexing worked. This time the man's response was even more dramatic than initially. Again he resumed his activities and was free of symptoms for two more months. But he was hexed again, this time by a report by the American Medical Association that "nationwide tests show Krebiozen to be a worthless drug in treatment of cancer." He was admitted again to the hospital a few days after the report was released. Two days later he died. Klopfer's appraisal: "To use a symbolic analogy, while he was floating along on the surface of the water under the influence of his optimistic autosuggestion or suggestion, he was transformed into a heavy stone and sank to the bottom without any resistance at the moment when the powers of this suggestion expired."

Penn State psychologist Howard Hall, in his review of this celebrated case, points out that the bidirectional effects in this patient are very important: It is not just a case of being suggestible, but of being suggestible in *both* a positive and a negative direction, *serially*.[24]

PROGNOSES AND CURSES

Dire predictions are commonplace in medicine and can occur anytime a physician gives a prognosis or outlook to someone. If the prediction is extremely negative or is delivered in a morbid way, it can function as a lethal curse by encouraging the patient to "die on time." Every physician knows patients who expired on schedule after being informed of how long they could expect to live.

The delivery of every serious prognosis should be considered a potential curse, and steps should be taken to limit its power over the patient. In fact, the negative effects of dire predictions are so commonplace, so well known and predictable, that I believe it is reckless for physicians to provide morbid prognoses without offering to the patient, on the same occasion, some form of protection. This could take several forms. For example, if it fits with the beliefs of both patient and physician (both must be considered!), prayer could be offered—for wisdom and guidance of both parties, for strength and healing, for the empowerment of medication or surgery, and so on. Even if the physician chooses not to pray with the patient, she might pray privately instead. In either case, she might emphasize the importance of spiritual support in the task that lies ahead and inquire as to the adequacy of the patient's resources. She might convey empathy and compassion in no uncertain terms, such as by reassuring the patient and his family that she will be with them no matter what. The worst approach is to ignore the importance of the prognosis altogether, such as by engaging in banalities about "being positive," building false hope for cures that are "just around the corner," and so on.

SPOOKY SURROUNDINGS

An intimidating environment has always been useful in casting spells and hexes. It is not surprising, therefore, that the radiology department is one of the sites in the modern hospital where medical hexes most commonly occur. Dim lighting, whirring noises, robotlike machines, gowned figures whispering to one another in an indecipherable language while wearing lead-lined protective shields, and ghostly, luminescent screens are everywhere. Before their X rays or scans are taken, patients are instructed, "Don't breathe! Don't talk! Don't move!"—which in any other context might be considered hexes. These commands are delivered by scurrying technicians who have retreated behind barriers designed for their protection, an obvious clue to the patient that the environment is dangerous. Most patients in these surroundings are apprehensive, many are terrified, and some die—as if they have been cursed by their fear.

Dr. Anthony Lalli of the Cleveland Clinic proposes that the negative emotions patients experience during invasive X ray tests may account for *all* the known causes of death associated with these tests. Lalli studied 248 fatalities that occurred as a result of the use of contrast media, the chemicals injected intravenously to obtain X rays of various organs (kidneys, bladder, liver, lungs, heart, brain, and so forth). He examined all the causes of death including heart attack, ventricular fibrillation, respiratory arrest, pulmonary and cerebral edema, rapid clotting of the blood, inability of the blood to clot normally, and various other causes. He was searching for a unifying, comprehensive explanation that might account for all these various fatalities. His conclusion: "The most important factors in the production of contrast media reactions are the patient's fear and apprehension."

Lalli does not deny that the chemical that is injected is involved, but the drug, he states, is always used against an emotional backdrop that often includes anxiety, even terror. Thus his down-to-earth advice: "I would recommend that [physicians] injecting [contrast] materials adopt the [advice of] Sir William Osler [the "father of American medicine"], treat their patients with gentleness and inapparent concern and not arouse their anxieties or increase their fear. . . . The physician-patient dialogue should not center on possible reactions but might best be devoted to the weather."[25]

COMING TO TERMS WITH ILLNESS

In shamanic cultures, it is generally believed that there are certain moments or situations when individuals are susceptible to being hexed, and any good sorcerer knows how to take advantage of these. In modern societies, it is during the early stages of illness, when people are trying to understand what is happening to them, that they are uniquely liable to being medically hexed.

I received a letter from a woman with AIDS that illustrates the vulnerability to medical hexing of individuals who are newly diagnosed. She had contracted the disease from her husband and was being treated at monthly intervals by an expert in infectious diseases. The doctor was a stern, no-nonsense fellow who fit the classic picture of the cool, dispassionate scientist. He believed in presenting a "realistic" picture to all his patients. He would remind the woman on each visit that since AIDS is "uniformly fatal," it was critical that she follow her treatment to the letter. The doctor's beliefs were a hex. She said,

> I began to realize my doctor doesn't *believe* I'm going to live. . . .
> It takes me two weeks to recover from a visit to him. He leaves
> me depressed and feeling sick. But after two weeks have passed, I
> always begin to feel terrific. Then, when it's time to return for an

appointment, a feeling of dread overwhelms me. I have to make myself keep my appointment. After the visit the cycle repeats itself. . . . Why do I feel like my own physician is *killing* me?[26]

After carefully weighing her options, this woman decided to change physicians in order to avoid the negativity that was interfering with her healing.

THE UNINTENDED CURSE: ANESTHESIA AND THE UNCONSCIOUS

Some of the most potent medical curses take place when no one—neither the perpetrator nor the recipient—is aware they are being made.

Dr. Rachel Naomi Remen, of the University of California San Francisco Medical School, and cofounder and medical director of the Commonweal Cancer Help program in Bolinas, California, had a patient who experienced severe depression for no apparent reason following a minor operation on his knee. He was recovering well physically, but became obsessed with the idea that he would die. Dr. Remen referred him to a hypnotherapist who was skillful in regressing people to the state they were in during anesthesia. When in hypnotic trance the man remembered hearing someone say during the operation, "Well, I've done everything. There's no need for me to come back." To the young man, this meant that the surgeons had done their best to help him but that it wasn't enough and that he was going to die.

Dr. Remen checked with the operating team. Sure enough, during the operation there had been a change in anesthesiologists, with one signing off to the other. Although nobody remembered the exact words, both doctors felt it quite possible that the physician going off duty said to his replacement precisely what the young man recalled. The misinterpreted words found a home in the patient's unconscious mind. When he awoke, he began to cooperate with the inadvertent curse.[27]

A similar case was related to me years ago by another physician. It involved a twenty-three-year-old man recovering from an abdominal operation for an incarcerated hernia.

Several days post-op, he was experiencing a series of complications. A fever had developed, he could not urinate without a catheter, and signs of infection had developed around his incision. His surgeon was baffled why these developments had arisen; the case was routine. When the patient told his nurse he was certain he would die, a psychiatrist was called in as a consultant. He found the man to be severely depressed, although the patient was unable to say why. The psychiatrist decided to use hypnosis in an attempt to uncover the source of his hidden fears. During hypnosis, the patient was able to recall the events of his operation. With great anxiety he described a surgical assistant saying, "This is the worst case I have ever seen!" The assistant was a first-year medical student, who meant his comment as a joke: It was the *first* incarcerated hernia he had ever witnessed. During hypnosis, the psychiatrist assured the patient of the insignificance of the statement. The medical student was summoned, and told the man his comment had been made in jest. Within forty-eight hours he was discharged from the hospital, a well man.

The power of anesthesiologists to influence our healing is not limited to what happens during anesthesia. Pre-op behaviors count, too. In a 1966 study at Massachusetts General Hospital, surgical patients were divided into two groups. Those in the control group received a cursory "hello" visit from their anesthetist the night before surgery. In the experimental group, the anesthetists purposefully engaged the patients in a warm, understanding, and sympathetic conversation for five minutes. These patients required only half as much medication post-op as the controls, and they were discharged 2.6 days earlier.[28]

TURNING MEDICAL CURSES AROUND

Creative physicians have begun to realize that if the mind can store negative suggestions during general anesthesia, it can store positive ones as well.

At a rehabilitation hospital in Chicago, a group of researchers tested the effects of a spoken message on patients undergoing back surgery. The patients were unconscious, under total anesthesia, and presumably had no awareness that a message was being spoken.

The commonest complication following surgery of this type is the inability to urinate voluntarily, which is treated by the temporary insertion of a urinary catheter. To avoid this, the researchers tried another solution. Toward the end of surgery, while the patient was still asleep, the surgeon spoke to the patient by name and said, *The operation has gone well and we will soon be finishing. You will be flat on your back for the next couple of days. When you are waiting, it would be a good idea if you relax the muscles in the pelvic area. This will help you to urinate, so you won't need a catheter.*

The results were impressive. Not a single patient given this suggestion required a catheter after surgery. More than half those in a control group, not given the suggestion, needed catheterization.[29]

Linda Rodgers, a social worker and classically trained musician, describes how the negative interpretations we make of ordinary events can result in great harm to our health. "In 1945," Rodgers relates, "I had my tonsils removed, and several days later, Franklin Delano Roosevelt died. For me, these two events have always remained inseparably linked: my first surgical experience and his death."[30] Many people, like Rodgers, carry unconscious assumptions about the connection of surgery and death, and they fear they will not survive an operation should they require one. In this process, nobody "out there" is hexing us; we hex ourselves through our beliefs, which are often irrational, as in Rodgers' case.

At one point in her career, Rodgers attended open-heart surgical procedures at a major hospital in New York City. "It was a stunning experience," she found.

More than anything else, I was startled by the cacophony of sounds: the sharp clang of metal instruments hitting metal pans; the banging, knocking, clatter of other equipment and instruments being readied for the next procedure; insistent throbbing, thumping beats of all the operating room machinery, each with its own distinct rhythmic level of auditory intensity; the piercing, ringing of the alarms, and jarring noise from other monitors; and the sound of Frank Sinatra piped in over two loud speakers because the surgeon liked Sinatra. . . . I often thought about the patients I had worked with [who had undergone surgery]. . . . I had been haunted by [those] who, following their surgery, expressed near panic as they struggled to recall something they couldn't quite remember . . . maybe a dream, maybe not. And then there were patients who thought they heard something during their surgery, and they were clearly terrified.[31]

Rodgers remained fascinated. Her subsequent research revealed,

The reality is that patients [under general anesthesia] can hear. The auditory pathway, unlike all other sensory systems, has an extra relay. Auditory fibers are not affected by anesthetics, so they continue to transmit sound. Simply stated: *We never stop hearing!*[32]

Rodgers reports a 1965 experiment to test auditory perception under general anesthesia. The researcher used a stray cat who was about to be destroyed. After electrodes to measure brain waves were implanted in the skull, the cat was progressively anesthetized until it died. Before death, a dog was brought into the laboratory; on seeing the cat it began barking ferociously. At that moment, the cat responded dramatically in an alarm reaction on all the brain wave channels.[33]

PROTECTION FROM MEDICAL CURSES DURING ANESTHESIA AND SURGERY

Any good shaman knows that methods of protection are essential when one is vulnerable to the intentions of others. The ultimate form of protection during anesthesia and surgery is to be healthy enough not to need these interventions in the first place. Failing this, several steps can help.

- Discuss your concerns with your surgeon and anesthesiologist. You won't be the first patient to bring up these issues. Ask for their suggestions about what can be done to make things go smoothly for you. Most important, tell them what *you* want to happen during surgery in terms of their comments and behaviors.

- Before surgery, consider making an audiocassette tape of self-suggestions for a smooth recovery, which you can listen to unobtrusively on a small tape player while surgery proceeds. This gives you a chance to play a positive role in your own healing and not be just a passive bystander while experts do things *to* you.
- Select a music tape for listening before, during, and after anesthesia. You can intersperse the above suggestions with the music of your choice. This will prevent you from being a hostage to the surgeon's musical taste, which you may deplore.
- Make use of resources that already exist. Many progressive hospitals have audiocassette libraries that lend music and instructional tapes to patients facing surgery. To inquire, contact the nursing department of your hospital. Commercial tapes are available for use before and during surgery, and many excellent books are available.[34]
- Should you wish to work with a professional, there are more than five thousand registered musical therapists (R.M.T.s) in the United States who can assist you. The National Association for Music Therapy sponsors two journals: the *Journal of Music Therapy* and *Music Therapy Perspectives*. An electronic database of medical music therapy (Computer-Assisted Information Retrieval Service System, CAIRSS) has been established with citations from more than one thousand journals, including empirical studies, case reports, and program reviews.
- Be hopeful, positive, and determined. If this proves impossible, consider delaying surgery—if it is elective—and explore the reasons behind your apprehension until you make peace with them.
- Allow yourself to have *some* anxiety. Some degree of apprehension is not only normal but desirable. In fact, there is evidence that people who permit themselves to be appropriately anxious before surgery do better afterward than people who are totally placid.[35]
- Don't forget to laugh. Humor can always be found in grim situations, even in serious illness. Andrew Weil recalls one old woman who had survived uterine cancer years before who told him, with a toothless grin, "That doctor told me I had less than a year to live, and now he's dead and here I am!"[36]

- Remember those who have come through. You are not the first person, nor will you be the last, to face this situation.
- Consider using specific forms of protection against medical hexing, such as prayer. Many people find comfort in the "protection clause" of the Lord's Prayer, "Deliver us from evil."
- If you achieve rapport on these issues with your surgeon and anesthesiologist, you can look forward to a fulfilling experience. If not, consider replacing the members of your health care team with individuals who understand your concerns.
- Following surgery, if you believe you may possibly be suffering from some form of medical hexing, deal with these concerns decisively. It may suffice to discuss this with an understanding friend. Professional counselors can help as well, such as the above therapists who used hypnosis to break the spell of negative suggestions inadvertently implanted during anesthesia.

REVERSING MEDICAL CURSES THROUGH PRAYER

A dramatic method of breaking medical hexes and dispelling the power of chronic disease is through prayer, described by psychologist Sandra Ingerman in her book *Welcome Home: Life After Healing*.[37] She describes her experiences with a painful condition she endured for years, which medical specialists declared untreatable. "You'll have to learn to live with it," she was invariably told—one of the classic forms of medical hexing described by Weil. Desperate for a solution, Ingerman prayed every night before going to sleep for healing to come to her in a dream. Nothing happened initially. Months later, however, as she continued her nighttime prayer ritual, she dreamed she was in her house when suddenly a Native American shaman appeared from behind her couch. He told her not to be afraid and declared that he had always been around, only Ingerman had been unable to see him. The dream image was vivid and detailed; the handsome young shaman was dressed in denim and held a rattle covered with a translucent blue material. He pointed with it to the place where Ingerman experienced her pain, told her she had a problem there, and shook the rattle vigorously over the area. At that moment Ingerman felt the pain leave her body and knew, while dreaming, that she had experienced a cure. When she awakened the pain was gone, and for more than a decade it has not returned.

Ingerman's experience raises several issues in dealing with medical hexing. Although the pain was chronic and had been declared incurable by specialists, she was unwilling to accept their dismal pronouncements as final. She recognized that cures are not always "out there" and that she had nothing to lose by following her own wisdom. Importantly, she realized she needed to transcend the workings of her rational mind, which she chose to do by venturing, through prayer, into dreams. She was patient; her healing dream required several months to arrive. She accepted the delay gracefully, without giving up, and waited patiently to see what her unconscious mind would deliver of its own accord.

Following her healing, Ingerman was drawn even more deeply into service for others—a step following healing that most people forget to take—which was perhaps a major reason why the problem did not recur.

THE POWER OF CURSES TO HEAL

It is a wise doctor and patient who always remember that thoughtless words, like curses, can kill. But let us conclude this chapter on a happier note—the power of curses paradoxically to trigger good health, not bad.

Dr. Andrew Weil once had a patient with a severe blood disease called ITP (idiopathic thrombocytopenic purpura) and hemolytic anemia. The treatment being urged on him by his physicians involved blood transfusions. The young man reacted angrily to this suggestion, and the focused rage appeared to trigger an immediate healing response. "I particularly like this example," Weil states, "because anger is perhaps the most stigmatized of the 'bad' emotions . . . , seen as wholly destructive and interfering with mind-body healing and immunity."[38]

If the knowledge that one has been cursed or hexed triggers anger, might this set in motion physiological changes that can be protective or even healing? Like Weil, I like this idea because it makes sense from the perspective of evolutionary biology. If we can be harmed by the thoughts of others, we almost certainly would have developed countermechanisms against them, just as we have developed immune responses against infections. We should *expect* the existence of a psychospiritual immune system.

Yet if anger is to provide protection, we must *know* that a negative prayer, curse, or hex exists, and thus the need to be alert to the malevolent intentions of another. Could this cause us to live our lives in a state of chronic paranoia? It need not. In cultures where negative, nonlocal mental influences are taken for granted, fear and suspicion do not get the upper hand. These events are accepted as a natural part of life, as are the protective measures that go with them.

THE DEATH WISH

> Much of psychiatry . . . concerns itself with the effect
> of hatred upon the hater. Too little time has been
> given to examination of . . . the effects upon the
> object . . . , especially when the target is unaware that
> he is, in effect, under fire. . . . Hate can destroy.
> —*Olga and Ambrose Worrall*

For some people, the most shocking moment in their life is the realization that they may have killed someone with their prayers.

I once treated a woman who was afflicted with chronic fatigue syndrome so severely that she could not attend to the requirements of daily living. She was extremely manipulative and controlling before becoming sick, and these traits intensified with her illness.

Her husband was one of the most unassertive individuals I have ever known. Although he had long contemplated divorce, he was too indecisive and weak willed to follow through. He resented his wife before she became ill; now he hated her. He believed she did not want to recover and that she was using her illness to dominate him totally. The couple refused to enter therapy or marriage counseling, preferring instead to wallow in their unhappiness.

The husband found an outlet in religion and returned to the church after years of absence.

One night following a bitter argument, he stormed out of the house. On returning, he found his wife dead, presumably from a heart attack. The man was overcome, not with sorrow but with guilt. Although he was certain that his intense hatred had killed his wife, he continued to refuse to enter psychotherapy to deal with his guilt. After a typical period of doing nothing, he made two choices. He remarried—to a neurotic woman very similar to his first wife—and he left his church in favor of an extremely fundamentalist sect that believed in a wrathful God of absolute power. This allowed him to deny any responsibility whatever for his wife's death and to believe without doubt that God, not he, had punished her.

For a fleeting moment, this man came face-to-face with the intensity of his hatred. He saw that he might possibly be capable of killing his wife with his thoughts, and this awareness terrified and shamed him so severely that he quickly put the lid back on things. He found a surrogate for his hatred—God—and buried his confused feelings even deeper in his mind.

IN THE BEGINNING: THE ORIGINS OF
NEGATIVE PRAYER

This man's experience may mirror a scenario that, some experts say, may have existed early in human history.[39] In our attempts to understand the roots of negative prayer, let's probe what may have happened when our ancestors first encountered these same feelings.

It is often said that early humans, faced with a menacing world they could neither comprehend nor control, concocted gods and demons to account for the events that threatened them. These imagined beings could be propitiated and manipulated to one's advantage through ritual, supplication, and prayer. However, according to psychoanalyst Jule Eisenbud, our ancestors may have followed another path. "Various data suggest that what occurred [first] was [not the invention of external gods but] the alienation of man from certain aspects of himself rather than from nature. . . ."[40] Eisenbud proposes that the thing that most threatened early humans may not have been a menacing world outside but a power from the inside—the gradual recognition that one contained the capacity to harm and perhaps even kill others, even when the remote individual was unaware of the attempt.

Early humans, Eisenbud proposes, responded to these capacities the same way the man reacted in the above incident—with extreme revulsion. In order to cope with this unease, these powers were psychologically repressed, denied, and projected outward onto an increasingly diverse pantheon of spirits, gods, and demons—perhaps the greatest giveaway of human potential in history. This is precisely the path followed by the above individual when he took refuge in the belief that a vengeful god had killed his wife.

We are not yet finished with the old fears. When skeptics revile the idea that the mind can act at a distance either to help or harm others, without bothering to consider the evidence, could they be experiencing the horror our predecessors felt about these same powers? Skeptics can always, of course, find plenty of reasons to justify their objections—for example, the nuttiness that always keeps company with belief in these powers in contemporary society. But the main reason for rejecting the mind's powers may be fear.

And also guilt. Eisenbud proposes that our ancestors felt deep "stirrings of uneasiness" about their mental capacity to harm others, a feeling that this was deeply wrong. As the fear and guilt were experienced by an increasingly greater number of individuals, there may have arisen a moment in history when these twin emotions of fear and guilt became intolerable, triggering humankind's first attempts "to absolve himself from culpability for any harm that may have come from such power."[41]

THE DEATH WISH

What is the evidence that our predilection for negative prayers and curses may be rooted in the remote past, along the lines of the above scenario? Many psychoanalysts believe we can get a glimpse of the mental life of early humans by probing the modern psyche. Contemporary cases, such as that of the above individual, may indicate what our ancestors felt in similar situations.

This was essentially Sigmund Freud's position in his 1912 work, *Totem and Taboo*, in which he described how his neurotic patients dealt with their hostile feelings, particularly their death wishes for others. These individuals could not admit to themselves that they wanted to kill another, so they transformed these desires through the psychological processes of repression, displacement, and projection. We need not dissect how these processes work in the psyche; basically, they are ways of avoiding the truth about oneself.

Freud believed that these psychological defense mechanisms were not recent developments but rather analogues of emotional reactions in early humans. The death wish, while most obvious in neurotic individuals, was universal.

For both early humans and us, Freud implied, the desire to harm others originated in infancy, in the earliest stage of psychosexual development. During this time, when the infant is wholly dependent on others for sustenance and gratification, it does not distinguish between itself, the mother, and the outside world. When complete gratification is not forthcoming from the mother, or if it is delayed or withheld, hostile feelings can develop. Although the infant may not act out these negative wishes in an obvious way, they do not disappear. They endure into later stages of psychosexual development and sooner or later are displaced from the mother onto objects or others who are more permissible to hate. If harm actually befalls them, one confronts the possibility that one's thoughts and wishes may actually hurt or kill another.

For early humans, displacing one's negative feelings onto others may not have been easy. In the small clans and family units of early humankind, survival depended on mutual cooperation and harmony of purpose, and hatred surely got in the way. Hating one's mother, the source of life, was irrational; hating one's kin, with whom one had to cooperate in order to survive, was impractical. How were they to deal with hostile impulses? One way of resolving this dilemma was to project the desire to harm or kill others onto gods, demons, ghosts, and spirits. Let them be the agents of the death wish; let them do the dirty work. By displacing one's destructive wishes onto an external entity, the emotional uneasiness associated with this power could be tolerated.[42]

IS THE DEATH WISH ONLY A WISH?

But there is a gap in the psychoanalytic theories. They may tell us *why* we want to harm or kill others with our thoughts and prayers, but they don't tell us whether these powers are real or not. Was the death wish only a wish, or were our ancestors—and ourselves—actually capable of harming others with thought?

Evidence that humans have the power to harm others mentally is not limited to theories originating from the armchairs of psychoanalysts. For this we turn to the evidence that is included in this book—sources as varied as anthropology, psychology, the experiences of individuals past and present, and, importantly, actual laboratory experiments.

INFANCY: THE CRADLE OF TELEPATHY?

While psychology can't give final answers, this field can nonetheless shed light on why humans believe so strongly in prayer and distant mental intention.

Physician-researcher Jan Ehrenwald believes that humans can indeed communicate with and affect one another at a distance. He shares with Eisenbud the belief that these capacities are rooted in our physiology and that the mother-infant relationship is a key to how these abilities develop.

The ways in which a mother and infant communicate, Ehrenwald observes, are rudimentary. They are limited to unconscious expressions, vocal intonations, body language, empathy, intuition, and what child psychiatrists and analysts call "mental cueing." At this stage the mother-child unit is symbiotic; boundaries between the two have not yet formed, and the respective egos of the mother and child are still merged. "The baby is the direct extension of the mother's body image," Ehrenwald states. "Although separated from each other in spatial terms, they form a closely knit functional whole. Indeed, the continued postpartum symbiosis of the two organisms has been described as extrauterine gestation." Some observers have suggested that connections between the mother and infant are so profound that they extend to the level of the unconscious, so that "one unconscious" may be able to communicate with "another unconscious."[43]

How does this communication take place? Every mother knows that something extraordinary goes on between her and her baby— something that materialists would consider outrageous. Ehrenwald suggests that we bite the bullet and call this form of communication telepathy—communication between minds. "Telepathy," he states, "in this case [of mother and infant], far from being a mere psychological curiosity without an apparent goal or discernible purpose, is well suited to fill whatever communication gap exists between the two in the symbiotic phase." But with the gradual maturation of the infant's central nervous system, the infant's cooing and babbling are gradually supplanted by speech, and the child "emerges from the period of partial communication blackout." The fusion with the mother gradually begins to dissolve. "His ego boundaries, until now sharply fused with those of his mother, become sharply delineated; he sets up a barrier separating his mental processes from those of his mother." As this process continues, telepathic communication between the two is no longer necessary, and it fades away by becoming repressed in the process of individual development.[44]

The telepathic maternal infant bond, however, may bend but not break entirely. Hundreds of cases have been reported by skilled observers, such as neurologist Berthold Schwarz, who coined the term "telesomatic events" to describe long-distance, mental communications between parent and child later in life. *Telesomatic* seems apt; it comes from words meaning "the distant body."[45]

A classic example is that of the mother who experiences a suffocating feeling and "just knows" that something is wrong with her young child. She rushes home to pull her from the swimming pool just in time. In cases like these, it is not difficult to imagine that the mental intimacy the mother and infant shared in the first months of life has not fully dissolved and is reawakened in a crisis when needed.

Some telesomatic events suggest that the link between mother and infant may never totally dissolve. In one case, a mother was writing a letter to her daughter, who was away at college. Suddenly her right hand began to burn so severely she was unable to hold the pen and continue. Less than an hour later, she received a phone call from the college telling her that her daughter's right hand had been severely burned by acid in a laboratory accident, at the same time the mother had felt the burn.[46] Sometimes the bond involves more than two people. In a case reported by psychiatrist Ian Stevenson of the University of Virginia, a woman had the distinct impression that her mother was seriously ill and needed her. Against the protests of her husband, she set out to see her mother, only to meet her sister as she approached the mother's house. The sister had the same impression and was acting on it as well. The women found their mother dying, asking for her daughters.[47]

MODERN CHILD-REARING PRACTICES: ARE WE FOSTERING CURSES?

Many people believe the infantile period is easier and gentler today than in prehistoric times. But in some ways, it may be more difficult. Modern obstetrical and child-rearing practices place increasing distance between infants and mothers. Babies face formidable barriers to their mothers, from incubators and cribs to plastic bottles, rubber nipples, and artificial milk. As a result, today's infants may have more cause for ambivalence, negativity, anger, and hatred toward their mothers than in primitive times. Consequently, one wonders if the death wish may be more virulent today than in earlier eras. If infant hostility is on the rise as a result of modern child-rearing practice, and if negative prayer is one way we vent these hostilities later in life, does this mean that we are fostering curses by the way we rear our infants?

In summary, our desire to harm others may originate in earliest infancy as hostile feelings toward our mother, which are projected onto others. If pronounced, these feelings may constitute a death wish, the desire actually to kill another. Moreover, mothers and infants appear to share a telepathic ability as part of the maternal-infant bond. The ability to connect mentally with another person may persist and may manifest later in life not just as the capacity to *communicate* with someone at a distance, but the ability to *influence* them as well.

In adulthood, if these distant mental abilities combine with the death wish, the result is a curse, hex, or spell. But it is not culturally acceptable to curse another. Therefore, the urge to curse often fuses with an activity that is acceptable, such as prayer.

THE POWER TO HARM: A SURVIVAL ADVANTAGE

Why does the power to harm another mentally still exist? Why would it not have died out in humankind's long evolutionary history?

According to the tenets of evolutionary biology, those traits that help an organism survive and reproduce are perpetuated genetically across generations. It is not difficult to imagine how the power to harm another mentally might have given an evolutionary advantage to those bold enough to employ it. This ability would have been a formidable weapon against not just the humans one hated, but also against beasts and predators that were constant threats. Even if these powers were not real, merely the belief that one possessed them might have conferred greater aggressiveness, therefore a competitive edge, to the believer. Moreover, the belief that one could harm others would likely have carried with it the worry that one could be harmed as well. This would likely have created a greater sense of alertness and caution and thus an advantage in the life-and-death game of survival.

MAKING DEMONS

PEOPLE WHO USE PRAYER to harm others often have highly vivid imaginations.

Consider, for example, the furor over witches in Europe in the sixteenth and seventeenth centuries, during which thousands of individuals, mostly women, were tortured and burned at the stake. The witch-hunts were essentially heresy hunts, and the hunters were deeply pious and prayerful. Although there were doubtless a few witches who actually believed they flew through the air to sabbats, had sexual orgies with demons, and feasted on the flesh of babies, the real source of these images were the imaginations of the inquisitors, bishops, and magistrates who secured their "confessions."[48]

The vast majority of those who confessed did so under torture and were willing to say anything the inquisitors wanted to hear. It was their only hope of escaping death, and they knew that if they withdrew their confession they would be tortured again. Still, in spite of the sheer unbelievability of almost all the evidence, there are a few instances that make one wonder.

One strange case was reported in 1591 by a magistrate at Louviers, near Rouen, involving a local girl, Francoise Fontaine, who periodically suffered from fits and had to be restrained.

> When she was brought before him, in the presence of the clerk, her gaoler, and a number of other witnesses, she suddenly rose off the floor, and then was dumped down and hauled around the room as if some invisible hand was dragging her. The magistrate tried to read the gospel, with a view of exorcising the demon responsible; but all at once the body of the said Francoise was raised off the floor, three or four feet high, and borne horizontally, face upwards, along the court, without anything to support her. When we saw the said body making straight at us, thus

suspended in mid-air, it threw us into such fright that we with-drew into the office of the court, locking the door behind us and reading the Gospel of St. John down to the end. But the said body kept following us through the air up to the office, against the door of which it struck with the soles of its feet, and then was carried back through the air, with the face upmost and head foremost, out of the court; which gave such a fright to the gaoler, his servants, our archers and many prisoners who were present, with several inhabitants, that they fled.[49]

Francoise might have taken advantage of the confusion by trying to escape, but she did not. She was discovered lying on the ground by the prison door and was carried to a church by five or six people. While they held her, the curé administered the sacrament—or tried to—but before he could complete it "she was snatched off the floor, higher than the altar, as if she had been taken up by the hair."[50]

According to modern rules of evidence, we cannot take this account at face value. The record may have been fabricated, or the event may have been a collective illusion. Still, it may be unwise to reject accounts such as this out of hand.

We often say that people see what they want to see. The crowd investigating Francoise Fontaine believed that witches flew, so they saw her fly. But could there be more to it? *Can our mental images, under certain conditions, actually create reality?*

This question is important in our exploration of the negative effects of prayer. For example, if we believe that the world is haunted and controlled by the devil, and if our prayers are continually filled with diabolic images, do we run the risk of actually *creating* demons? If I am so fearful of getting cancer that that's all I can think of in my prayers, am I actually creating the problem I want to pray away? Is this one way prayer becomes negative? If images actually create changes in the physical world, we should be careful what we pray for.

Can our imagination bring into existence something that is not now present? One group of people who took this question seriously was shocked by their success, because the entity they created was a ghost. The story of Philip follows.

CONJURING UP PHILIP

In the 1970s, eight members of the Toronto Society for Psychical Research formed a group that tried to create a totally imaginary character they named Philip.[51] They seemed an unlikely group to do such a thing—engineers, housewives, nurses, accountants—and were supervised by Dr. A. R. G. Owen, a British mathematician.

"Philip Aylesford," they simply decided, was born in 1624 in England. He followed a military career, was knighted at the age of sixteen, and enjoyed an illustrious role as a Royalist in the Civil War. He became a close friend of Prince Charles (later Charles II) and entered his employ as a secret agent. Philip's undoing resulted from his dalliance with a gypsy girl. His wife found out and accused the girl of witchcraft, and she was burned at the stake. Despairing, Philip committed suicide in 1654 at the age of thirty.

None of the participants in the Toronto group were considered psychically gifted. They would file into a normally lit room and sit on folding metal chairs around a card table. On the table they placed a pair of fencing foils and a dish of candies, items they declared to be of special fondness to Philip. They would meditate on Philip and try to visualize the details of his life, and they'd greet him and chat with him as if he were actually present. The project was not a typical Victorian séance. As parapsychology researcher Richard S. Broughton explains, "Unlike their Victorian counterparts, the Toronto group was not interested in communicating with someone on 'the other side'; they wanted to re-create the *physical* phenomena so often a part of the Victorian séance. Philip was simply a means to this end."[52]

As the séances proceeded, some participants occasionally felt a presence in the room and others had vivid mental pictures of Philip, but no apparition appeared. Then on one occasion, after the social amenities were concluded, all hell broke loose. The table shifted slightly, began to tilt, and then slid across the floor. In order to keep up with it, the sitters had to leave their seats to keep their hands in contact with the surface. When the table was finally still, they began to urge Philip to levitate the table—which happened, but with only *one* leg. Then the tabletop began to twist out of shape, with sounds of straining wood and metal coming from it. One leg and corner of the table continued to lift; it required four of the sitters to push it back down. Although the room was normally lit and it was obvious that nothing was under the table, it felt as if someone were resisting their efforts.

When things settled down, candies were passed around. When someone reached to take Philip's candy, the table again tipped to a forty-five-degree angle, but the candy remained stationary—as did other types of candy when they were placed beside Philip's. To test this puzzling event, after the session the participants placed candies on the table once again and tilted it; they slid off well before the table was elevated to forty-five degrees.[53]

The participants called these effects "PK by committee"—psychokinesis, or mind over matter. They believed they somehow *produced* the phenomena and that Philip was entirely the product of their imaginations. Was the Philip experiment a gigantic contrivance? You decide. If the reports are accurate—levitation and movement of the table were recorded on film in 1974—the implications are sobering. They suggest that human will, imagination, and expectation can bring about physical manifestations, some of which may not be "nice."

SÉANCES AND CHURCH SERVICES

I have never been to a séance, but, growing up, I spent a lot of time in gatherings that resembled them: church services. There are striking similarities between the two. In both, people are drawn together by a common set of beliefs and expectations. Both séance sitters and worshipers believe in an unseen world with which they can make contact, if they follow the proper procedures. Both often see entities such as angels and demons that are denied to be real by others.

If séance sitters such as those in Toronto can conjure the objects of their visualizations and expectations, what about worshipers? If Philip can manifest, why not the devil?—who, as one wag said, has always received more attention in church than God. What role might prayer play in this process? By focusing the concerns of worshipers on sin, evil, and the devil, does prayer become a tool of the devil, helping him come to life?

In search of answers, let's examine a provocative series of experiments that predated the Philip research.[54] In the 1950s Kenneth Batcheldor, a British clinical psychologist, was struck by the common observation that the physical phenomena associated with séances appear to decline in proportion to the increased scientific and often skeptical attitudes of those who investigate them. The beginning intentions of many so-called skeptics have been to discover fraud behind these events. While this may have increased the scientific rigor of the séance, it does not nurture the psychological conditions that most mediums or seers have considered important for their work.

Batcheldor believed that almost anyone could produce ESP (telepathy and clairvoyance) and PK-type ("mind over matter") events but that the psychological conditions present at the time of their elicitation are crucial. "Batcheldor's basic idea was that doubt and suspicion hinder the production of psychic phenomena, whereas belief and expectation facilitate it," notes parapsychology researcher Broughton. "This is a common notion, of course, but Batcheldor's version was more specific. Not only was a general belief and expectation helpful, but conditions had to be such that the persons involved felt an almost tangible expectation that a miracle was about to take place."[55]

According to Batcheldor, two factors commonly inhibited successful PK production. One he called "witness inhibition"—the initial surprise, shock, or actual fear one experiences on witnessing a paranormal event. The other factor he called "ownership resistance," which is the fear that one might actually be responsible for causing the happening. If one could reduce these factors, Batcheldor reasoned, one stood a better chance of producing a paranormal event such as those described in Victorian séances.

To test these possibilities, Batcheldor and a few friends launched a series of "modern" séances, with none of the Victorian trappings, in an ordinary room with a plain table. The participants maintained an experimental approach combined with as much lighthearted playfulness as objectivity would allow. To avoid ownership resistance, they did not try to "make" the table move. Rather, they addressed requests to the table, which would allow them to avoid responsibility for whatever movements might take place. In the course of ten sessions, the table tilted, rocked, slid, and even hopped. These motions, however, were hardly convincing; "all of [them] could be attributed to the normal but unconscious muscle action of the sitters," Broughton observes. These minor effects, however, built the sitters' confidence—and during the next session, the eleventh, the forty-pound table actually rose off the floor, while the hands of all participants were on its surface. The table also levitated during the twelfth session, but after that nothing was noted. The reason, Batcheldor believed, was that the rather violent activity aroused too much anxiety in the sitters.[56]

An electrical engineer named Colin Brookes-Smith was intrigued by Batcheldor's work and began a similar series of experiments, along with his colleague, D. W. Hunt. They also experienced a host of dramatic events, including the switching on and off of a distant, unattended light switch. Brookes-Smith designed a specially constructed table from which pressure from any direction could be monitored. Strong PK activity was recorded, and the recordings indicated that normal forces were not being used.

While every other scientist has tried to eliminate cheating from his experiment, Brookes-Smith devised a way deliberately to include it. He came up with the idea of the "designated cheater"—a sitter who was chosen beforehand by drawing lots and whose job was to "get the ball rolling" by discreetly using normal means to do so. He would stop when paranormal movements took over, and later he would identify himself and describe what he'd done normally. His actions were easily distinguished from the paranormal actions by the electronic recordings.[57]

It was too bad the Philip group in Toronto did not initially know about Batcheldor's research. They might have saved themselves a lot of trouble, because they spent almost a year in a fruitless attempt to conjure Philip using a meditation technique. When they heard of Batcheldor's work, they redesigned their experiments to resemble the séance motif and incorporated his advice about the right attitude of the sitters. By inventing Philip, they circumvented the problem of ownership. Even though fictitious, he, not they, could be credited (or blamed) for whatever happened.

What are we to make of these reports? Researcher Broughton wisely states,

Even though all of the groups, especially the Philip group, demonstrated phenomena to visitors, we must ultimately rely on their own affidavits of good faith as fellow investigators. Films exist of both the Philip group and Batcheldor's group, but these ultimately depend on the good faith of the filmmaker. We must recognize, however, that evidentiality was not the goal of these groups. They wanted to learn something of the psychology behind the séance and how this might lead to the production of physical phenomena. In this respect they have gained some important insights.[58]

FURTHER RELEVANCE TO PRAYER AND WORSHIP

Insights from the parapsychology experiments might shed light on the dynamics of prayer, belief, faith, and worship.

We have already addressed the most obvious area of relevance—whether we can create mischief by focusing on it, vividly and imaginatively, through prayer.

In addition, let's consider the factors of "witness inhibition" and "ownership resistance." These are problems for religious groups as well as for séances. Today, a great number of churches are dominated by rationalists and intellectuals who are skeptical about anything out of the ordinary. These churches seem cold; there is no fire in their belly. The atmosphere in them can be so depressing that one wonders whether Prozac instead of bread should be served at communion. People who affiliate with congregations such as these would probably be shocked to see prayer working—a result that they, bless them, never intended. These groups pray hesitantly, as if to avoid confronting events that their worldview could not explain. If Batcheldor's research is valid, these collective attitudes are leading to "witness inhibition" on a grand scale. There may be practical consequences of this phenomenon. For example, the psychology of these churches may be smothering the physical manifestations of prayer, such as the healing of the sick.

"Ownership resistance"—the fear that one has somehow caused the unexpected event to happen—is also a factor in these congregations, because the pray-ers have no wish to own what they didn't desire or expect in the first place. If healing *were* to occur in this situation, the congregation would probably dismiss it as a chance event—just "one of those things"—anything to avoid attributing it to the power of prayer.

In other types of congregations, however, participants really do expect a miracle. It may be that the free-wheeling, lighthearted atmosphere of these congregations is one reason why their prayer seems more potent. In these upbeat settings, witness inhibition is replaced by witness enhancement, and ownership resistance is overcome by owner-ship pride.

IF PHILIP, WHY NOT THE DEVIL?

Again: What if worshipers expect bad or evil events instead of good ones? What if the devil instead of the divine is expected to make an appearance? If people can conjure Philip, why not the devil? We cannot avoid the issue by insisting that the devil is not real. Neither was Philip, but he managed to raise a ruckus in the séance chamber.

"[T]he most dramatic realization to come out of the group-PK research is that quite ordinary folks can produce some amazing phe-nomena *if the psychology is right*," Broughton concludes. "Believing that the phenomena are possible, expecting that something might happen *right now*, and not worrying about who is 'causing' it all, seem to be part of the recipe."[59]

In comparing the séance chamber and the worship service, I do not wish to trivialize or demean prayer. I believe strongly that prayer is not PK and that worship is not psychokinesis by committee. I do feel, however, that common psychological factors operate in both prayer and the anomalous events studied by parapsychologists, factors that we would be foolish to ignore.

MAKING EVIL STRONGER?

The implications for how we pray are sobering. Prayer is one of the most powerful methods of mental imagery known to humankind, and most people who pray invoke images. Praying against something we fear and hate may involve more powerful imagery than praying for something friendly; images of danger always seem more real than benign ones. What are the consequences of prayers and highly vivid images that focus on eradicating evil and denouncing the devil? Are they empowering evil, like the Toronto group empowered Philip?

Most people who pray fervently for the defeat of the devil or the antichrist believe he is getting stronger, not weaker. Is this evidence that our prayers may be part of the problem? Are we *making* Satan?

THE DEATH PRAYER

WHEN EUROPEANS FIRST CAME to the Hawaiian Islands, they encountered a practice literally called the "death prayer," or *ana-ana*. They developed a horror of this practice, which came to be "the most feared phenomenon in old Hawaii."[60] Eventually, laws were drafted prohibiting it.

One of the most interesting accounts of this practice comes from psychologist Max Freedom Long, who arrived in Hawaii in 1917 and took a job as a teacher in the area near the Kilauea volcano. Long, who had an intense interest in comparative religion, became fascinated with the native shamans, the *kahunas*, or "Keepers of the Secret." Long managed to gain their trust, and they eventually revealed to him much of their lore.[61]

After four years of research, he met William Tufts Brigham, the curator of Honolulu's Bishop Museum. Brigham was a respected scientist in his field, a contributor to the British Museum, and was listed in *Who's Who in America* for 1922–1923. "He looked like Santa Claus," said Long, "eighty-two, huge, bald and bearded." Brigham had studied the kahunas for forty years. Not only did he confirm Long's impressions that the kahunas could kill people at a distance with negative mental intent, even when the victim was unaware, he also described how the curse could be fatal to the individual who perpetrated it.

Soon after the Bishop Museum was built, Brigham climbed Mauna Loa on a three-week expedition to collect indigenous plants. He stopped first at the village of Napoopoo to recruit men and pack animals. He set out with four Hawaiians and eight horses and mules. The weather was favorable, and they made good progress, although trails were virtually nonexistent. When they encountered the barren country above the rain forests and were making for the summit and crater of Mauna Loa, one of the Hawaiians, a strong youth of twenty, became ill. Brigham thought it must be the altitude that was troubling him, and he left him behind with a man to care for him. Brigham continued on his journey, spent the next day in the crater, and returned to the lower camp by early evening that day. By now the youth was stretched out on a blanket, too weak to rise. Brigham, still concerned about altitude, resolved to move him to a lower altitude the next morning. Eventually the other Hawaiians revealed that they believed the youth was being prayed to death. Brigham went to the youth and asked his opinion. He protested, "No! No!" but was obviously terrified. He denied knowing why anyone would want to kill him. Brigham made a more thorough examination and confirmed the "slow paralysis of the lower limbs and threatening general collapse," the symptoms of the death prayer. At last he convinced himself that some kahuna was at work. When he announced this, all the natives in his party became frightened, fearing the whole party might be killed.

One of the Hawaiians questioned the youth more thoroughly. He lived in a tiny, isolated village on the windward side of the Big Island. There was little to attract the white people. The old kahuna wanted to keep the village isolated and commanded the villagers to have nothing to do with the *haoles* (whites) under penalty of being prayed to death. The youth had gone to live in Kona a few months and had nearly forgotten the prohibition. When Brigham had come through Napoopoo, recruiting men and pack animals, the youth joined him without a second thought. He did not realize the command to avoid whites still held outside his village.

Brigham was furious. While he was nursing his anger, one of the older Hawaiians politely told him that the natives respected him as a powerful kahuna himself. Had they not seen him participate in the firewalk across hot lava, along with them? They suggested that Brigham pray for the youth and reverse the curse. Said Brigham,

I decided there and then to try my hand at sending the death prayer back to the kahuna. The spell had been initiated and the trained spirits sent out. All I had to do was to put up the usual big arguments to talk [them] over to my side, and then exert all my will to send them back and make them attack the kahuna. I felt this would be fairly easy as the boy was guilty of no actual sin. . . . I got up and said to the men: "You all know that I am a very powerful kahuna?" They agreed most enthusiastically. "Then watch me," I growled. With that, I went over to the boy and set to work.

His strategy was to convince the spirits that their master must be a devil to send them to kill one so pure and innocent. "I knew that if I could win them over and get them worked up to a high emotional state and ready to revolt," he said, "I would be successful."

The traditional way the kahunas protected themselves from the spirits they were manipulating was by a ceremony using *ti* leaves. Brigham thought it improbable that the old kahuna had invoked this protection, as he would have no fear that Brigham or the other men would send back the death prayer. According to the account, Brigham put on quite a show on the slopes of Mauna Loa that night. He stood over the youth and pontificated at length to the spirits. He praised and flattered them, assuring them they were deserving and clever. He gradually got around to saying how sad it was that they had been enslaved by a kahuna instead of being allowed to go to heaven where they belonged. And was not the youth pure and innocent? Did this not mean the old kahuna was evil and vile? Finally, Brigham believed he had sufficiently riled the spirits and that they were ready to pull the kahuna limb from limb. Then he let forth a "bull roar" and gave the command for the spirits to return to the shaman with ten times the punishment he ordered for the youth. Brigham frightened the pack animals and terrified the men and the youth. "I put every particle of will and concentration into that command," the museum curator said. "It was a supreme effort, mentally, emotionally and physically." Brigham kept his mind intently dedicated to the command. Amid the stars, he felt he could feel the air tremble with "the fury of some unearthly conflict of forces." Suddenly Brigham felt an odd sensation, as if the tension in the air had vanished. A few minutes later the youth whispered, "Legs . . . good." Brigham watched as the youth's feet began to twitch and his lower limbs began to move. The men timidly offered congratulations. "It was the high point in my career as a kahuna," Brigham acknowledged. In an hour the youth was up and eating.

Brigham had the feeling that he had killed something deadly. He cut short his trip and went down to the youth's village to see what had happened to the kahuna. When they finally straggled out of the mountains into the village, an old woman and a girl working in a *taro* patch spotted them and ran away screaming. Brigham and his crew followed them to some grass houses. They were deserted. Brigham made himself at home outside the hut where the kahuna lived, while the youth went to see if he could find someone.

Soon he came back with news. On the night Brigham had sent back the death prayer, the old shaman had been sleeping. He awoke with a scream and rushed about to get some *ti* leaves and began to fan himself with them to ward off his evil spirits. But it was too late. In a very short time he fell to the ground and began to groan and froth at the mouth. By morning he was dead.

The villagers were terrified, certain that Brigham had come to destroy the entire village. Brigham asked the youth to tell them he had taken his revenge. Soon they were all great friends; nobody seemed concerned he had killed their shaman. "That was all a part of the game for them," Brigham sardonically observed. They treated Brigham's party to a *luau,* a feast.

Brigham puzzled over why the kahuna, if he were psychic, could not have known Brigham was sending the spirits back to him. He concluded that the kahuna was simply not as skilled as others who could see clearly into the future, and that "he was not up to that."

Why did the young man become paralyzed? Was this an effect of negative prayer, or was it due to negative suggestion, expectation, and hysteria? Did the spell have an effect independently of these psychological factors, or was the young man merely cooperating with a curse he already knew about?

I had been fascinated by these questions for years, and I asked anthropologists about them every chance I got. They acknowledged that the events were real, but almost all of them believed they were explainable in psychological terms. The term *death prayer* was simply a fanciful expression for the power of belief in the victim. On one occasion, however, I found myself across a dinner table with Professor Michael Harner, the noted anthropologist and authority on shamanism, whose book *The Way of the Shaman* remains a classic.[62] Harner had spent extended periods doing fieldwork with the Jivaro Indians in the Amazon drainage. He learned their language, penetrated their culture, and witnessed firsthand the intimate details of Jivaro life. I asked him if the shamans he encountered could harm someone at a distance with their thoughts, without the victim knowing they were doing so.

"In Jivaro culture distant hexing is taken for granted," Harner said unhesitatingly. "Many of the shamans I've studied on the Amazon have claimed to be very good at it. I have no reason to disbelieve them."

"Why do they hex others at a distance?" I asked.

"Their rationale is simple," he responded. "If the victim is unaware he's being hexed, he won't take measures to counteract the hex or take revenge on the shaman. As an added safety measure, the Jivaro shamans perform distant hexing as a team of two or three, not alone. If the victim tries to get even, there's safety in numbers. Distant hexing is a security measure."[63]

Harner's view that negative mental intentions can cause harm in distant individuals, outside their awareness, is shared by Serge Kahili King, a modern authority on the kahuna tradition. King believes, however, that suggestion was also commonly added to the negative prayer to make it more potent, for if the victim *knew* he had been cursed, the potency of his belief would have combined with that of the prayer.[64]

It is difficult to decide scientifically whether negative intentions can harm others remotely, because it is unethical and illegal to perform on humans experiments whose goal is harm. But, as we shall later see, experiments have indeed been performed on nonhumans showing that thought can harm at a distance. These experiments strongly suggest that, in principle, negative intent does have distant effects, whether we call these intentions prayers, curses, hexes, or spells.

TAKING ON THE ILLNESS OF ANOTHER

Brigham's experience with the offending sorcerer suggests that an illness, when it departs an individual, can strike those who are unprotected from it. This reflects a universal belief that a disease is not neutralized merely by being cast out of an individual. It remains potent and can rebound and cause harm.

This is not just a "primitive" view. We find it in our own culture in certain religious groups that employ prayer for healing. For example, folk medicine researcher Dr. Loudell F. Snow conducted the following interview with a sixty-four-year-old evangelist in the Holiness Church:

> "I don't pray for 'em [sick people], though, cause I picks up their [ailment]. See, you could have something wrong with you and I could pray for you, and I'd take it!"
>
> "Would I get well?" [Interviewer]
>
> "Yeah, you'd be all right. But I'd be sufferin' with it! It'd go in *me!* And then somebody's have to come along and pray it out of me! Lots of times people won't accept it; it's the way you have to pray for the sick people to keep from takin' it. Reverend _____, he stopped me from prayin' for people down there. Ever' *time* I'd take it. Pick it up, take it like that. And they had to come right on and pray it off of me. And so they kind stopped me."[65]

This attitude reflects the Legion Principle (p. 47)—the idea that illness or misfortune is never totally eradicated but is conserved, by becoming displaced from one person to another.

Fortunately, not every healer believes she or he will take on the illness of the patients; otherwise healing traditions might totally disappear. Protection is always possible. This is illustrated in the views of a Pentecostal evangelist Snow interviewed who spends much time at the hospital praying for the sick. "She understands," Snow states, "that there are illnesses caused by microorganisms but believes that while she is making her hospital rounds God puts an invisible barrier around her that germs cannot penetrate."[66]

AVOIDING THE DEATH PRAYER

Let's examine another example of the death prayer, which illustrates how the victim may escape its influence.

Long relates the case of a young Irishman who came to Honolulu at about the time the first modern taxicabs made their appearance. He was "rough and ready, his hair was red and he was afraid of nothing." In a short time he became romantically involved with a Hawaiian girl, who was so enamored she broke off her engagement to a Hawaiian boy. The girl's grandmother was furious and did her best to break up the new affair, believing the young Irishman was up to no good. She even made veiled threats that heaven would punish him if he did not leave her granddaughter alone.

The young Irishman had no fear of heaven or of anything else, and the threats didn't work. One day, however, his feet became numb, and as the prickling numbness began to creep upward he lost the ability to walk. By the end of the day he had seen two doctors and had wound up in the hospital. No cause for the problem could be determined. Within four days the numbness had reached his waist. Finally an elder doctor, who had practiced long in the islands, was called in. He immediately recognized the symptoms as those of the death prayer.

The physician began to question the young man in earnest. He learned of his Hawaiian girlfriend, and more questioning brought back the memory of the grandmother's threats. The young man still found the threats laughable. Even so, the old doctor set off to visit the grandmother.

The physician, a friend of Long's, later revealed the conversation:

"I know that you are not a kahuna and have had nothing to do with this case, Grandma," said the doctor. "But, just as a friend, will you tell me if you think anything could be done to save the man?"

"Well," said Grandma, "I know nothing about the matter, and I am no kahuna—as you know. But I think that if the man would promise to take the next ship for America and never return or even write back, he might recover."

"I will agree that he will do just those things," said the doctor.

"All right," said Grandma imperturbably.

These events were revealed to the stubborn young Irishman, who became terrified and willing to agree to any terms. By night his symptoms had resolved enough for him to stand and walk, and he caught a Japanese ship for the States.[67]

We should therefore not be forlorn. Although murderous thoughts are universal, it is obvious that they do not invariably kill, otherwise no one would be alive. The kahuna tradition we've just examined shows that a lot more is involved than merely *having* a negative intention for another person. The thought must be empowered, like the arming of a nuclear warhead, which is accomplished in many cultures through ritual and ceremony. And even when armed, destructive thoughts are not destiny; as we saw in Professor Brigham's defensive measures, they can be neutralized or reversed.

GUILT: A CONNECTION BETWEEN THE DEATH PRAYER AND WESTERN RELIGIONS?

The kahunas, Long discovered, believed that the death prayer worked through a sense of guilt over wrongs done to others. Guilt functioned as the hole in one's armor that allowed the negative influence to penetrate. If no sense of guilt existed, the intended victim's subconscious mind would successfully ward off the menacing intentions. Therefore, to prevent being cursed in the kahuna tradition, one should not behave in ways that engender guilt. Or, having done so, one should absolve the guilt by making restitution.

The similarity between the dynamics of the kahuna death prayer and the way prayer is often used in our culture is striking. Like the kahuna shamans who perpetrated the death prayer, those religions in our culture that preach original sin and the fall also foster and capitalize on a sense of guilt. In the kahuna tradition, the guilt arises from wrongdoing; in these religions, from wrong*being*. Simply being born is sufficient to merit eternal punishment unless certain conditions are met, which are laid out in the particular religion involved. This can create what has been called "the religious wound," a chronic, gnawing sense of shame and unworthiness.

In a sense, the curse associated with the doctrine of original sin seems *more* potent than the most virulent death prayer of the kahunas. At least the effects of the death prayer ended with the demise of the victim; the damnation and punishment associated with the fall are said to be eternal.

If the kahunas are correct—if a sense of guilt makes one susceptible to the malevolent thoughts of others—we must wonder whether some of our religious traditions are setting up people to be victimized by the malevolent intentions of others by promoting a sense of guilt.

Many people object to comparing our religious traditions with those we consider primitive. They maintain, for example, that the death prayer does not really involve prayer because it is not offered to God.

They often insist that "true prayer" cannot cause harm, let alone death. We should recall, however, that prayer frequently is not directed to a personal god. For example, prayer is central to Buddhism, yet Buddhism is not a theistic religion; Buddhists offer their prayers not to a personal god but to the universe. And even in the Christian tradition there is a thin line between prayers and curses, as we have seen (pp. 4–5).

NEGATIVE PRAYER IS NOT A PLAYTHING

Many people take curses and spells lightly and dabble in them for amusement. Yet negative prayers are not a plaything. As Brigham's experience showed, not only can negative intentions harm those to whom they are directed, they can be fatally turned against the person employing them.

Northern New Mexico, where I live, has long nourished an enchanting mixture of Native American, Hispanic, and Anglo beliefs and customs. For example, the use of medicinal herbs remains widespread and is divided loosely into two categories. There are *curanderos* who use them for healing and *arbularios,* or witch doctors, who use them for harm.[68]

Around 1900, Dolores la Penca was the most notorious *arbularia* in the Santa Fe area. She lived on Agua Fria Road, a charming street that now lies in the northwestern part of the city.[69] She became a fearsome living legend, and parents would invoke her name to keep mischievous children in line. *La Penca* means "the foundling" in Spanish, and reflects the fact that Dolores was abandoned as an infant and was raised by foster parents. Even as a child she seemed different, and people would comment on her mysterious behavior. By her late teens she was living alone in a small adobe dwelling. For weeks at a time she would roam the Sangre de Cristo Mountains outside Santa Fe gathering the medicinal plants and herbs that formed the basis of her potions. When she could not find the ingredient she needed for a concoction, she would trade with sheepherders to obtain it. Visitors to her house invariably came away sobered, with reports of drying herbs, antlers, hoofs, and horns dangling from the rafters, and bags of dried leaves littering the floor.

As Dolores's reputation grew, she became a source of immense anxiety for her neighbors and acquaintances—until her witchcraft finally turned against her in a bizarre sequence of events. On one occasion she took a wedding gift, a bar of handmade soap, to a young girl who was about to be married. Although the girl's mother warned her against using it, the bride ignored her and washed her hair with the sweet-smelling soap that very night. She awoke the next morning with a florid red rash and was fearful that a spell had now been cast on her marriage. "Who wants to enter their wedding day looking like a smallpox victim?" she lamented. But on the day of the wedding the rash had disappeared, and she was married without incident.

The week the ceremony was to take place, the brother and cousin of the bride were working with a survey party in southern New Mexico. The night of the wedding, they were sitting around a camp-fire wishing they were in Santa Fe for the festivities. Then an owl began hooting in the surrounding piñon trees, and Antonio, the cousin, remarked, "Ah, there is Dolores la Penca. She has come all this way looking for trouble or for news to carry back to Santa Fe." When the brother appeared incredulous, Antonio explained how witches can take any form and travel immense distances instantly. "See if I am not right," he said, as he marked a cross on a bullet, loaded it into his rifle, and killed the owl with a shot through one eye. When he examined the bird he found the right eye gone, the left wing raised and almost torn away, and the left foot folded up under the owl's body.

On returning to Santa Fe, the cousin and brother paid a visit to the adobe house of Dolores la Penca and found it locked and vacant. Then they went to congratulate the new bride, where they learned that the witch had been slain mysteriously on the night of the wedding. A sheepherder had seen her alive shortly before, having stopped by to deliver herbs. The next morning a neighbor discovered her dead body—a bullet through the right eye, her left arm raised and nearly torn loose, and her leg doubled up against her chest. As they listened to the account, the two young men exchanged knowing glances and made the sign of the cross.

Common sense says, of course, that the deaths of an owl and a human cannot be causally related. Yet linked events such as these are not rare in the lore surrounding curses and spells. They suggest that sorcerers can be victimized by the power they try to manipulate and that their death can be mediated by the death of an animal.

To the experience of Dolores la Penca can be added the cele-brated case of Grace Pett in eighteenth-century England. Grace was the sixty-year-old, pipe-smoking wife of a poor Ipswich fisherman. Some of her neighbors believed she was a witch. When a local farmer named Garnham noticed that some of his sheep were getting sick, he decided Grace had cursed them. A local "white magician," a Mr. Winter, advised Garnham to intentionally burn one of them to break the spell. Although the farmer considered the suggestion silly, his wife decided to give it a try. She made one of the farmworkers bind the four legs of the sheep and lay it in the hearth and set it on fire while still alive. As the bonds burned through, the poor animal tried to escape but was forced with a pitchfork to remain in the flames until dead.

Sometime that night—April 9, 1744—Grace Pett died. The following morning her daughter found her remains in the kitchen. She was lying on her right side, her body stretched across the hearth, her legs extended onto the wooden floor. Her trunk was incinerated and resembled coals covered with white ash, and her head and limbs were burned also. Because the body was still incinerating, the daughter threw water over the remains, causing a fetid odor to permeate the house, almost suffocating her and the neighbors, who by this time had gathered to lend their assistance.

No one could explain how Grace Pett caught on fire. There was no fire in the grate. A candle was close by, but it had burned down completely in the candlestick. The heat had been intense. The melted fat from her body penetrated the hearth and could not be scoured out, but the wooden floor was not even discolored. A paper screen and some clothes were nearby, but these had not been damaged by the intense heat. Oddly, no one in the house that night had been aware of a conflagration or even of smoke. According to various books and documents, the disease afflicting Garnham's sheep abruptly ceased after the poor sacrificial sheep and Grace Pett burned to death.[70]

Was Grace the English equivalent of Brigham's kahuna and Santa Fe's Dolores la Penca? Were they all victims of returning curses?

PRECOGNITION, CURSES, AND PRAYER

Is the death prayer an exotic ritual performed in Hawaii by a shaman, or could it be a general phenomenon that is expressed in other cultures in different ways?

Suppose we are worried about a loved one—their future health, finances, and so on. We mentally make an image of what might befall them, and we instigate a prayer to avert these possibilities. Prior to the prayer, when we "see" harm befalling them in the future, are we functioning as the shaman who also "sees" the harm he intends toward his victim?

Sorcerers who attempt to pray an individual to death try vividly to "see" the future death of the intended victim, as if it were a fact that will undoubtedly happen. The sorcerer's vision resembles the experience of precognition—knowing an event will happen before it does—because he or she is filled with certainty that the malevolent happening will take place in the future. If we, like the shaman, imagine or "see" that another person will die, and the event happens, have we killed them? Are we capable of committing "future murder" with our dreams, visions, thoughts, and prayers? What if we see our own death? Have we hexed ourselves?

Perhaps everyone has thought of murdering or harming another person, sometimes to the extent of seeing this event in our imagination. These desires may take the form of impulsive wishing, impetuous statements, or dreams. What if the event really happens? Has our "seeing" played a role in causing the future occurrence?

Seeing into the future and knowing an event will occur before it happens is called precognition, and surveys show that this experience is quite common. Setting aside the issue of whether or not these are mere coincidences, let's ask a question that concerns researchers in this field: Does seeing a future event in our imagination, visions, or dreams influence the future? Or is our current knowledge only a passive reflection of what will happen anyway?

One of the most celebrated examples of the precognition of death took place in the life of Abraham Lincoln. Shortly after he was nominated for the presidency, Lincoln began having frightening dreams in which he saw himself dead. He revealed them to his wife and his most intimate friends. Ward Lamon, his former law partner who subsequently served as marshal of the District of Columbia during Lincoln's administration, wrote an account of these death dreams in his biography of Lincoln:

> [T]he most startling incident in the life of Mr. Lincoln was a dream he had only a few days before his assassination. To him it

was a thing of deadly import, and certainly no vision was ever fashioned more exactly like a dread reality. . . . After worrying over it for some days, Mr. Lincoln seemed no longer able to keep the secret.

"About ten days ago," said he, "I retired very late. I had been up waiting for important dispatches from the front. I could not have been long in bed when I fell into a slumber, for I was weary. I soon began to dream. There seemed to be a death-like stillness about me. Then I heard subdued sobs, as if a number of people were weeping.

"I thought I left my bed and wandered downstairs. There the silence was broken by the same pitiful sobbing, but the mourners were invisible. I went from room to room; no living person was in sight, but the same mournful sounds of distress met me as I passed along. It was light in all the rooms; every object was familiar to me; but where were all the people who were grieving as if their hearts were about to break? I was puzzled and alarmed. What could be the meaning of all this?

"Determined to find the cause of a state of things so myste-rious and so shocking, I kept on until I arrived at the East Room, which I entered. There I met with a sickening surprise. Before me was a catafalque, on which rested a corpse wrapped in funeral vestments. Around it were stationed soldiers who were acting as guards; and there was a throng of people, some gazing mourn-fully upon the corpse, whose face was covered, others weeping pitifully.

"'Who is dead in the White House?' I demanded of one of the soldiers.

"'The President,' was his answer; 'he was killed by an assassin.'

"Then came a loud burst of grief from the crowd, which awoke me from my dream. I slept no more that night; and although it was only a dream, I have been strangely annoyed by it ever since."

"That is horrid!" said Mrs. Lincoln. "I wish you had not told it. I am glad I don't believe in dreams, or I should be in terror from this time forth."

"Well," responded Mr. Lincoln, thoughtfully, "it is only a dream, Mary."[71]

What are we to make of Lincoln's dream? Philosopher Stephen E. Braude, of the University of Maryland, describes several different ways of thinking about precognitions such as Lincoln's:

1. The "passive analysis." According to this interpretation, our knowledge of a future event is a form of retro- or backward causation. For example, tomorrow's plane crash was the cause of today's precognitive dream of such. Braude describes the passive analysis as a counterclockwise form of perception or information-acquisition.

2. The "active analysis." By contrast, this is a clockwise form of knowing. It takes two forms.

a. Inference, based on considerable information about the current state of affairs. For instance, the precognizer might infer the likelihood of the plane crash from information obtained paranormally or normally about developing weather patterns, the level of maintenance of the airplane, the mental state of the crew, passengers, and air traffic controllers, all of which might manifest in the dream content.

b. Causal, meaning that the subject, quite simply, for any number of very deep reasons (presumably unconscious), might cause the plane to crash.

The philosophical reasoning underlying Braude's analysis of the passive or counterclockwise form of precognition (tomorrow's plane crash caused today's dream) and the active or clockwise interpretation (today's dream caused tomorrow's crash) is too complex to describe here and is discussed elsewhere.[72] His personal conclusion is that "we have no choice but to accept the reality of pervasive, and apparently extremely refined and extensive, clockwise psi."

Braude clearly believes that precognition may function as a curse—a possibility that many find horrifying. He comments,

[It] is particularly difficult to accept [the causal, clockwise version of psi] warmly . . . [because of] the grim nature of many ostensibly precognized events. Hence, unpleasant though it may be, we may have to repudiate much of what we think we know about the world, and return to a belief in processes very much like the evil eye, hexing, magic spells, and divination. [73]

When we see future difficulties for ourselves and others, are these harmless thoughts and images, or are we influencing the future according to the clockwise process described by Braude?

I have known individuals who devote themselves continually to prayer because they are burdened with a pervasive sense of impending tragedy. They ruminate continually about catastrophes that have not yet happened and focus constantly on the worst-case scenario. I have often wondered if these people are sorcerers in disguise, because their doom-and-gloom outlook is so infectious that it is difficult to be around them for any length of time. In their presence, one *feels* hexed. And if seeing catastrophe in the future makes it more likely, are these people agents of disaster? Is prayer a veneer that hides their negative influence from everyone, including themselves?

AVOIDING GUILT

The fear that prayer can cause death casts a long shadow in our culture. For example, when people pray for the relief of suffering and the person dies, they may worry that they prayed the individual to death. One woman, whose husband suffered from severe Alzheimer's disease, began to offer a daily "Thy will be done" prayer. When her husband died shortly thereafter, she was overcome with a sense of guilt because she believed she was responsible for his death. With counseling from her minister and friends, she was able eventually to accept a different view—that her husband's death was a blessing.[74]

We must be careful not to regard empathic, well-intended prayers that are followed by death as death prayers. A healthier response is illustrated in the following accounts:

> Sometimes answers to prayer for healing end in death. Like the time . . . we visited a lady who had been in agony for days. She got no sleep from the pain. The doctors didn't seem to be able to do anything for her. We prayed for relief from the disease. Immediately her breathing became normal, and she lapsed into a peaceful sleep. The next day she woke up, and spoke of the wonderful rest she had, and then died. It was indeed relieved pain.[75]

✦ ✦ ✦

> In my family growing up, love was abundant. My parents, brother and sister, and I were always extremely close. Following the death

of my mother, my father, then in his eighties, began to change. He lost all interest in life and became extremely negative about everything, even hostile at times. The doctors could find nothing wrong, and medications did not help. He lived for a while with my brother, then my sister, but he upset their households so much that we began to consider a nursing home, which I opposed. I was single and lived alone and was convinced Dad could live with me. It didn't work. Dad would greet visitors at the door and curse them for calling. He would answer the phone with tirades of abuse. Every effort to please him failed miserably. I again sought the advice of my physician, who referred Dad to a neurologist and a psychiatrist. Once again, no one could find anything specifically wrong—just the changes of "old age."

Things continued to deteriorate. My father would reject every offer of kindness and invariably respond to compassion with contempt. I realized he could not help how he was behaving, and I was heartbroken. This was not the father I knew.

After six months I was an emotional wreck. I felt I was losing control and did not know what to do or where to turn. Never in my life have I felt so desperate. One night, following one of Dad's typical outbursts, I suddenly began to cry and heard myself say, without any forethought whatever, "Please help us. Take him or me—I don't care which—but please help us." I cried for an hour, and a feeling of peace descended. Three nights later my father died serenely in his sleep.

A negative prayer? Not in the opinion of the woman who related this account. She loved her father so deeply that she put her own life on the line—"Take him or me—I don't care which"—and she was certain that her father's death was a benevolent answer to the spontaneous cry from her heart.

When our prayers are answered with the death of a loved one, it can be difficult to see the wisdom in such a response. At such moments it is often best to suspend our verdict, set our judgments aside, and just be with the answer. If we do, our understanding of death may be transformed—death not as tragedy but as a stepping stone to another world. Then we can see that our prayer was answered not with death, but with another form of life.

THE DEATH PRAYER IN THE MAJOR RELIGIOUS TRADITIONS

Using prayer to kill others is not limited to so-called pagan religions. As we saw in chapter 1, this practiced surfaced in Christianity in the form of the black mass, in which priests prayed for the death of specific individuals.

According to Hindu scholar Georg Feuerstein, a variation of the death prayer is also found in Hinduism in the form of *marana,* which is one of the six *siddhis,* or paranormal powers, recognized in the sacred tantric religious texts. *Marana* means "killing" or, literally, "death-ing." Through *marana* one can bring about the death of an enemy through purely mental means, but only if one has perfected the required state of consciousness. *Marana,* then, is not something that can be employed casually by amateurs. The practice of *marana* is not highly valued in the Hindu tradition. Although those who employ it may be successful, it is said that this practice will prevent them from attaining liberation.[76]

THE EVIL EYE

He that hasteneth to be rich hath an evil eye.
—*Proverbs 28:22*

PRACTICALLY ALL TRADITIONAL SOCIETIES have believed that good and bad influences can be transmitted through the eyes. When a gaze is used to convey harm, the term *evil eye* is commonly used.

"We know from the study of both human and animal behavior that intentions are frequently aimed with the eyes and at the eyes," British anthropologist Francis Huxley notes. "A newly caged lion will eat its meat happily enough in the presence of human beings, but it will snarl defensively if you stare at it. . . . Both animals and humans can fight battles of will by staring at each other, the first one to drop his eyes admitting defeat. . . ."[77] Huxley's observations are often affirmed in politics. For example, we often hear that at a summit meeting a particular statesman "blinked first" when a touchy issue was being discussed, indicating that he was the first to give in.

GAZES GOOD AND BAD

A look is not always negative. In his book *Seven Experiments That Could Change the World*, English biologist Rupert Sheldrake discusses the benefits of another's gaze:

> The positive effects of looks, especially loving looks, are also widely acknowledged. In India, for instance, many people visit holy men and women for their *darshan*, literally their look, which

is believed to confer great blessings. Perhaps an unconscious survival of the same kind of belief is involved in the popular desire to see in person the Queen of England, the President of the United States, the Pope, pop stars, or other luminaries. Although they can be watched more conveniently on television, there is something about their real presence which has an enormous appeal, motivating people to spend hours waiting in crowds to catch a glimpse of them—and, better still, to be seen by them ("The Queen waved at me!"). Such people are, as we say, "in the public eye.". . . the idea that influences can pass out of the eye is practically universal. This implies an implicit belief in the extension of the mind, capable of influencing what is seen.[78]

During my medical training I had two experiences of the power of a look—one positive, the other negative—that I shall never forget.

Toward the end of my internship, the demanding year of clinical work following medical school, I felt my spirits lifting as the end was in sight. One Sunday when I was not on duty at the hospital, I discovered at the very last minute that the famous Russian ballerina, Natalia Makarova, would be performing *Swan Lake* that very afternoon. The performance was to begin in one hour, so I hurriedly dressed and sped to the performance hall. "There is only one seat left," the ticket saleslady informed me, "front row, center." I gulped. Although practically penniless, I decided on an impulse to reward myself for the year's difficulties, purchased the single remaining seat, and was ushered forward at the very last moment.

Makarova's beauty, power, and grace were enchanting. Only a few feet away, I was so completely captivated I felt she was dancing for me alone. In the final movement she glanced at the front row, and her gaze fleetingly met mine. I felt suddenly transformed, as if I were experiencing a numinous, joyful epiphany—the positive power of a look.

The flip side of this experience took place a year earlier in my third year in medical school, during the daunting period of instruction on the internal medicine service. Each week a particular student was chosen to present a complex case to the chief of the department, a world-renowned scholar and researcher who was famous for his intimidating style of teaching. Students had been known literally to break down emotionally and run from the classroom under his "instruction."

The day before our first weekly conference with the chief, all the students, including me, were hoping they would not be chosen to present the case of the week. By day's end, however, no one had been selected. That night, around midnight, I received a call from the chief resident informing me apologetically that I had been selected to present one of my patients the next day and that he had forgotten to let me know. The case involved a man who suffered from acromegaly, a rare disorder of the pituitary gland. Sick with anxiety, I returned to the hospital and stayed up almost all night reading about the disease and familiarizing myself with the most intimate details of the patient's clinical history, physical examination, and laboratory results. By the time the conference began the next morning, I was exhausted but ready.

The professor stalked dramatically into the room and nodded grimly, his trademark signal that the conference was to begin. Although extremely nervous, I confidently presented the case without a flaw. Within ten minutes I was finished and stood silently for the chief to take up the discussion. Instead, he stood and fixed me with his gaze from across the room. I was terrified and immobilized by his look as he began slowly to walk toward me. As he closed the gap between us, he extended both arms fully and positioned his hands in front of my neck as if he were going to strangle me. I was trembling and faint with fear. At the very last moment he rotated his palms downward, away from my neck, and clapped me vigorously on the shoulders. "My, my! What a crisp young lad! What a crisp young lad!" he announced with a faint smile. Then, having terrorized me sufficiently, he turned his attention to my fellow students, who by then were also quaking. The professor insisted he used these techniques out of genuine concern and caring. This was unconvincing; we students felt caught in the dilemma psychologists call the double bind, in which authority figures talk one way and behave another.

THE EVIL EYE AROUND THE WORLD

When the professor paralyzed me with his gaze, it was as if I were receiving the evil eye—the *malocchio*, the *jettatura*, the *mal ojo*, or the "fascination" that the ancients spoke about. In the Talmudic language of the Jewish tradition, the evil eye is known as *ein bisha* or *ein rah*.

Throughout history, the look is often combined with other forms of hexing, such as pointing of the shaman's finger, stick, bone, or wand. Although the evil eye may be employed deliberately, the act may also be unintentional. It is particularly apt to wreak havoc when an individual admires or is envious of someone else's circumstances, such as another's children, animals, or possessions. According to some beliefs, one is unusually susceptible to the evil eye when at the peak of prosperity and happiness.

The earliest records of the evil eye date to about 3000 B.C.E. in the cuneiform texts of the Sumerians and Assyrians. The ancient Babylonians, Egyptians, and Greeks believed in it, and the Romans were particularly fearful. Many tribal cultures continue to respect the evil eye to this day. It remains a part of the black magic or voodoo rituals of Vodoun, which spread from Africa to the Caribbean and now exists in many urban centers in the United States. Also in Mediterranean Europe, Mexico, and Central America, the belief remains prevalent.

The capacity to cause harm through the evil eye exists even in mainstream religions, whose adherents frequently believe that one can be cursed from birth and not realize it. Pope Pius IX and Pope Leo XIII were both said to be afflicted with the power of the evil eye, and their look was feared.

According to the lore surrounding the evil eye, one must be always on guard and take immediate precautions to ward off or negate the ill effects. One way is simply to avoid those who possess the power. One of the telltale signs, it is said, that someone is capable of harming others through their gaze is eyebrows that are grown together in the middle.

A variety of protective actions have predictably arisen. When a child or a treasured possession is being praised, which is believed to be a context for the evil eye, the Irish and Italians say, "God bless it!" or "God love it!," and the Jews say, "Keinahora" (no evil eye). In Italy men grab their genitals if hit with the evil eye, and spitting is said to annul its effects. The most common amulets used to ward off the look are the *corno*, a curved horn, and the "fig," a clenched hand with the thumb stuck through the middle and fourth fingers. In ancient Rome, phallic amulets honored their phallic god, Priapus, also known as Fascinus, from which *fascination*, or bewitchment, is derived. The spectrum of amulets is broad—shamrocks, garlic, eyes, bells, brass, red ribbons. When these fail, victims often rush to a sorcerer, wise woman, or witch for a counterspell.[79]

THE EVIL EYE AND ANIMALS

Animals as well as humans can be affected by the evil eye, as in the following reports collected by Angelos Tanagras, a physician and admiral in the Greek navy:

> The shepherds in Crete are profoundly convinced that it is not the fastest among them who succeed in catching sheep and goats which have strayed from the flock, but those who have the "eye" and who are therefore able to cast a spell on the animals.

✦ ✦ ✦

> In the gang [of brigands] to which I belonged and which for years terrorized the provinces of Rethymno and Heraklion, we had a comrade who was indispensable when it came to carrying out an action which involved the necessity of *bewitching* dogs. . . . In Greece the dogs in the villages and sheepfolds are particularly fierce. . . .
>
> Whenever we approached the house or sheepfold where we were going to operate, the comrade in question would put a small pebble under his tongue and remained motionless for some time, while concentrating. . . . We then set to work. We leaped over the walls and smashed in the doors without being disturbed in the slightest by the dogs, who either appeared to be asleep or looked at us without moving. This effect only *failed when the comrade was drunk or if a woman approached him*. [Emphasis in the original.]

✦ ✦ ✦

> Mr. Zannas, former Air Minister [of Greece] in the Venizelos cabinet, [reported] that during the Greek-Turkish war of 1912, when his soldiers entered a village, the men had to confront dogs who were particularly ferocious. When this occurred, they only had to call on one of their comrades who was known as a

"healer" . . . and who had the gift of bewitching dogs. He went up to them and concentrated; and as he did so, the most savage dogs drew back, tails between their legs, and fled without even barking.[80]

"THE LOOK" IN MEDICINE

Like prayer, medical interventions are used for benevolent reasons. And medical interventions, like prayer, can be contaminated by an element of the evil eye, though in a different way.

Modern medicine is an exercise in looking. Physical exams, blood analyses, X rays, scans, and scopes have become the eyes of the physician. Although we doctors are enchanted with the diagnostic power of these tools, patients often are not as impressed. Some of them are more focused on the side effects and potential harm of the tests than on the benefits they may bring. I have often wondered whether these objections may reflect a primal fear of being looked at by another, of being harmed by the evil eye of someone they do not fully trust.

But it is also possible that physicians might be able to use the evil eye therapeutically—hexing a disease through the power of "medical looking" and stopping it dead in its tracks.

Consider the history of tuberculosis, one of the great scourges of humanity. As biologist Lyall Watson notes, skeletal evidence for tuberculosis has been found in graves in Germany dating back ten thousand years and in Egypt's Old Kingdom. Engravings from 2500 B.C.E. show spinal deformities that, along with hieroglyphic descriptions, provide clear descriptions of death from tuberculosis. The disease was common in ancient China, India, and Greece, where it was described by Hippocrates five centuries before Christ.[81]

As cities grew larger and people moved about more freely, tuberculosis became pandemic. Waves of the "white plague" spread across the world, devastating cities in its wake, competing with the "black death" in ferocity. The last and greatest European epidemic began in England during the sixteenth century and peaked in London around 1750. The capital cities of western Europe were affected in turn through 1870. Then, Watson states, "There was a sudden, marked and inexplicable decline in TB everywhere that records have been kept—beginning, it seems, in Germany in 1882."[82] Why? It has been suggested that the population may have become more resistant to infection, but this almost certainly was not the case. Were medical advances the reason? It seems unlikely. Surgical interventions in tuberculosis did not begin until 1912, and antibiotic therapy in this illness was unknown until 1944. "But something did happen in Germany in 1882 that could be very significant," Watson observes—the discovery by Dr. Robert Koch of the cause of tuberculosis, *Mycobacterium tuberculosis*. Almost overnight physicians and researchers could actually see the organism for themselves, and common citizens could visualize it from illustrations. "Almost immediately," Watson states,

> there was a marked decrease, not only in the incidence of the disease, but also in its mortality. Deaths fell from 600 per 100,000 to around 200 in less than a decade. . . . The recent improvements can all be attributed to better medical care, but nothing comparable happened to account for the sudden and rapid decline which is evident in Hamburg and Berlin during the 1880s. Nothing, that is, except Koch's discovery and a spreading awareness of what lay behind the disease that had come to be called "Captain of all the Men of Death."[83]

Watson acknowledges that there is clearly room for more prosaic explanations for the dramatic decline of tuberculosis than just knowing about its cause. But in view of recent experiments showing that human beings can inhibit the growth of bacteria, fungi, and other microorganisms at a distance by merely thinking negatively about them (pp. 167–170), perhaps we should take seriously the possibility that something like an evil eye on the disease may have occurred in 1882 as a consequence of Koch's discovery, as biologist Watson suggests.

Is it possible that the effectiveness of today's "medical looking" with various scans, probes, and tests is due, at least in part, to the ability of physicians to negatively affect diseases through "the look"? Are doctors using the evil eye therapeutically without realizing it? Might medical schools of the future teach medical students how to hex illnesses purposefully using the evil eye? Might they also instruct students of the *dangers* of their look and how to avoid damaging their patients with their gaze?

THE DANGER OF BEING NOTICED

Particularly in Mediterranean and Middle Eastern societies, a look of admiration is believed to blight a thing because of the destructive power of envy. In fact, the word *envy* comes from the Latin *invidia*, "a looking upon." One way of counteracting envy for a particular object is to give that object to the person who remarks upon its beauty. The gift overwhelms or neutralizes the envy and puts the envious individual into a dependent, indebted position in relation to the giver. In this way, generosity functions as a form of protection.

But what if the object of envy is a person, who cannot be given away? In this case, other forms of protection come into play. "In Mediterranean countries, to compliment a mother upon the beauty of her child is the height of bad manners, and she will either beg you to criticize the shape of its nose, ask you to spit on the ground as a combined insult and gage of good intentions, or ward off the evil eye with [an] obscene gesture," British anthropologist Francis Huxley observes.[84]

Why do admiration and envy function as a curse? To praise a child's beauty or intelligence is to bring it to the attention of Fate. And Fate can become jealous, because perfection is for the gods, not for humans. This may cause Fate to reconsider its apportionments and take back what it gave. Praising a child is a way, then, of placing it in danger.

Many societies believe that being too perfect or too powerful can anger the gods. It is best to fit in and not draw too much attention to oneself. One way of managing this danger is to hold sumptuous feasts at which food, drink, and material wealth of the fortunate individual are given away to others. This is a way of maintaining the social system and power structure by circulating wealth and taming envy. In a classic case reported by Darwin, two Fuegians were taken to England, taught good manners, English, hygiene, and a smattering of the Bible, and then sent back to Tierra del Fuego to exert a healthful influence upon their fellows. "But as soon as they disembarked," Huxley recounts, "their compatriots stripped them of their possessions so completely that within two days they were indistinguishable from their neighbors, and, because they occupied no [privileged] social position, the missionary hopes that had been fixed on them remained unrealized."[85]

How different is the situation in our culture! We have enshrined personal achievement and individuality, and we consider standing out from everyone else to be highly desirable. But if there is wisdom to these widespread beliefs, perhaps we should reconsider some of our most common prayers, such as those for success and prosperity. Highly successful people stand out in a crowd and are envied by millions. Does this mean they are being cursed through the envy directed toward them? Is this a factor in their frequently unhappy, chaotic lives? If marked success and prosperity make us stand out as targets of envy, should we reconsider praying for these developments? Are prayers for success self-imposed curses, a form of the evil eye?

PRAYER, ENVY, AND THE EVIL EYE

The evil eye may contaminate prayer when we admire the good fortune of another and pray to be blessed in a similar way. If the ancient lore is valid, such a prayer, as an exercise in envious looking, may be a subtle form of the evil eye and a curse in disguise

Dee Brown, in his delightful book *Wondrous Times on the Frontier,* describes an incident in New Mexico in 1887 in which prayer for rain began sincerely, shaded into envy, then degenerated into a downright curse for a neighbor's good fortune. This example may seem quaint, but it could serve as a warning for a lot of contemporary praying.

At the time, cattlemen in the Sulphur Springs valley were enduring a spotty but serious drought. When things reached the dangerous stage, the cattlemen elected one of their number to intercede with the Almighty for rain at a public meeting. Dan Ming, the elected individual, first reminded God that he was not making excessive demands, as he had never asked for anything before. But the range was in a terrible condition, and the cattle and horses needed water desperately.

"Oh, Lord, if you do not grant us our prayer," he went on, "for Christ's sake stop it raining on Joe Hampson's range, for all our cattle are going over there. Hampson, oh, Lord, is a powerful sinner and undeserving of such goodness from you. . . . Yes, oh, Lord! we pray you to stop the rain on Hampson's range. . . ." In spite of this curious mix of prayer and cursing, results weren't long coming. According to the local newspaper, the *Chloride* (New Mexico) *Black Range,* which reported Dan Ming's prayer, three days later the Sulphur Springs valley was deluged with one of the heaviest rains on record.[86]

THE EFFECT OF THE EVIL EYE ON
SPIRITUAL PRACTICE

The belief in the evil eye is so ancient and pervasive that it may have influenced our methods of spiritual practice in ways that have long been forgotten.

For example, why do we frequently close our eyes when we pray? As an expression of humility and reverence, as commonly believed? As an aid to concentration? Or might closed-eyes prayer have developed as a safeguard against the harmful influence of looking on another with envy during prayer, thereby cursing them with the evil eye? Are the prayers of the blind, who are unable to look, liable to cause less harm than those of sighted persons?

Jesus advised, "When thou prayest, enter into thy closet, and when thou hast shut thy door, pray to thy Father which is in secret. . . ." (Matthew 6:6) Why did Christ advocate solitude? Merely as a way of avoiding the dangers of pride and ostentation that contaminate public prayer? Could this also have been a way to prevent looking on others with envy while praying, thereby blighting them?

Could this be one reason why solitary prayer is highly valued in many religious traditions? Why have so many spiritual seekers sought isolation in remote places such as deserts and caves? Could they have been trying to distance themselves from the malevolent effects of another's gaze?

HEXING OURSELVES: THE POWER OF NEGATIVE BELIEF

MOST PEOPLE THINK negative prayers are directed exclusively toward others, but the commonest victim of negative prayer is probably the pray-er.

A negative prayer involves a negative belief—that someone is unworthy, deficient, or evil; that someone must be made morally better; or that someone deserves to be punished. These beliefs are often nothing more than projections—the displacement onto others of the qualities we hate in ourselves. An example is someone who condemns his neighbor for racial intolerance but cherishes his membership in a whites-only club. Projection means, "I can't hate myself, but I can hate you."

Therefore, when we turn our negative attitudes and beliefs against others, we often are really turning them against ourselves. This means that if I pray to manipulate or harm you, I am really praying to harm myself. This may be one reason behind the universal belief that curses and spells can rebound and injure the person making them.

Negative beliefs, therefore, are not as outer directed as we often think. Now let's explore how these beliefs, if turned inward, can harm.

HARMING OURSELVES: NEGATIVE BELIEF TURNED INWARD

One the most memorable moments of my childhood came in third grade when a dozen of us kids were rehearsing the annual school play. During a rare moment of discipline, while we were standing dutifully on stage, I heard a dull thud. I looked around and saw the biggest boy in the class lying on the floor, out like a light, with an egg-sized abrasion on his forehead. Then there was another crash as a nearby girl hit the deck—then another and another. Kids were falling like timber, and classmates were screaming like magpies. These were not gentle swoons but full-body crashes that would have been a credit to any movie stuntman. The facial abrasions were swelling into sickening lumps, some of which had started to bleed. The poor teacher was frantic. As soon as she would haul off one kid, another would topple. We were terrified. It was as if some invisible monster were stalking us, slashing right and left. Someone ran for the principal, a stern disciplinarian who could put an immediate stop to any nonsense. He got there in time to catch a falling body and prevent another casualty. Realizing this was a medical emergency, the shaken teacher finally abandoned her station to call the town doctor. By the time he arrived, the kids had begun to recover. They looked terrible—ashen, scared, and bruised. Nobody had ever seen anything like this. Theories abounded to explain things—poor ventilation, a silent gas leak, and the inevitable "something we ate"—but nothing panned out.

I wasn't aware of it at the time, of course, but this elementary school epidemic was a classic example of mass hysteria or sociogenic illness, both of which are calamities based on the power of a negative belief turned inward. In all such instances, the negative effects come not from someone "out there" but from ourselves, in the form of a negative expectation. This process is indistinguishable from a self-hex.

These episodes are not rare. A similar incident on a larger scale was described in 1985 by author Norman Cousins, the former editor of *Saturday Review*. He described a football game at which it was announced to the entire stadium that six or seven people may have suffered food poisoning from soda purchased from a particular concession stand. Following the alert, more than two hundred people had to be hospitalized with symptoms of nausea and vomiting, although many of them had not gone near the concession stand in question. When it was reported the next day that the soda was not contaminated, everybody suddenly got well.[87]

A Canadian researcher reviewed seventy-eight outbreaks of mass hysteria that had been documented in Quebec from 1872 to 1972 and found that the greatest proportion, 44 percent, occurred in schools.

They were most common during periods of uncertainty and social stress. Convulsions were reported in one-fourth of the outbreaks. The episodes were not uncommon, occurring annually in one of every 1,000 schools in Quebec. Researchers calculated that they affected on average ten people per 100,000 each year—a rate similar to that for common infectious diseases.[88]

"A classic example [of this sort of thing] is voodoo death," says Herbert Benson, M.D., president of Harvard Medical School's Mind/Body Medical Institute. "It comes about when people believe a hex was placed on them." Benson cites animal studies that show there is an area in the insular cortex of the brain that, when stimulated, causes the heart to experience ventricular fibrillation and sudden death. This can occur anytime we experience extreme fear, even in a dream.[89]

Benson recalls the time he essentially hexed himself through the effects of memories stored in his unconscious mind. It happened during his internship, as he was about to examine an Asian man. As the patient came into the examining room, Benson says he "absolutely panicked." He performed the exam in a cold sweat, his heart racing. When he finished, he explained to the patient his fears. The Asian man was delighted. "Ha, ha, ha, Yank. Now you die!" he said, recreating his Tokyo Joe film role from World War II–era movies. Benson had responded to the sight of the former actor with the same emotions he experienced while watching the movies as a boy. "Wired in me was this fear," he observed. "When I saw him, although I couldn't identify the fear, it expressed itself."[90]

BELIEF BECOMES BIOLOGY

We physicians often deny the reality of hexes, spells, and curses, but we have a version of the same thing: the *nocebo* effect. The nocebo and placebo effects are opposites. The latter refers to the *positive* physical effects that occur as a result of belief, expectation, and suggestion. In contrast, nocebo effects are the *negative* results of negative beliefs, feelings, and emotions. Nocebo effects are essentially self-curses.

Robert A. Hahn, an epidemiologist at the Centers for Disease Control and Prevention in Atlanta, believes nocebo effects are a matter of life and death. People who feel hopeless—the psychological state most often associated with those who are hexed and cursed—have greater disease and mortality rates. "More than 5 percent of US ischemic heart disease mortality, or 26,000 deaths a year, are attributable to depression, independent of other known risk factors," Hahn states. In the Framingham Heart Study, in which thousands of residents of Framingham, Massachusetts, have been followed over decades, women aged forty-five to sixty who *believed* they were likely to suffer a heart attack were 3.7 times more likely to die from coronary conditions than women who didn't consider themselves particularly coronary prone.[91]

BELIEF AND HEALING: LESSONS FROM SURGERY

The impact of belief on healing was demonstrated in patients with retinal detachment at Columbia-Presbyterian Medical Center in New York City.[92] When the retina detaches from the back of the eye, a blind spot in the visual field occurs. Retinal detachment can be a frightening situation because the person faces the possibility that his or her blindness may be permanent.

Dr. Graham Clark, an eye surgeon, reviewed several hundred of his retinal detachment cases and found a 400 percent difference in healing time between the most and least rapid healers. Healing time in this situation is the number of days from surgery to the appearance of pigmentation in the retina, which indicates completion of the process of reattachment and recovery of vision. Normally, the variation in biological processes of this sort is around 20 percent. Clark noted that the state of mind of some of the patients seemed to correlate with poor healing. One woman whose operation was a failure was so tense before surgery she required an extraordinarily large amount of anesthetic. Before the operation was repeated, Clark asked the hospital chaplain to help her deal with her anxieties. For the second surgical procedure, she required the smallest amount of anesthesia in Clark's experience, and she healed rapidly.

Another woman had not begun to heal six days after surgery. Clark arranged for chaplain Robert B. Reeves, Jr., to visit her, but the woman cut him off with meaningless chitchat. When he returned the next day, she tried the same thing—but then suddenly switched gears and began, with broken voice, to pour forth incredible stories of bitterness, hatred, fear, and guilt resulting from the failure of almost every personal relationship in her life. Clark reexamined her the next morning. He found that, overnight, she had caught up on her healing; her retina was just as it should be.

Why the 400 percent variance in healing? Clark's team analyzed five hundred cases of retinal detachment, searching for physical indicators that might explain the differences. They found no correlation in healing rate with age, sex, severity of the eye damage, the type or extent of surgery, the type and degree of anesthesia, body chemistry, or even the presence or absence of other diseases. Their impressions from dealing with patients such as those above led them to believe that psychological factors were more powerful in healing than they had believed.

The research team designed two studies, involving fifty-one and forty-six patients, respectively, with detached retinas. They found strong statistical correlations between psychological states and the speed of healing following surgery, all of which was done by the same surgeon, Dr. Graham Clark. Patients who healed quickly confronted their situation directly, were trusting of the surgeon, were optimistic about results, were confident about coping and doing things for themselves, were willing to accept their situation without special concern, and accepted the bad with the good in life. Those who healed slowly tended to feel trapped in life with their back to the wall. They were suspicious of others and pessimistic. They felt they could not cope well, and they acted as if they were entitled to the services of others. They were angry about being dependent on others and avoided personal contact. They often felt helpless—"It's God's will, so what can you do?" or "It's a dirty trick."

In classic forms of hexing seen in premodern societies, hexed individuals demonstrate many of these features. They know something terrible has befallen them, and they feel trapped with no place to turn. They cooperate with the hex, give up, and often die.

Looking at specific individuals in the research study who healed slowly, it appears as if they had hexed themselves. Often the self-curse took the form of guilt and punishment. "A woman of Christian Science faith failed to heal despite the relative simplicity of the surgical procedure. Afterwards, she indicated to the surgeon that having surgery was in conflict with Christian science beliefs." Before reoperating on her, the surgeon made clear to her that he was only doing a mechanical task, like setting a broken bone, and that her faith was the major factor in her actual healing. He helped her reconcile her Christian Science beliefs with the need for surgery, and she healed quickly after the second operation. A married man involved in a sexual affair felt he was being punished in the form of blindness for his deeds. The speed of healing of his surgery increased sharply when he decided to end his infidelity. "As strange as it may seem to the scientifically sophisticated," the researchers observed, "even well-educated people, on an emotional level, still believe that blindness may result from sin." They noted that some people, rather than facing up to their own tangled feelings about themselves, often project them onto their physicians. Psychiatrists call this "negative transference." For example, a patient headed for surgery may tell everyone who will listen that he's been railroaded against his will and that his surgeon has a bad record. When patients predict failure, this can turn into a self-fulfilling prophecy.

The Columbia-Presbyterian researchers concluded that some types of religious faith were healthy and some were not. Those patients who healed and regained their sight quickly following retinal surgery tended to demonstrate a "transcendent" belief:

> These are people whose world view is such that they are sincerely convinced that life will continue to be meaningful whether they see again or not. The faith aroused by their ideology permits them to be relatively unconcerned about the exigencies of their situation. . . . These patients affirm in either secular or religious language: "Whether I see or go blind, life will continue to be meaningful and rich."

In contrast,

> most patients appear to have been taught that faith is believing intensely that you will receive what you wish, and that if you believe and pray sufficiently, reality can be changed. . . . This type of faith is usually quite brittle, easily destroyed or challenged by adverse circumstances. Any negative word about the surgeon, his methods, or the outcome of the surgery becomes an immediate

source of concern. . . . This kind of faith is [a] distortion of the nature of faith certainly in the Christian tradition and probably within most religious traditions.

Patients who demonstrated the transcendent religious perspective—who said that life would continue to be meaningful and rich, no matter what—were not common. They made up only 1 or 2 percent of the retinal detachment population. More common were people who demonstrated a "split ideology: they were enough influenced by the scientific culture to acknowledge the necessity of the scientific medical procedures, but also felt that to regain their vision they needed to trust God in a way that did not include the surgeon and his methods."[93]

THE ASTRONAUT'S MOTHER

Apollo 14 astronaut Edgar Mitchell is one of only twelve human beings who have walked on the moon. Following his adventures in outer space, Mitchell began to explore the inner space of the mind. In the early 1970s he founded the Institute of Noetic Sciences in Sausalito, California, which is dedicated to investigating the mysteries of human consciousness.

In 1972, just prior to opening the doors of his new institute, Mitchell was asked to deliver a series of lectures at a conference in Little Rock, Arkansas. The occasion was special for Mitchell because his mother, who lived in neighboring Oklahoma, would be able to drive to the meeting and spend time with him. But there was a problem; his mother, then in her sixties, had developed severe difficulties with her vision because of glaucoma. She considered surgery too risky. By now she was legally blind without her glasses, which through the years had grown progressively thicker, and without which she simply could not see.

During the conference Mitchell met several remarkable men and women. Among them was Norbu Chen, an American who had studied a form of ancient Tibetan Buddhism that embodied a great deal of shamanistic practice. Norbu Chen purported to be a healer.

One evening Mitchell introduced him to his mother. He wanted to determine if Chen was "real or just talk" and to see if Chen could help his mother with her vision. Mitchell was skeptical anything would come of it. He also was uncertain about how Mrs. Mitchell would respond to Chen. "My mother," he said, "a fundamentalist Christian all her life, had definite and traditional ideas about how the mind was capable of influencing matter through healing—either by the hand of God, or by that of Satan. There was no middle ground."

Chen was convinced he could help, but he made no promises. He merely suggested they try and see what would happen. Mitchell's mother proved to be a good sport about the whole thing and agreed that something good might result.

The next day Mitchell, his mother, and Norbu Chen met in Mitchell's hotel room. Chen asked her to sit in a chair and relax, and then he appeared to enter a meditative trance through singing his mantra. Soon his hands floated over Mrs. Mitchell's head and rested over her eyes. Mitchell felt that his mother was accepting and trusting. After a few minutes, Chen announced that he was finished and suggested that Mrs. Mitchell go to bed, get some sleep, and treat herself gently, as if she had been through major surgery. He suggested that she consume grape juice and broth for nourishment.

Although Mitchell was exceedingly curious and wanted something to have happened, at the same time he was trying to be the detached, clinical observer. Nonetheless, he had the sense that he had witnessed something extraordinary. He was not wrong. At 6 A.M. the next morning his mother rushed into his room and exclaimed, "Son, I can see, I can see!"

To prove it, she grabbed her tattered Bible and began to read from it, while holding her glasses in hand. Then she said quietly, "I can see. Praise the Lord, *I can see!*" As if to demonstrate her faith, she dropped her glasses to the floor and ground the thick lens into shards under her heel. "Needless to say," Mitchell states, "I was impressed."

Mitchell could neither deny nor explain what had happened. He conceded that this was not science—no careful before-and-after exams had been conducted on his mother's eyes and visual acuity—but he knew her reaction was authentic and believed she had not been duped. Besides, she drove back to Oklahoma alone, a distance of several hundred miles and she did it without her glasses, which she was incapable of doing before.

Then an event happened that confirmed for Mitchell his growing conviction in the power of belief. His mother had returned home and assumed her routines, still unassisted by contact lenses or eyeglasses. One day she called Mitchell to inquire whether or not Norbu Chen was a Christian. She realized that his name sounded Asian, which meant that his religious ideas probably did not coincide with her beloved faith. Though Mitchell did not want to pursue this, she was adamant in demanding to know the faith of the man whose efforts had helped restore her sight. "Reluctantly, and perhaps ominously," Mitchell relates, "I told her Norbu was in fact not a Christian, and the moment I did so the deep pain of regret was clear in her voice."

Mrs. Mitchell insisted that her new sight was not the work of the Lord but of the darker forces of this world. Norbu Chen, she was absolutely certain, was an instrument of evil. No matter what her son said to her, she would not be dissuaded. Her restored vision was the work of Satan. "Hours later, the gift slipped away and thick new glasses were required."[94]

Mrs. Mitchell's healing seemed real. She had been legally blind, and overnight her vision was restored. The improvement continued until, through a change in belief, it fizzled. Suspicious of the healer's Asian roots, she became convinced she had come under the influence of Satan. In her mind her healing was transformed into a demonic act. As she became convinced she had been victimized by evil forces, the miracle of sight was retracted.

These events raise important questions. Where do curses come from—from some disembodied, evil force in the world, from our own mind, or both? How often do we sabotage our own healing? Are our religions, in their attempts to carve the world into the divine and demonic, actually *causing* illness and disease by condemning healers outside that particular faith as agents of darkness? Are our religions so out of touch with healing that their believers sometimes prefer disease to getting well? By obstructing the work of compassionate healers such as Norbu Chen, can religious beliefs become a curse?

Our Western religions in general acknowledge that the ability to heal is divine, not demonic, and that healing is not restricted to any particular creed. But a few religious folk contend that healers outside their camp are bogus, fraudulent, and satanic. Although this point of view masquerades as deep religious insight, it is religious intolerance in disguise. It leads to a great irony—that, in the name of Jesus, the Great Physician, healing is often rejected.

PART 3

THE BIOLOGY OF CURSES

We are going to need a lot more than fig leaves to protect us . . . especially now when it is becoming obvious
that the enemy we face is not a chill wind or a fire-
breathing demon, but something already inside us. . . .
It's not the devil who is to blame, but that part of us
that operates its own agenda, ruthlessly ignoring the
possibility of suffering and very real pain for the rest.
—*Lyall Watson*, Dark Nature

THE BIOLOGY
OF CURSES

WHEN I FIRST ENCOUNTERED the evidence that 5 percent of Americans admit they have prayed for harm for others, I was stunned. I realized that this was only the percentage who were willing to admit to the Gallup pollsters that they have done so; the actual number of people who use prayer negatively is surely much higher.[1] Who would do such a thing? I do not believe that those who use prayer to harm others are diabolical individuals who spend their time hatching plots to do in their neighbors. For the most part, they are normal, well-behaved citizens. I am also convinced that they are not fully in charge of what they are doing—that they may be using prayer negatively against their will; that they are, in effect, under a curse.

THE URGE TO CURSE: OUR GENETIC SHADOW

We have all had the experience of being unkind to another person before we knew what we were doing—for example, the unkind remark that slipped out that we later wished we could retract. These moments suggest that we have an inner compulsion to injure others, that we are not in control. Are we compelled to cause harm? The answer may lie in our biology—our genes, our DNA.

One of the premises of evolutionary biology is that our genes are programmed to reproduce and perpetuate themselves by any means possible. Ethical and moral behavior is not part of our genes' strategy unless these activities serve their quest for survival. As Robert Wright states in his book *The Moral Animal,* "We are designed not to worry about anyone else's happiness, except in the sort of cases where such worrying has, during evolution, benefited our genes."[2]

Most evolutionary biologists consider genes the ultimate expressions of selfishness. According to biologist Lyall Watson, their strategies have evolved into three basic genetic laws. The first is: be nice to insiders. This means behaving kindly toward our offspring and blood relatives who share our genes, because if their genes survive, so do ours, since our genetic makeup is similar. This is the basis of the adage that "blood is thicker than water." Although we may feel good about behaving altruistically toward our kin, we should not flatter ourselves about our motivations. We are really being nice to ourselves, because it is our genes that are benefiting.

The second genetic law is the mirror image of the first: be nasty to outsiders. An outsider is anyone who is genetically different from us. Being mean to outsiders helps us capture scarce resources for ourselves, which helps perpetuate our genes, not theirs.

The third genetic law is: cheat a lot. Be deceptive and cruel, and do whatever is necessary to maximize our own chances of survival. Summing up the effects of these three laws, Watson states,

> The behavior [of our genes] is designed to interfere with the happiness of others. If genes were capable of having emotions, [they] would say things like: "Happiness is making others unhappy.". . . [Their] strengths depend upon billions of years of selection for selfishness.[3]

The Swiss psychologist C. G. Jung described the shadow, that part of the mind that is the storehouse for everything we dislike about ourselves and do not want to accept consciously. Watson considers this more than a psychological concept and contends that the shadow is rooted in our biology. The shadow, he feels, is ultimately genetic:

> Everything Jungians believe about the shadow—that it is dangerous, disorderly, fugitive, distasteful, sensual, stupid and lacking in spirituality—is true also of the genes. Every time we laugh when someone slips on a banana peel, it is the shadow showing. Every time we take pleasure in the pain of a rival, it is a genetic pleasure. Each time we become impulsive, display exaggerated feelings about others, feel humiliated, find excessive fault, display

unreasonable anger, or behave "as if we are not ourselves," we are seeing the genetic shadow in action.[4]

Modern psychology has ignored the genetic roots of the shadow and considered it only a psychological phenomenon. But unless we make a place for the biological origin of the shadow, we will continue to underestimate its power. We will be unable to understand our compulsions to harm others through malevolent thoughts, negative prayers, and curses, and we will remain unprotected from them as well.

Many people resist the idea of a genetic shadow. They feel that if our tendency for wickedness is rooted in our genes, then we are biologically evil and therefore innately depraved and hopeless. This means we are not morally responsible for the pain we cause others. Because we can't yet change our genes, we are victims of forces beyond our control and without hope of moral improvement. If widely accepted, these beliefs would play havoc with our legal system and would lead to a breakdown of individual and social responsibility. Because this scenario is too horrible to contemplate, it is more convenient to ignore the possibility of a genetic shadow.

One way of getting ourselves off the genetic hook is to invent surrogates for our evil ways, such as an external devil. This shifts the blame for our bad behavior to an outside entity. But claiming that we are controlled by the devil instead of our genes is no solution to the problem of evil actions toward others. Whether I am under the influence of my genes, or whether "the devil made me do it," the end result is the same.

DARWIN AND SIN

Let's take a closer look at the main themes of modern evolutionary theory.

1. All living organisms are constructed by groups of genes whose purpose is to leave more copies of themselves. They are the ultimate examples of selfishness.
2. The inherent selfishness of our hereditary material compels organisms to compete with others in the game of survival of the fittest.

3. In their attempt to become fitter, organisms are always struggling to adapt to their environment, which is always changing. This means that the struggle for fitness never ends.

4. Humans, of all the organisms, can paradoxically develop altruistic qualities in opposition to the selfish dictates of their genes, through educational and other cultural efforts.

"Does this list look familiar?" asks biologist Brian Goodwin in his book *How the Leopard Changed Its Spots.* "Here is a very similar list of principles from another domain":

1. Humanity is born in sin; we have a base inheritance.
2. Humanity is therefore condemned to a life of conflict and
3. Perpetual toil.
4. By faith and moral effort humanity can be saved from its fallen, selfish state.[5]

Goodwin is struck by the resemblance of Darwinian theory to the legend of the fall. "Darwinism . . . has its metaphorical roots in . . . the story of the fall and redemption of humanity," he observes. "Darwinian metaphors are grounded in the myth of human sin and redemption, . . . so selfish genes, struggle, progress, good works, and the possibility of altruism for humans are precisely the right images to use in conveying the meaning of evolution from this perspective."[6]

If Goodwin is correct, no wonder Darwinian evolutionary theory is repellent to so many people. It maintains not only that we evolved from simpler organisms—the usual reason for its rejection—but also, to make matters worse, it implies that we are utterly unworthy beings spawned in sin and condemned to a life of horrible struggle unless we muster the courage to repent. It isn't surprising that millions would shun such an unattractive image of themselves.

But Darwinian theory does help us understand why we curse others and pray negatively against them. Evil acts are just the sort of thing you'd expect selfish genes to promote in their stop-at-nothing quest to compete and survive. Cursing others would help the genes meet their goal in an environment where resources are often limited.

Some scientists see images of the fall not just in our own biology, but throughout the entire universe. Science reporter John Horgan writes,

Some physicists have speculated that the cosmos had its beginnings in symmetry-rich particles called superstrings. Those almost infinitely malleable loops of ur-stuff allegedly gave rise to all matter, forces, space and time. "In the beginning," [journalist George] Johnson writes, "was a world of mathematical purity that shattered to give birth to the world in which we find ourselves. How is this belief different from the Fall from the Garden of Eden. . . . ?"[7]

Are remnants of the fall lodged in the primordial matter that was spewed forth in the Big Bang, which eventually formed the stuff of our genes? Does the entire universe have a shadow, cast from the first moment of its beginning? Are even our genes fallen?

SUICIDE FROM THE INSIDE: OUR CELLULAR CURSE

Biologists have discovered that a "cellular curse" is taking place millions of times every day in our bodies. Unlike most curses, however, this one has benevolent consequences. Our cellular curse is a natural phenomenon without which we could not survive. It is the process of cells dying off, which takes place in rhythm with the formation of new cells.[8]

Without cell death we certainly would not look human. Consider the development of the human hand before birth. At a certain stage of the embryo, webbing exists between the fingers. Cellular death is believed to remove the webbed tissue, allowing the emergence of distinct fingers.[9]

Life depends on the multiplication and division of cells. We require, however, a delicate balance between cell division and cell death; otherwise we would die as a result of the spiraling overproduction of our own cells and the development of cancers of all sorts. That is why massive cell death is normal in all living animals.

Normal cell death is called apoptosis, from the Greek word for falling, as in the falling away of leaves in autumn. Only recently have biologists begun to appreciate how extensive and important cell death is.

Martin C. Raff, professor of biology at University College, London, and fellow of the Royal Society, estimates that as the brain develops, about half of the nerve cells die off soon after they are formed, and that this process takes place in other developing organs as well.[10] Large-scale cellular death continues into adulthood. Before you finish reading this chapter, hundreds of millions of the one hundred trillion cells in your body will die. The simple reason we don't shrink away to nothing is that a new cell arises for every one that dies.

To Raff, cell death appears to be a kind of suicide. And its occurrence depends on what the neighbors say. "Suicide among some cells is a social phenomenon," he says. "Many developing nerve cells, for instance, kill themselves unless they get signals from the cells they contact."

Raff explored whether all cells are actually programmed to kill themselves unless their neighbors continually tell them to stay alive. He found that if he removed a type of brain cell called an oligodendrocyte from the brain and placed it in a culture dish, it underwent apoptosis within a day or two, even when supplied with all the nutrients it needed. But if neighboring cells in the brain were added to the dish, the oligodendrocytes survived, and they survived if the signaling molecules made by the neighboring cells were added to the dish. Obviously the neighbor cells were sending a message to the oligodendrocytes to live. When the message was cut off, the cells shut down. Raff and his colleagues tested other types of cells as well. "In every case the cells committed suicide unless signaled by other cells," they found. There was only one exception—blastomeres, cells generated by a fertilized egg, which survive and divide without encouragement from other cells.

It is as if our cells contain a ready-made "poison pill," Raff states, that "is already embedded under the skin, poised to release its deadly works unless something actively interferes." The curse, it seems, is innate. Whether or not it is deactivated depends on a second-level message, a kind of whisper from the neighbors that says, "Live!"

Gruesome? Hardly. Life depends on the curse contained in every cell and the willingness of normal cells to die. "Such a mechanism could ensure that any cell that ends up in the wrong place is automatically eliminated: isolated from its life-affirming partners, it quickly dispatches itself," Raff states. And, "If too many cells were generated by cell division, some would not receive enough signals to resist suicide, which would bring the population back to its proper size. Such a system, in short, would ensure that cells survive only when and where they are needed."

How can cancer cells, which defy normal suicidal tendencies, be encouraged to be willing victims of the intrinsic biological curse and die like normal, well-behaved, "good" cells? The answer could transform the treatment of cancer in general. It could also yield answers to diseases such as multiple sclerosis in which some cells are destroyed or die too willingly—cells like oligodendrocytes, which normally function as the insulation around nerve cells in the brain and spinal cord.

THE CELLULAR CURSE AND PRAYER

The normal tendency of our cells to commit suicide has consequences for how we pray. Because this process is crucial for our survival, to pray that all the cells in our body live and flourish is a negative prayer. If such a prayer were answered, it would be fatal. At the cellular level we need death as much as life; our existence depends on a delicate balance between the two. This means that every prayer for life is also a prayer for death, for if only life prevailed at the cellular level, no cells would die and the delicate balance of survival would be fatally upset. At the level of our tissues, "May the Almighty slay and preserve me equally!" is a more rational prayer than asking for life alone.

In order to be healthy, we need just the right amount of the cellular curse. Too little cellular suicide is as fatal as too much. Rather than agonizing about what the right balance may be, the best solution may be to pray, "May the cells in my body behave normally," and leave the details to our cellular wisdom and that of the Almighty. Any other approach may not work or may actually backfire as a curse in disguise.

Is there any evidence to support this approach?

PRAYING FOR NORMAL

No one would have predicted that Dr. Leonard Laskow would become a spiritual healer. He trained as a traditional obstetrician and gynecologist at New York University School of Medicine and Stanford Medical Center and became a fellow of the American College of Obstetrics and Gynecology. In the course of his medical practice, however, he discovered that if he allowed himself to experience deep, unconditional love for his patients, healing responses would occur, and he began to cultivate this talent. His experiences are detailed in his book, *Healing with Love*.[11]

Laskow was trained in scientific medicine and has immense respect for the traditions of science. He was therefore willing to subject his healing abilities to scientific testing by Dr. Glen Rein, a biophysicist at the Quantum Biology Research Laboratory in Palo Alto, California. Rein was interested in Laskow's ability to influence the biological function of cells with his thoughts, images, and intentions. The growth of tumor cells in culture dishes was chosen as a test subject, because this process could be monitored quantitatively using state-of-the-art techniques and also because this biological process is relevant to real life. The actual protocol involved measuring the synthesis of DNA by the cancer cells, as indicated by the amount of radioactive thymidine, an amino acid they incorporated, and determining the rate of cell proliferation by standard methods.

Laskow shifted into a specific state of consciousness and mentally focused on three petri dishes containing cancer cells held in the palm of his hand. A nonhealer in an adjacent room was performing the same activity while reading a book to minimize any effect his mental activity might have on the cells. All six dishes were evaluated blindly for their growth characteristics. The results indicated that different ways of focusing mentally were associated with different biological responses from the cancer cells. Of the five methods Laskow employed, only two showed significant effects. The most effective intention was "return to the natural order and harmony of the normal cell line" (39 percent inhibition). Asking for God's will to manifest was half as effective (21 percent inhibition). Adopting unconditional love for the cancer cells was neutral, neither stimulating nor inhibiting cell growth.[12]

Both Rein and Laskow believe these results have important implications for healers and the way people pray. But they do not recommend these methods as a universal approach. Perhaps they are "healer specific," meaning that they work better for some people than others. Or they may be "target specific," meaning that they are more effective for some problems than for others. These questions are amenable to further scientific study. They show that good science not only answers questions, it raises them as well.

Other experimental studies support the idea that healing methods vary in their effectiveness from healer to healer. What works for one healer may not work for another. Spindrift, Inc., a research group dedicated to the scientific evaluation of prayer-based healing, found that in studies involving lower organisms and plants, a Thy-will-be-done, nondirected approach was more effective than one in which specific outcomes were requested.[13] For Laskow, however, this approach was not the most effective. These findings suggest that there is no formula for prayer in healing, no one best way.

Even the simplest bodily processes are dauntingly complicated. In view of our appalling ignorance of the human body, asking for a "return to the natural order and harmony" appears to be a sound strategy in praying for healing. This approach does not require us to know the ins and outs of apoptosis. We can let the body figure out which cells should live and which should die. Our role may be to set the process in motion, not to tell the body in detail what to do. If we forget this, we may find ourselves inadvertently participating in negative prayer.

CURING AND CURSING: A FINE LINE

BETWEEN *curing* AND *cursing,* there is only a letter's difference. Curing often involves cursing, and vice versa. The fine line between the two often makes it difficult to determine what, exactly, constitutes a negative prayer.

My earliest lesson in how curses can cure took place when I was five years old, on a small cotton farm in central Texas where I grew up. In the 1940s, life on those bleak blackland prairies was an endless round of bank foreclosures, boll weevils, and drought. As an additional nuisance, during the summertime the few head of cattle owned by every small cotton farmer were in constant danger of attack by screwworms, *Callitroga americana,* a devilish pest that was particularly well named. Female blowflies would lay their eggs in any open wound of an animal, and the eggs would develop into small white maggots. These would bore like a screw through the animal's tissues, tearing away the flesh and leaving gigantic holes in their wake. As a consequence the animal could be maimed for life or, not uncommonly, would die of the accompanying infection.

Like physicians making rounds, farmers continually surveyed their cattle during the summer, looking for any cut or wound that had become infected. Treatment was gruesome. The animal had to be captured and immobilized while the squirming mass of maggots was scraped from the infected site. Then as the animal writhed in pain, the blood-raw cavity was doused with a concoction of foul-smelling chemicals to cauterize it and destroy any remaining screwworms and unhatched eggs. But sometimes the treatment didn't work.

One day, after multiple attempts, my father gave up on treating a young calf with a gaping wound on its flank. It could not walk, was in constant agony, would not eat, and was slowly dying. Looking at the calf, my father simply said, "Let's go get Maria."

I had never heard of Maria and had no idea what my father had in mind. We drove for miles down a narrow unpaved road into the prairie countryside, eventually turning onto a lane that led to a small, rundown shack situated conspicuously in the middle of a small cotton field. Maria, who spoke little English, lived here with her Mexican family, who subsisted as farm laborers. After a lengthy conversation I could not understand, she followed my father back to the car and returned with us to our farm and the dying calf, saying nothing the entire trip.

Maria, I later discovered, was a *curandera*, a folk healer. The local farmers kept her in reserve for the really tough cases. They frequently preferred her to the expensive local veterinarian who, in those preantibiotic days, was often as helpless as they against overwhelming screwworm infections.

Maria got out of the car without a word and began walking to the barnyard where the sick calf lay.

"What's she going to do?" I whispered to my father.

"She's going to talk out the worms," he said.

I was completely confused by his reply and was stunned to think that worms could actually converse with humans. I tried to coax an explanation from my father, by nature a reticent man, but could not. I began to trail after Maria, not wanting to miss anything, but my father, towering above me, placed his hand on my shoulder and said, "Son, we can't watch her. She has to be alone."

Disappointed, I viewed Maria from a considerable distance. I saw her dark figure kneel before the calf, which was on its side. It seemed curiously unafraid of her. She made several passes with her hands over the animal, and then, after being completely still for many minutes, her lips began to move.

After a half hour the ritual ended, and this mysterious woman signaled to my father that she was finished by simply raising her head slowly and fixing her gaze on him. He nodded to me that it was okay, and we both walked slowly in her direction. Curiously, my father paid almost no attention to the calf; he seemed to have no doubts whatsoever about the results of her therapy. Maria walked with us to the car, and we retraced the country roads on the long drive back to her house. My father escorted her to the front porch of the shack, where they began to converse. After several minutes he paid Maria and we left once more to return home.

"What did she say to you, Dad?"

"Maria knows why the calf is sick. She says it has a strong will and is always misbehaving. It got the cut on its flank from barbed wire when it tried to escape the pasture and the rest of the cows. She says the infection is the price it has paid, but that it is a very smart calf and has learned its lesson. She made a bargain with the worms. She told them they have succeeded in teaching the calf a valuable lesson. But if they stay the calf will die, and they will eventually die with it. It would be better for everyone if they leave now and spare the calf."

"But what if they don't?"

"She threatened them with stronger measures if they stay. She says the worms listened and are afraid. They are leaving now and the calf is going to be all right."

"But how does Maria know all this?" My father, sensing my pained confusion, looked at me and smiled.

"Maria," he said patiently, "knows what things mean."

It was late when we arrived home, and while Dad finished the chores in the moonlight I grabbed a flashlight and ran to the barnyard and the calf. I had to have a look for myself. The calf was standing, the first time in days, eating from a trough. There were no worms in sight in the gaping wound, which—did I imagine it?—was smaller. In a few days the wound had healed completely and the calf was fine.

Was Maria engaging in curing or cursing? As we saw earlier, it depends on which side of the fence you're on—whether you're the calf or the worms. This issue can bedevil our attempts to categorize prayer—to say, for example, that a positive prayer is one that is loving and compassionate and that a negative prayer is always malevolent. Prayers and curses can't be put in a box.

I didn't know it at the time, of course, but "talking out worms" is a universal phenomenon. It is relevant to our exploration because it clearly shows that the distinctions between curing and cursing, positive and negative prayer, can be exceedingly blurred.

The following episode, reported in 1967 by the Greek physician Angelos Tanagras, would not have surprised Maria. In addition to being a doctor, Tanagras was a highly decorated admiral in the Greek navy and a scholar on Greek history and legend. He was keenly interested in what he termed psychoboly, the action of "man's impulses . . . upon living or inorganic matter." As an example, he reported the following case, which involves the experiences of Monsieur A. Laforest, "a French literary man," in the jungles of Colombia.

Laforest begins by acknowledging the fabulous nature of his account but insists that he "was witness to a genuine miracle. . . . This is not an invented story, nor is it a trick," he asserts. "I guarantee the absolute truth of the facts I am about to describe, as I saw them. . . ."

Laforest went into the jungle to hunt wild pigeons, and en route he met the beadle, a minor parish officer, of the church of Simiti. The beadle volunteered to guide him to a spot where game was plentiful, which happened to be on the path he was traveling. When Laforest inquired about the purpose of his journey, the beadle replied, "I am going to Joselito's to get rid of his fish worms. It is an exorcism. I go here and there in the countryside ridding fish of worms. I am the only one in the whole country who can do this."

Laforest, not comprehending, remained silent and went along to see what would happen. They soon arrived at Joselito's wood cabin, and Joselito explained to the beadle that the white worms had invaded his store of salted fish. He showed them about a hundred infested fish hanging on an iron wire. The beadle examined them, saw they were full of worms, and shook his head. "They will only disappear by exorcism," he announced. Then he stepped back a pace and began repeating in a low voice, "Le conjuro animal inmundo. . . . Salga! . . . Salga! . . . Salga! . . . Creo! . . . Creo! . . . Creo!"

"He had hardly finished when the worms began to drop from the fish like iron filings," Laforest reported. Joselito then thanked the beadle, as if this event were the most natural thing in the world.

"I approached the fish to examine them," Laforest said. "Not a single worm remained. A few words from the beadle had been sufficient to loosen them from the flesh in which they had been buried." Laforest continued, "I could not understand it at all, but the miracle had been carried out before my own eyes. Was it witchcraft? . . . prestidigitation? It hardly matters!"

Laforest, stunned, returned to Simiti, where he hastened to see the priest and tell him what had occurred. The good man shook his head:

"No, it is not witchcraft," he said, "it is simple exorcism . . . accompanied by great faith. My beadle is the simplest and most devout of all my parishioners. The words themselves are meaningless. . . . Be like my beadle and you will possess the same power." The beadle's powers surprised no one in the region. "Sometimes flies lay their eggs in the wound of a horse, thus making the wound fatal But my beadle heals the wound from a distance of several kilometers, provided he is told in which part of the animal's body the wound is situated."[14]

Plants can also be invaded by worms, and the worms apparently can be driven away by the methods that are effective in animals. Tanagras reports a case in which a priest in the Caucasus was invited to visit a Russian farmer, whose field of sunflowers was infested by worms that were causing great damage. The priest began to recite with great fervor prayers composed for such occasions by Saint Basil and others saints of the Greek Orthodox Church. The worms, present in great numbers, "began to drop off the plants and flee like a minor torrent in the opposite direction."[15]

Similar methods appear to work on insects. Tanagras reports that in 1920, during the Greek occupation of Asia Minor, a Greek professor journeyed to the village of Eskisehir for the purpose of examining the local antiquities. For his accommodation, an empty house was requisitioned, but in the door of this house, at a height of about six feet, a swarm of bees had built their nest. Every effort was made to dislodge the nest, without success. The maidservant, very disturbed by the proximity of the bees, advised calling in a local *hodja,* a Turkish priest, who had the ability of exorcising and would therefore be able to solve the problem. "[T]he hodja . . . came in the evening and stayed for some time in order to pray. The bees were not seen again and no dead bees were found, as would have been the case if fumigation or a poison had been used."[16]

Sometimes the bees get the upper hand, as in a disturbing account concerning one of Brazil's most famous psychic surgeons. As reports of the man's healing ability grew, so did his ego. He became increasingly arrogant and prideful, traits generally considered by genuine healers to be incompatible with their calling. At the height of his fame—and hubris—he and a friend were paddling a boat in the middle of a wide river when they were attacked by a swarm of killer bees. Oddly, the bees attacked only the healer, leaving the other boatman unharmed. "They want only me!" the man shouted as he tried in vain to fight off the bees. "They are punishing me because of my pride! I have been untrue as a healer!" The man dived into the river to escape the bees, but he was unsuccessful. As his horrified companion looked on helplessly, they stung him to death.[17]

"SOFT" CURSES

I am fond of accounts such as that of Maria the *curandera*, because they show a softer side to cursing than we ordinarily imagine. Maria bargained with the offending organisms and steered away from unnecessary violence in favor of a live-and-let-live policy. Curses don't have to be loosed in full fury to be effective. Aggression and violence can be held in reserve until lesser measures fail.

I have known people who are so opposed to violence that they reject praying, imaging, or visualizing the death of their cancer or whatever their disease may be. They choose instead a strategy like Maria's—bargaining, striking a deal, making a tradeoff that will benefit both parties. One patient I knew decided not to harm her cancer but to try to love it to death. There is evidence supporting this approach. As we saw earlier, Leonard Laskow, a physician whose ability to retard the growth of cancer cells has been verified experimentally, has found that his most effective technique is not actually to kill the cells but to focus mentally on their return to normality and balance (p. 144). This suggests that prayers for healing need not involve destruction or killing to be effective but may be tailored to the temperament of the individual involved.

Most people with cancer, however, would not be so polite; they would use any means that worked—surgery, chemotherapy, radiation, and a curse thrown in for good measure.

Which approach is better, the aggressive or the compassionate? Sometimes healing requires killing, as when surgeons kill cancerous tissue by resecting it from the body or when we pray for the cure of an infectious disease, which requires the death of millions of microorganisms that are causing the problem. In these situations, we don't say that surgery or prayer is negative.

The bottom line is that a variety of methods work. We should not close the book on what may appear to be negative prayer. Someday we might need it.

Negative Prayer as Ambush

After the publication of my book *Healing Words,* as I've mentioned, I discovered that a few people considered my views on prayer blasphemous and were using prayer to convert me to their way of thinking. I considered these prayers to be negative because, from my perspective, they were exercises in manipulation and control. Sometimes the prayers actually conveyed meanness and hate. I was surprised by these events. I had generally associated prayer with love and compassion, and I was used to people praying for me, not against me. I felt, in a word, ambushed, and I began to see that ambush is a helpful concept in understanding the dark side of prayer.

AMBUSH: A UNIVERSAL TACTIC

Ambushing others is part of the natural order. Every entity, from the simplest to the most complex, is capable of it. Even atoms do it. If a stray electron wanders too close, an atom may suddenly capture the electron and hold it in its field. In the same way, planets capture hunks of solid material and make moons of them—enslavement on a celestial scale. The grandest form of cosmic ambush may be by black holes, highly condensed forms of matter whose gravitational pull is so great that any form of matter wandering too close is sucked in, without any hope of escape.

Ambush is most obvious in the world of living things. Viruses, which are unable to survive and replicate on their own, are perhaps the master ambushers. For a virus, the rule is ambush or die. They have become masters of stealth, having learned how to penetrate the cells of other organisms and steal the components they need for reproduction.

Plants are also masters of stealth. Flycatcher plants lie in wait, capturing unsuspecting insects who happen innocently into their traps. Pools of rainwater collect in pitcher-shaped plants, in which insects drown. Barbs and spikes allow entry into the flowering parts of some plants but prevent insects from exiting.

Ambush tactics are also part of the behavior of an astonishing variety of fish, birds, and animals, made possible by their stripes, dapples, and camouflage patterns.

The history of medicine reflects our attempts to avoid being ambushed by viruses, bacteria, fungi, and other infectious agents. Our fear of being bushwhacked by these organisms is built into the metaphors of medicine, which are overwhelmingly military in nature. We must be vigilant against attack, and we must continually develop smart weapons with which to shoot back—for example, the antibiotic that will seek and destroy the invader. We declare unending wars against diseases such as high blood pressure, heart disease, and high cholesterol. High blood pressure is called "the silent killer," an enemy lying in wait, who can ambush us at any time via a stroke, heart attack, or kidney failure. Curiously, some of the deadliest viruses, AIDS and ebola, originated in regions of the world we most associate with ambushes—the tropics, where thick foliage encourages deception and hiding. This is a reminder of the origin of the word *ambush*—"in the woods" or "in the bush."

How did humans become ambushers? Chimpanzees, our nearest relatives, may have started us on the road. Howard Bloom, in his book *The Lucifer Principle,*[18] hypothesizes that a quantum leap in the art of predation took place when our simian predecessors learned to go beyond hand-to-hand encounters. At some moment millions of years ago, one of them managed to throw a rock or stick, which hit its mark and resulted in more food. This led to a tendency to repeat the act of throwing and to refine it by combining stealth and distance: the ambush.

Ambush has been a human ability for as long as we have anthropological records. Ambush sites have been discovered on several continents where primitive peoples surprised herds of bison and other game and drove them over cliffs or into bogs, killing them en masse.

The use of the ambush by humans probably evolved in stages. Its earliest form was perhaps short-range—surprising game or an enemy at close quarters and killing with one's hands, fists, a rock, or club. Then, when the bow and arrow were invented, a major advance in the ambush took place. Stringed weapons made it possible to ambush from a greater distance, maximizing the element of surprise and also the ambusher's opportunity for escape if the arrow missed and the animal or enemy retaliated. The long bow made it possible to ambush from hundreds of yards. The discovery of gunpowder and the development of rifles and cannon extended the range even farther. Today, ambush can be done at global distances through a variety of means. Modern warfare, in which we kill enemies without ever seeing them, is essentially an exercise in distant ambush. High-altitude bombing, laser-guided missiles, smart bombs, and artillery that shoot beyond the horizon are the tools of the modern ambush.

Sorcerers, who have practiced their art for at least fifty thousand years, are perhaps the greatest ambushers the human species ever produced. They practice a form of distant ambush that puts modern military technology to shame—hexes, curses, spells, and negative prayers sent at a distance without using any intervening physical object.

Negative prayer usually takes the form of an ambush. Those who use prayer against others are spiritual snipers who select their victim, fire, and fade into the background.

An example of prayer-as-ambush occurred in the experience of researchers at Spindrift, Inc., a prayer research organization. Spindrift's efforts were considered by some religious believers to be attempts to "test God" and for this reason were believed to be heretical and blasphemous. During a particular phase of their research, opponents of the prayer experiments, rather than confront the Spindrift researchers openly, organized a prayer ambush by forming a prayer group whose purpose was to pray secretly for the failure of the tests. The spiritual saboteurs were unsuccessful; Spindrift's experiments worked anyway.[19]

AMBUSH SURVIVAL STRATEGIES

When it comes to negative prayers, there are no gun control laws. Negative prayers are available to anyone at any time, no background checks required. Negative prayers are exceedingly sinister; unlike a

Molotov cocktail or a handgun, they are invisible and difficult to detect. They are the perfect guerrilla weapon.

In spite of this, we are not helpless against ambushes by negative prayers and malevolent pray-ers. Every good warrior knows that the best precaution is simply to avoid ambush sites. This involves keen intuition and a finely honed sense of danger. Survival also entails methods of protection—the spiritual equivalent of the bullet-proof vest—and also requires the skill to respond immediately and effectively once an ambush has occurred. This is a topic we will soon address.

Rain Man:
The Danger
of Being Obvious

> Natural selection is simple. It makes just three
> assumptions. First, that individuals vary in their
> hereditary traits. They do. Second, that some of these
> traits will be better than others for ensuring reproduc-
> tive success. They are. And third, that such successful
> traits will become more widespread in the population.
> They have. And that is all there is to it. Vary, multiply,
> and let the fittest survive. But there are, of course,
> hidden complexities.
>
> —*Lyall Watson*, Dark Nature

NEGATIVE PRAYERS AND CURSES serve a valuable purpose: they help
an organism survive. In order to see how, let's look at a capacity we all
admire: luck.

Richard S. Broughton is director of research at the Rhine Research
Center in Durham, North Carolina. He bears an uncanny resemblance
to William James, the founder of American psychology, who, like
Broughton, was keenly interested in parapsychology. In his insightful
book, *Parapsychology: The Controversial Science*, Broughton disagrees
with those who claim that long-distance mental abilities such telepathy and clairvoyance are exotic traits possessed by a few rare souls.[20]

He proposes, rather, that these "psi abilities" are widely shared and that being human means being "psi effective," at least to some degree. These traits are highly variable, to be sure, concentrated in some people, nearly absent in others, just as there are a few four-minute milers among all the millions of plodding joggers. Parapsychology researchers naturally delight in discovering psi superstars and experimenting with them in their labs, just as every NBA coach dreams of finding a Michael Jordan for his team. But this level of talent is rare, whether in professional sports or in parapsychology.

Broughton is a science fiction fan. He refers to Larry Niven's 1970 sci-fi classic, *Ringworld*, in which a young woman, Teela Brown, is sought by an alien who is forming a crew for an extremely hazardous space exploration mission. Teela is valued as a crew member not because of her skills in spaceflight—she has none—but for her luck, which the alien race has discovered that only humans possess. Teela Brown is the product of six generations of winning gamblers. Luck runs in her blood. Having her on board the spacecraft will help ensure success, like wearing a charm or amulet.[21]

In *Ringworld*, luck is taken for granted. Like most human abilities, it can be enhanced genetically through breeding. People who have it notice that things turn out in their favor, and lucky people appear as if they can actually influence the course of the natural world.

Unlike the aliens in *Ringworld*, many of us deny that luck exists because we have been heavily influenced by the scientific outlook. We attribute all fortunate coincidences to randomness or to the operation of selective memory, which causes us to forget unlucky or unfortunate happenings and remember only the lucky or positive ones. But Broughton and other contemporary researchers in parapsychology have produced compelling evidence, which is too extensive to review here, that the *Ringworld* aliens may be right. There is a robust line of research showing that some individuals can influence the probability of events, whether we want to call it luck, ESP, psi effectiveness, intentionality, or something else.[22]

When Broughton was president of the Parapsychological Association, he was obliged to deliver a speech about parapsychological abilities in humans. He chose as his title, "If You Want to Know How It Works, First Find Out What It's For." In his speech he followed the logic of natural selection. Any organism possessing luck or psi

effectiveness would have an advantage in the high-stakes game of surviving in nature, in which the winner often takes all and the loser van-
ishes without a trace. Broughton's thesis is simple: "The purpose of psi
ability is survival."[23]

LUCK, PSI, AND SURVIVAL

If psi abilities evolved to help us survive, what would they look like by
now? They probably would not be flamboyant but would be quite
ordinary, perhaps even unnoticeable. We would use them without
thinking much about it, like using our eyes or our legs. They would
probably "look much more like what we call intuition and . . . luck—
just what is required to get the job done, and no more. . . . Intuition
would not be limited to occasional creative flashes but would include
the act of acquiring the information to guide the mass of petty decisions that go into being in the right place at the right time, or avoiding
the wrong place at the wrong time"—which is what natural selection
is all about. "[L]uck would not be simply winning lotteries or card
games. Luck . . . would be a generalized success factor—getting more
than one's share of life's breaks." In short, "The psi component of luck
would be . . . shifting the odds in one's favor. . . ."[24]

A barely discernible advantage, an edge in the competition of
staying alive—this is the sort of factor that makes or breaks a species
in the long haul of evolution. And when we look at the evidence, we
discover that a slight shift in odds is precisely the type of effect that
has been proved to exist in hundreds of careful parapsychology experiments dealing with sophisticated electronic devices.[25]

Most critics of psi research do not appreciate this point. They
tend to reject experiments in parapsychology because they do not produce colossal, large-scale effects. Yet small effects may be better suited
for favoring survival in the process of natural selection than effects of
much greater size. The magic may be in the minimum.

THE DANGER OF BEING NOTICED

Low-level luck is invisible, whereas big luck isn't—and invisibility is a
valuable quality in natural selection, where deception counts. "The
most effective psi might be imperceptible psi, since if it became too

obvious, one could get into trouble," Broughton states. Who can doubt it? "It was only a few centuries ago that witches were burned. Ostentatious displays of psi ability could severely limit one's chances of reproductive success." Adds Broughton, "It could even be that psi has evolved to be deliberately self-obscuring because it works best when it is unhampered and unnoticed by the individual it is serving."[26]

In the movie *Rain Man*, the Dustin Hoffman character is a genius-savant who appears to be mentally retarded. His prodigious powers of memory and mathematical calculation are totally unsuspected—except by his brother, the Tom Cruise character. Together they invade the gambling casinos of Las Vegas. They put Hoffman's undetected skills to work and are wildly successful at the tables. But they become greedy and go too far. Hoffman's advantage becomes noticed, and they are run out of town. If he had held his ability in check at a low level, it might have been tolerated. But when it became exaggerated, he was finished.

In the course of evolution, too much luck might have been treated in the same way. We don't like those who are excessively lucky; their good fortune seems unfair. People can "know too much for their own good"—and for ours, too. When they do, we often put them in their place.

IS NATURE MORALLY BANKRUPT?

In spite of the widespread sentimentality about nature, the biological world is a bloody mess. George Williams, whom biologist Lyall Watson calls "the godfather of evolutionary biology," wrote in his 1966 book *Adaptation and Natural Selection*, "Natural selection really is as bad as it seems. . . ."[27] Watson drives the point home:

> Courtship in animals, which once seemed to be simply a matter of stately dances and colorful displays, can now be seen to be a web of intrigue full of deception, coercion, desertion, rape, and sometimes lethal violence. . . . Even a tank of tropical fish, once a popular refuge for those looking for relief from human stress, has been revealed to be a scene of never-ending underwater sexual harassment. And bird songs, those "profuse strains of unpremeditated art," stand revealed now as fragments of an ongoing

domestic argument based on male suspicion and female protesta-
tions of fidelity. . . . Among mallard ducks, aggravated sexual
assault is such a normal part of reproductive behavior that an
unguarded female may be gang-raped so persistently that she
drowns. Man-eating male blue sharks seem to be unable to mate
until they have made injurious attacks on their own females.
Rape is an established pattern of behavior in many insects, frogs,
and turtles; and can even be homosexual in some parasitic
worms. . . . Cannibalism has now been recorded in just about
every animal that isn't strictly vegetarian. . . . Fighting between
rival males ought to be ritualized and largely risk-free, but the
sad truth is that it can also quite often be lethal. As many as one
in ten red deer stags dies each season from such injuries. . . . The
conclusion to be drawn from this unhappy catalog of unpleasant
things is obvious. . . . Nature is morally bankrupt and stands condemned. Worse than that, . . . in the light of recent discoveries,
nature is clearly and grossly immoral. [Said George Williams:]
"Natural selection . . . can honestly be described as a process for
maximizing short-sighted selfishness. I would concede that moral
indifference might aptly characterize the physical universe. But
for the biological world, a stronger term is needed." The only one
that will do, it seems, is evil.

A WAY OUT

In emphasizing the nastiness in nature, I do not wish to demonize it. I
wish only to point out that competition in the biological world is
widespread, intense, and often lethal—and that any individual who
gains an advantage in the business of staying alive will be favored in
the process of natural selection.

Harmful prayers, curses, and spells confer such an advantage. They
make sense in the context of evolution, because they help an organism
survive and reproduce. But, as we've seen, to endure and be effective,
these activities must operate mainly in the background, like luck. This
permits them to be used without being noticed, which protects the
individual employing them.

All of which suggests that we are hardwired for negative prayer.
This ability is ours whether we like it or not—our built-in, biological

inheritance from those who came before us, and our legacy to those who come after.

Humans are presumably the only species capable of being aware of the power to harm others through their thoughts. What should our response be?

I feel we should think twice before repudiating our capacity to harm others mentally. Even if we could do so, it does not make sense to disown a power, like vision and hearing, that has helped us survive as a species. Who knows—perhaps we may need it again in the future.

The important realization is that awareness of this power brings with it choice. If we have the courage to face up to our dark side, we can decide whether we will harm others with our thoughts.

PART 4

THE
SCIENTIFIC
EVIDENCE

The facts beat me.
—*Alfred Russel Wallace (1823–1913),*
co-discoverer of the theory of evolution,
referring to distant mental events

SCIENTIFIC STUDIES

> It is the responsibility of scientists never to suppress
> knowledge, no matter how awkward that knowledge
> is, no matter how it may bother those in power. We
> are not smart enough to decide which pieces of
> knowledge are permissible and which are not. . . .
>
> —*Carl Sagan*

I~T IS ILLEGAL AND UNETHICAL~ to conduct human experiments that
involve the deliberate attempt to cause harm. Therefore, studies that
examine the effect of negative intentions have employed nonhumans such as microorganisms, seeds and plants, animals, and human
tissue.

I know of only one formal experiment in which one human tried
deliberately and openly to kill another. It is reported by anthropologist
Joan Halifax in her classic paper, "Hex Death." A professor who taught
a course in parapsychology and the occult had a student in his course
who claimed he had the ability to perform hex deaths. For his term
paper, he wanted to demonstrate his talent. The professor agreed.
"[B]ut . . . we couldn't have him try to kill just anyone—that wouldn't
be fair or nice," the professor said. "So we agreed that he would
attempt by hex death to kill me." The professor left a sealed envelope
with the registrar, on which he wrote, "Open this upon my death if it
occurs within the next year." Inside the envelope a note instructed the
registrar to give the student an "A" if the professor died. The student
agreed that if the professor did not die, he would receive an "F." The
student flunked. Said the professor, "I think there are a lot of people

around who would be willing to be targets for people who claim they can perform hex deaths, myself included . . . we can test [this.]"[1]

I disagree with the professor's sanguine prediction. I believe there is a deep psychological resistance on the part of researchers to studying the effects of mental influence on humans. Psychologist and researcher William G. Braud, professor and director of research at Palo Alto's Institute of Transpersonal Psychology, agrees and suggests reasons why these objections exist:

> Fears of the possibility of "evil" mental influence may indeed be responsible for the dearth of studies of distant mental influence of human subjects, even in the context of healing. . . . Success at distant mental influence may trigger conscious or unconscious thoughts or feelings about the possible abuse of such "powers."[2]

ETHICAL CONSIDERATIONS

Before reviewing the actual experiments, a word about ethics. Some people believe it is unethical and immoral to harm *any* living creature, human or nonhuman, including microorganisms. It is unclear how anyone could be totally true to this conviction. Those holding this position would presumably never bathe because of the killing effects of soap and water on skin bacteria. They would never bake bread, because the baking process kills the yeast cells that make bread rise. We all make compromises on this issue in daily life, because we cannot take a step, brush our teeth, or eat a meal without killing *something*.

I personally believe it is ethical to use nonhumans in experiments involving potential harm, but for reasons seldom offered in discussions of this controversial issue.[3] I feel that informed consent and compassion are the key. How can informed consent be obtained from nonhumans? This question has been answered in the experiences of native peoples over untold millennia. For example, Australian aborigines used to "ask ahead" while wandering, requesting respectfully that an animal or plant make itself available for sacrifice later in the day at an appointed site for their sustenance. Native Americans prayed to an animal's spirit for permission to take its life for food and offered thanks after the killing.

Laboratory experiments involving harm to living creatures could similarly be conducted as sacred, reverential exercises. Their permission could be sought prior to the beginning of any study. We humans volunteer as subjects in medical experiments involving great risk; non-humans would volunteer as well. Indeed, stories of pets putting their lives on the line to aid or rescue humans are legendary. How would we know their decision? By cultivating the sensitivity to hear their response, as native tribes did routinely. Therefore, in addition to the usual institutional review boards that govern the use of human subjects in scientific testing, every research institution might need a Non-human Permissions Committee (NONPERC). The NONPERC would be made up of individuals who have special skills in sensing and listening to the responses of mice, rats, chimps, cats, dogs, rabbits, bacteria, fungi, yeasts, seeds, and plants. Good candidates for committee members would be Native Americans and other individuals who have not severed their communication skills with the nonhuman world.[4]

EXPERIMENTS WITH MICROORGANISMS

There are two major advantages to using microorganisms instead of people in studies of distant negative intentionality, aside from the potential harm to humans if the negative intentions succeeded. Skeptics who do not believe in the effects of distant intentions say that any observed result must be due to the expectations of the subject—the power of belief and thought. But if bacteria respond to outside intentions—if they grow more slowly than controls not receiving the negative influence—one cannot dismiss this result by attributing it to negative suggestion. Bacteria presumably do not think positively *or* negatively. The second major advantage of microorganisms in studies of distant mental intentions has to do with the control group. If the effects of intercessory prayer, for example, are being assessed in a group of humans who have a particular illness, it is difficult to establish a pure control group that does not receive prayer. The reason is that sick human beings generally pray for themselves, or outsiders pray for them, thus "contaminating" the control group, which by definition should not receive the treatment being evaluated. In studies involving microbes, this notorious "problem of extraneous prayer" is totally overcome, because one can be reasonably certain that the bacteria, fungi, or yeast in the control group are not praying for themselves and that their fellow microbes are not praying for them. If the study involved negative intentions instead of positive ones, the advantages remain the same: the thoughts of microorganisms do not influence its outcome. On balance, therefore, one can perform experiments of distant intentionality with great precision using microbes as the test subjects, without the problems posed by human studies.

Several experiments involving the effects of distant negative intentions on microorganisms have been performed.

Jean Barry, a physician-researcher in Bordeaux, France, chose to experiment with a destructive fungus, *Rhizoctonia solani*. He asked ten people to try to inhibit its growth merely through their intention, at a distance of 1.5 meters. Trying to retard this organism made sense to Barry, since it is destructive and causes a variety of diseases. The experiment involved control petri dishes with fungi that were not influenced in addition to those that were. The laboratory conditions were carefully controlled regarding the genetic purity of the fungus, the composition of the culture medium, the relative humidity, and the conditions of temperature and lighting. The control petri dishes and the influenced dishes were treated identically, except for the negative intentions directed toward the latter. A person who was blind to the details of the experiment handled the various manipulations. The mental strategy of the influencers is not described in the published report; they simply took their stations at the required 1.5 meters and were "free to act as [they] saw fit for [their] own concentration" for fifteen minutes, while disregarding the controls. Each subject was assigned five experimental and five control dishes. Of the ten subjects, three to six subjects worked during a session, and there were nine sessions. Measurement of the fungus colony on the petri dish was obtained by outlining the boundary of the colony on a sheet of thin paper. Again, this was done by someone who did not know the aim of the experiment or the identity of the petri dishes. The outlines were then cut out and weighed under conditions of constant temperature and humidity. When the growth in 195 experimental dishes was compared to their corresponding controls, it was significantly retarded in 151 dishes. The possibility that these results could be explained by chance was less than one in a thousand.[5]

Physician Daniel J. Benor, who has evaluated all the known experiments in the field of distant healing in his landmark work *Healing Research*, calls this study "highly significant" and "sound."[6]

University of Tennessee researchers William H. Tedder and Melissa L. Monty replicated Barry's experiment with the fungus *Rhizoctonia solani*. The goal of this study was to inhibit the growth of the fungus from a distance of one to fifteen miles. One researcher handled the cultures and had no knowledge of the subjects or the identity of experimental or control targets; the other researcher organized the influencers. Two groups participated. Group 1 was made up of Tedder and six others who knew him and had frequently interacted with him for the past year and a half. Group 2 consisted of eight volunteers who either did not know Tedder or who had infrequently interacted with him.

In order to assist the subjects in their intentions, they were shown six pictures that pertained to the target area, such as the outside of the Plant Sciences Building at the University of Tennessee, a view of the room and incubator that contained the target and control petri dishes, a view of the open incubator door, and so on. Subjects were separated from the petri dishes from one to fifteen miles and asked to concentrate on the targets for at least fifteen minutes a day for three days, day or night, using "any technique available to them." Both control and treatment dishes were subjected to identical conditions.

When the growth differential between the experimental and control dishes was compared, Group 1 was highly successful; the likelihood of explaining their results by chance was less than three in 100,000. Group 2 was less successful; their likelihood of a chance explanation was 6 in 100. Why was Group 1 more successful? The researchers theorize that the Group 1 subjects, because of their established rapport with Tedder, may have had greater motivation and expectancy of a positive outcome than the Group 2 subjects. On a post-experiment questionnaire, the Group 1 subjects indeed responded more positively to questions about how they perceived their ability to inhibit the fungal cultures at a distance.[7]

Carroll B. Nash, a researcher at St. Joseph's University in Philadelphia, conducted an experiment to determine whether the growth of a common bacterium, *Escherichia coli*, could be influenced by mental intent over a twenty-four-hour period. All sixty subjects were volunteers from the student body and were not known to be psychically gifted. Each was assigned nine test tubes—three marked with a "+," three with a "-," and three control tubes. They were instructed to try, by wishing during the following twenty-four hours, to cause the bacteria in the "+" tubes to grow at a faster rate and the bacteria in the "-" tubes to grow at a slower rate than the bacteria in the control tubes. Growth in the test tubes was measured by an electrophotometer, which determined the optical density of the liquid suspension. Proper precautions were followed, with the person measuring the bacterial growth being blind to the identity of all tubes. The subjects indeed demonstrated that they could both stimulate and inhibit growth, although they were more successful in their efforts to promote replication than retard it. Nash suggested that this was due to a psychological preference in producing a positive rather than a negative effect on living things.[8]

In assessing this experiment, Benor states, "This is an excellent experiment, rigorously performed and adequately reported."[9]

In another experiment, researcher Nash examined the ability of fifty-two unskilled subjects to influence the mutation rates of *Escherichia coli*. This microorganism normally mutates from the inability to metabolize milk sugar (lactose negative) to the ability to use it (lactose positive) at a known rate. Using nine test tubes of bacteria, subjects tried to influence three to become lactose positive, three to become lactose negative, and three to remain as they were. Careful precautions were taken to preclude the researchers from knowing which tubes were selected for which conditions. The results indicated that when the subjects urged the bacteria to become lactose positive, their growth was stimulated; the likelihood that this result was due to chance was less than 5 in 1,000. And when they tried to make them lactose negative, growth was inhibited; the likelihood of a chance explanation was less than 2 in 100. Whether the subjects were actually influencing the mutation rate of the bacteria or "merely" influencing their growth rate, as in the above experiment, is not known.[10] Benor's evaluation: "a carefully designed, executed and reported experiment."[11]

ARE EXPERIMENTS WITH MICROORGANISMS RELEVANT TO HUMANS?

These experiments may be more relevant to humans than we commonly think. Even though we are far more complex, we share many identical biochemical processes with microorganisms. If we can harm bacteria and fungi with negative intention from a distance, we may be able to harm humans as well.

Moreover, whether we realize it or not, every time we pray for someone to recover from an infection we are conducting a single case study in negative prayer, whose goal is to inhibit or kill microbes. This situation exists when prayer is used in any infectious disease, from athlete's foot and AIDS to measles and malaria. Seen from this perspective, the above are highly analogous to real-life situations.

ARE EXPERIMENTS WITH MICROORGANISMS RELEVANT TO PRAYER?

But is "wishing" or "concentrating"—terms used to describe the mental strategies of subjects in the above studies—related to prayer? For those who say no, just try praying *without* wishing or concentrating. This doesn't mean, of course, that prayer is *only* a matter of wishing or focusing; indeed, prayer is a complex activity that is much richer than the mental activities employed in the above experiments. But since prayer does involve wishing, focusing, and concentrating on a desired outcome, these studies are relevant to the act of prayer.

Some people believe experiments with microorganisms have no connection with prayer because there is no biblical injunction to pray for or against microbes. But, of course, the Bible is mute on this question because the concept of microbes did not exist in biblical times. Therefore, we must interpret for ourselves whether or not it is fitting to apply prayer to these creatures.

There are indirect biblical sanctions to pray both for and against microbes. For example, when we pray for the sick, as we are instructed to do, this often includes those suffering from infections. As already mentioned, a prayer *for* someone with an infectious disease is a prayer *against* the microorganisms involved, whether we realize it or not, and is therefore an exercise in negative prayer. Likewise, when we pray that our food, which is never sterile, be blessed, we are presumably asking that the bacteria it contains be put out of commission. A sanction to pray *for* microbes can be found in the Lord's Prayer. When we pray for our daily bread, this presumably includes praying for the yeast that makes it rise.

ARE EXPERIMENTS WITH MICROORGANISMS BLASPHEMOUS?

I often hear that prayer experiments involving microbes trivialize and debase prayer. This argument rests on the belief that the majestic act of prayer should be reserved for humans and that the Almighty is not terribly concerned with the welfare of creatures as insignificant as bacteria. This argument is egregiously anthropocentric and is based, in my opinion, in spurious theology and shortsighted biology. Many religious traditions believe that *all* of creation is good; why should any of it be outside the notice of the Almighty and off limits to prayer? Moreover, microbes are not insignificant when compared to humans. All ecological systems depend on them; without microbes, human life could not exist. How could prayer involving microbes be trivial, when our life is inextricably tied to theirs?

Another common complaint against prayer experiments in general—with or without microbes—is that these experiments "test God" and are therefore blasphemous. The blasphemy argument has even been used by skeptical scientists as a reason to oppose the empirical testing of prayer.[12] The fact is, however, that many scientists believe that the experimental approach can be a form of worship. For example, the Jesuit priest and paleontologist Pierre Teilhard de Chardin said that research is the highest form of adoration. Prayer experiments *can* be conducted irreverently, but they can also embody a sense of sacredness, as if the researcher is treading on holy ground. This approach characterizes the attitude of all the researchers I know who are currently investigating the effects of prayer.

BUT IS IT PRAYER?

When confronted with evidence that distant intentionality can indeed enhance or retard microbial growth, some religionists resort to a last-ditch objection—that these effects are really not due to prayer but to "mind over matter" or some mental force. They have never been able to clarify what this force might be. Others simply condemn these effects as the work of the devil and let it go at that. In addition, some objectors claim that true prayer can't be involved in these studies because the subjects are trying to demonstrate their personal power instead of God's, which is further evidence that these studies are corrupt and blasphemous.

Perhaps the strongest evidence that these studies involve actual prayer is the fact that spiritual healers, who often serve as the influencers, say they do.[13] Consider, for example, an experiment with the well-known spiritual healer Olga Worrall, who for years conducted prayer-based healing services at the New Life Clinic at Baltimore's Mt. Washington United Methodist Church.[14] Worrall was revered by all who knew her as a humble servant of God. On one occasion she accepted the invitation of physicist Elizabeth A. Rauscher and microbiologist Beverly A. Rubik to participate in an experiment with bacteria. The study originally called for Worrall to kill bacteria in a particular phase of the experiment. When she objected to using prayer to harm God's creatures, the study was redesigned to allow her to help, not harm, the microorganisms by protecting them from the killing effects of antibiotics. The results showed that she was able to do so.[15] It is difficult to dismiss this study as not involving genuine prayer, with which Worrall was intimately familiar and which she believed she was using during the study.

Are we to believe that these studies don't involve "real" prayer? Or that the prayers of spiritual healers are genuine in church but bogus in the lab?

Are the pray-ers in these experiments glorifying themselves instead of the Almighty? Are they putting their ego first? For all I know, this objection may have merit; but if it does, it surely applies to prayers offered in church as well as in the laboratory. We cannot fully know the heart of another person. This fact should make us hesitant to pass judgment on the prayers of others, whether they take place inside or outside the lab.

EXPERIMENTS WITH CANCER CELLS

Researchers studied the ability of the British healer Matthew Manning to influence cervical cancer cells in artificial cultures. Healthy cancer cells adhere to the surface of plastic flasks by means of an electrostatic force. With injury, death, or change in metabolism, their normal positive charge changes to negative, and they are no longer attracted to the negatively charged wall of the plastic flask. When this occurs they slough off into the surrounding fluid. Microscopic counts of the cells in the fluid medium are therefore an indication of the health of the cervical cancer cell culture.

Manning was able to exert dramatic influences on the number of cells in the culture fluid, from 200 to 1,200 percent, compared with appropriate controls. This effect occurred when he touched the flask by laying on of hands for twenty minutes, and also when he never touched the container—for example, when he was placed in an electrically shielded room and tried to influence the cancer cells at a distance.[16]

In another study, researcher Glen Rein explored the ability of Leonard Laskow, an American gynecologist and healer, to influence the rate of growth of cancer cells. (Although already mentioned on p. 43, a more complete description is offered here.) The experiment was well designed, with appropriate controls. The growth rate of the tumor cells was measured according to their uptake of radioactive thymidine, a standard index of DNA synthesis.

Laskow, wishing to be in a state of emotional connectedness with the cells, which he considers a vital component of his healing technique, tried to adopt a generally loving attitude toward the cells throughout the entire experiment. Achieving this feeling involves, he states, entering into a certain form of meditation. Once he accomplished that, Laskow then adopted a variety of attitudes toward the cancer cells, including: (1) asking that they return to the natural order and harmony of ordinary cell growth; (2) cultivating a certain type of Taoist visualization in which he visualized only three cells remaining in the dish; (3) letting God's will flow through his hands, without trying to direct the outcome; (4) offering unconditional love to the tumor cells, without giving specific instructions; and (5) dematerializing the cancer cells. Two forms of dematerialization were visualized—dissolving the cancer cells into the light and dematerializing them into the void. Laskow held the cancer cell dishes in his hands during each of these intentions. As a control, a nonhealer held identical dishes of cells in a nearby room while reading a book to distract his attention from the cells.

The different forms of intention were associated with drastically different effects. Most effective was asking the cultures to return to the natural order and harmony of the normal cell line (39 percent inhibition). Allowing God's will to manifest was about half as effective (21 percent inhibition). Unconditional love appeared neutral, neither stimulating nor inhibiting cell growth. The Taoist visualization technique, in which only three cells were visualized remaining in the dish, was associated with 18 percent inhibition. (Interestingly, when Laskow switched to visualizing many more cells remaining in the dish, an increased tumor cell growth of 15 percent occurred.)

In another phase of the experiment, Laskow focused his intention on the cells' returning to their natural, noncancerous state, with a 20 percent inhibition effect. Using imagery to accomplish the same result also resulted in a 20 percent reduction. When he combined intent and imagery, the inhibition rate doubled to 40 percent, suggesting additive effects from mentally intending and mentally imaging a particular result.

In a third phase of the study, Laskow focused on a container of water that would later be used in the cell cultures. He "treated" the water with the intention of returning the cells to their normal order and harmony. The result was a 38 percent inhibition rate, similar to that obtained from treating the cells directly. Also, when the water was treated with unconditional love and the intention of dematerialization, inhibition rates of 21 percent and 27 percent, respectively, were seen.[17]

EFFECT OF QIGONG ON LIVING SYSTEMS

"The Chinese consider qi to be the animating power that flows through all living things," writes Kenneth S. Cohen, in his masterful book, *The Way of Qigong.* "A living being is filled with it. A dead person has no more qi—the warmth, the life energy is gone. A healthy individual has more than one who is ill. However, health is more than an abundance of qi. Health implies that the qi in our bodies is clear, rather than polluted and turbid, and flowing smoothly, like a stream, not blocked or stagnant."[18] Other cultures have concepts similar to qi—spirit, mana, vital force, prana, and so on.

Over thousands of years the Chinese have evolved the practice of qigong—*qi* meaning "life energy" and *gong* meaning "work." The goal of this practice is to bring one's qi into balance and harmony or increase it if it is deficient.

Several scholars distinguish between internal qi and external qi. "Internal Qi helps develop good health and self healing by means of individual practice of Qigong exercises," writes Kenneth Sancier, Ph.D., and Bingkun Hu, Ph.D., of San Francisco's Qigong Institute of the East West Academy of Healing Arts. "There are a wide array of personal Qigong practices ... most [of which] contain ... breath exercises, deep relaxation, meditation, visualization, body postures, movements and certain self-applied massage techniques."[19] External qi, on the other hand, refers to the emission of qi by a qigong master, with the objective of affecting someone or something "out there."

The precise nature of "emitted qi" is not known, although researchers have reported observing low levels of photon emission,[20] infrared light,[21] and magnetic fields;[22] alterations in the discharge behavior of a Van de Graff generator;[23] and infrasound emissions when qigong masters attempt to emit qi.[24]

Qi has long been believed by the Chinese to have both positive and negative effects—what has been called "health-promoting" or "peaceful mind" qi, or "lethal" or "destroying mind" qi.[25] To test these two types, researchers at National Yang Ming Medical College and National Research Institute of Chinese Medicine in Taipei, Taiwan, studied both the positive and negative effects of emitted qi on cell cultures. In this experiment, a qigong master directed either positive or negative intent on two types of cells—human fibroblasts, which form connective tissue in the body, and boar sperm cells. Following "destroying mind" qi for two minutes, decreases from 22 to 53 percent were observed in growth rate, respiration rate, and the rate of synthesis of DNA and protein. Following ten minutes of "peaceful mind" qi, these measures increased from 5 to 28 percent.

Sancier and his colleagues are tracking the many studies now coming out of China and Taiwan dealing with the effects of emitted qi. They have assembled the Qigong Database™, an impressive computerized collection of published papers and information from international conferences.[26] For anyone wishing to explore the negative effects of prayer and distant intentionality, this body of information is a rich resource.

Are there parallels between the emitted qi of qigong masters and the intercessory prayer that is used by spiritual healers in our culture? Psychologist Lawrence LeShan, who has extensively researched the methods employed by contemporary healers in the United States, describes two basic approaches to healing—Type I, in which the healer senses that she is a conduit for divine healing energy, and Type II, which is less common, in which the healer believes she sends some sort of healing energy that originates within her.[27] Descriptions of emitted qi appear similar to LeShan's Type II healing.

Studies from China involving negative intent in the form of emitted qi have shown the following effects:

- destruction of human stomach cancer cells in vitro (in artificial cell cultures)
- destruction of chromosomes within human stomach cancer cells in vitro
- destruction of leukemia cells in mice
- inhibition of the growth of transplanted tumors in mice
- inhibition of formation of tumor metastases in mice
- inhibition of DNA synthesis and cell growth in human cell cultures in vitro
- decrease in the activity of the enzyme amylase
- decrease in the growth rates of the bacterium *Escherichia coli*

How reliable are these experiments? Many have not been replicated or published in peer-reviewed journals, so caution is required in interpreting them. Similar studies, however, are currently under way at respected research centers in the United States and elsewhere with qigong masters from China and Taiwan. These experiments will soon be subjected to the scrutiny of the scientific community, and the Chinese experiments will either be confirmed or refuted. Because of the evidence that already exists favoring the nonlocal, distant effects of consciousness, my prediction is that many of the Chinese findings will indeed be confirmed.

AN EXPERIMENT AT MT. SINAI SCHOOL OF MEDICINE

Consider, for example, a well-controlled experiment by researchers at New York's Mt. Sinai School of Medicine, in which two qigong masters tried to interact with a cell-free enzyme system involved in the phosphorylation of myosin light chains, a biochemical process involved in the regulation of smooth muscle contraction in the body. Standing five feet away, the qigong practitioners treated the enzyme samples for six minutes for nine trials. All but one qigong treatment affected the samples, decreasing the myosin phosphorylation from between 8.5 and 23 percent when compared with controls. For all the trials by both practitioners, there were fewer than 5 chances in 100 that the results were due to chance. The researchers then placed the enzyme samples inside a metal box, which shielded them from ambient electromagnetic fields, and conducted four additional trials. All four trials showed reduced phosphorylation activity compared to controls, two of which were statistically significant and two of which were not. The researchers concluded,

> The results of these preliminary experiments demonstrate that Qigong practice can consistently affect a biologically relevant enzyme system. This interaction requires no physical contact between the practitioner and the sample.... [H]ypotheses regarding mechanisms by which these effects may be understood are as yet unclear.[28]

A CAUTION

As investigations of qi continue, we should avoid a condescending attitude toward Eastern science, as if ours is the only science that counts. Recalling the Western encounter with acupuncture might provide a valuable dose of humility. Three decades ago, when news began to filter from China that profound levels of anesthesia could be obtained by sticking needles into human beings, enabling major surgical procedures to be done, Western scientists and physicians generally had a good belly laugh. The derision faded, however, as the clinical efficacy and physiologic rationale of acupuncture were demonstrated by careful research. Today, many physicians who were former skeptics routinely refer their patients for acupuncture.

The idea of emitted qi admittedly makes greater demands on the Western scientific mind than acupuncture, for two reasons. First, the nature and existence of qi remains in doubt; and second, the effects of qi suggest a nonlocal, distant action of the mind, which horrifies individuals dedicated to a materialistic interpretation of the world. But let us stay open-minded and treat our intellectual indigestion with good scientific studies, which are still the best medicine.

I do not wish to imply that qigong practitioners traffic mainly in "destroying mind" or "inhibiting" qi. Qigong is used overwhelmingly to bring about harmony, order, and vitality. But the intent of the qigong masters in the above studies was indeed negative—they really did try to destroy the cancer cells, and they apparently succeeded. It should be obvious, however, that the effect of this type of qi on someone with cancer is not negative: a negative impact on cancer cells is a positive result for a patient. As we saw earlier, whether a curse is positive or negative depends on which side of the fence you're on.

The "destructive qi" experiments suggest that an aggressive, negative attitude toward a disease entity such as cancer can be valuable. This approach contrasts with the prevalent idea that love alone is the key to healing. The "destroying mind" experiments imply, therefore, that there is no one right way or formula to follow in using mental intentionality to heal, and that our toolbox of healing needs to include negative, as well as positive, prayer.

MAKING CONNECTIONS

There may be a connection between positive qigong and the strategy that was found most useful by physician-healer Leonard Laskow above, in treating cancer cells in the laboratory. Laskow mentally promoted a return of the cells to their normal, natural function. Qigong practitioners also promote a return to one's "original nature" in using "nourishing" or "facilitating" qi, the most common type. Are Eastern and Western healers using similar strategies and calling them different names? My belief is that a common pathway underlies the various strategies used by healers worldwide and that these connections will become obvious as our knowledge advances.

THE EFFECT OF MOOD ON HEALING: THE GRAD EXPERIMENTS

At McGill University in Montreal, researcher Bernard Grad examined the possibility that mental depression might produce a negative effect on the growth of plants. This idea fits with the common belief that some people have green thumbs and others do not and that one's thoughts and emotional states may play a role in how vigorously plants respond. Grad theorized that if plants were watered with water that had been held by depressed people, they would grow more slowly than if watered with water held by people in an upbeat mood. A controlled experiment was devised using a man known to have a green thumb and two patients in a psychiatric hospital—a woman with a depressive neurosis and a man with a psychotic depression.

Each person held a sealed bottle between his or her hands for thirty minutes, which was then used to water barley seeds. The green thumb man was in a confident, positive mood at the time he held his solution, and his seeds grew faster than those of the others and the controls. Unexpectedly, the normally depressed, neurotic woman responded to the experiment with a brighter mood, asking relevant questions and showing great interest. She cradled her bottle of water in her lap as a mother might hold a child. Her seeds also grew faster than those of the controls. The man with the psychotic depression was agitated and depressed at the time he held his solution; his seeds grew slower than the controls.[29] Although not definitive, this study, states Benor, "suggests that emotions may influence healings," positively as well as negatively.[30]

NONLOCAL MIND: THE EMERGING PICTURE

Researchers are gradually piecing together a picture of how distant healing may take place without invoking the physicists' usual concepts of energy.[31]

For a decade, a research team led by Jacobo Grinberg-Zylberbaum at the Universidad Nacional Autónoma de México in Mexico City, has performed experiments examining the electroencephalograms (EEGs or brain wave tracings) of subjects who are far removed from each other—in some cases placed in metal-lined boxes that block ambient electromagnetic influences.[32] While the distant subjects are sitting quietly, there is no correlation in the pattern of their respective EEGs. But when they allow a feeling of emotional closeness or empathy to develop between them, the EEGs begin to resemble each other, often to a striking degree. No type of energy or signal can be detected to pass between the distant individuals. Moreover, the statistical correlations between the distant EEG patterns do not diminish when the subjects are moved farther apart. This defies one of the hallmarks of energy as defined in physics—its decrease in strength with increasing distance from its source. Also, the EEGs remain equally correlated if the subjects are placed in metal-lined boxes, which block ambient electromagnetic energy.

But if an exchange of energy is not involved, how do the EEG correlations take place? How do the distant brains communicate? How does one brain know what the other is doing? Grinberg-Zylberbaum's team, along with physicist Amit Goswami, of the Department of Physics and the Institute of Theoretical Science at the University of Oregon, propose that these "transferred potentials" between brains demonstrate "brain-to-brain nonlocal . . . correlations. . . ."

Nonlocal correlations have been a concern of physicists since they were proposed by Einstein, Rosen, and Podolsky in 1935.[33] From the moment they were hypothesized, these effects stretched the imagination of physicists to the limits. It isn't difficult to see why. Nonlocal correlations between distant subatomic particles are believed to take place instantly, regardless of how far apart they are. The fact that they occur simultaneously means there is no travel time for any known form of energy to flow between them. But if there is no signal from one particle to the other, how could their behavior be correlated? How could one particle know what the other is up to? For almost half a century, nonlocal events remained hypothetical until they were demonstrated experimentally in a celebrated study in 1982 by physicist Alain Aspect and his colleagues.[34]

Physicists assumed that nonlocal connections exist only between subatomic particles such as electrons and photons. But the pioneering work of Grinberg-Zylberbaum, Goswami, and their colleagues, which they have replicated, strongly suggests that nonlocal events occur also between human beings. Summarizing their findings in the prestigious publication *Physics Essays*, these researchers state,

> The data indicate that the human brain is capable of establishing close relationships with other brains (when it interacts with them appropriately) and may sustain such an interaction even at a distance. Our results cannot be explained as due to sensory communication between subjects . . . or due to low frequency EEG chance correspondence. . . . [N]either sensory stimuli or electromagnetic signals may be the means of communication. This point is further borne out by the fact that we have not seen any distance attenuation of the transference effect

compared to our previous measurement which involved a shorter distance between subjects. . . . As is well known, local signals are always attenuated, and the absence of attenuation is a sure signature of nonlocality.[35]

But the connections between distant humans are not automatic. The researchers asked the subjects to try deliberately to "feel each other's presence even at a distance." If they did not, the distant EEG correlations were totally absent. This implies that love and empathy are required for distant connections between people to take place, and it is consistent with the universal belief that distant healing depends on love, caring, and compassion.

Does this rule out the possibility of distant harm, such as in negative prayer and curses? Probably not. The researchers in the EEG experiments did not actually ask the distant subjects to experience love for each other but to "feel each other's presence" at a distance. We can feel the presence of another as keenly through animosity as through love. For example, when we intensely dislike someone, we feel their presence vividly. These studies suggest, therefore, that hatred as well as love might underlie the connections between distant individuals, and they may eventually shed light on how negative intentions cause harm.

THE "TOHATE" EXPERIMENTS

Are nonlocally connected human brains a laboratory curiosity, or are they relevant to healing and to real life? In search of clues, let's return to the world of qigong.

In 1996, a Japanese research team headed by Mikio Yamamoto, from the National Institute of Radiological Sciences in Chiba and the Nippon Medical School in Tokyo, performed three experiments dealing with a phenomenon called *tohate* or *taiki*, in which a qigong master makes an opponent who is several meters away step back rapidly without touching him. The two people involved are usually highly trained individuals who have their eyes fixed on each other. Is the *tohate* action caused by subtle sensory cues, the experimenters asked, or could the recoil response be due to emitted qi, as the qigong masters maintain?[36]

In a prior experiment, the researchers had separated a qigong master and his opponent in distant, shielded rooms and had observed a synchronized tendency between the sender's and the receiver's brain waves shortly after the master emitted qi.[37] Because sensory contact was impossible between the two individuals, these findings suggested that *tohate* cannot be explained by subtle cues and that a more complex explanation is required. They designed a subsequent series of studies to clarify this issue.

In the first experiment, the qigong master was stationed on the first floor and his opponent on the fourth floor of a ferroconcrete building in Tokyo, both in sensory-shielded rooms. Forty-nine trials were conducted under randomized, blind conditions. When the EEGs were compared, the *tohate* movements of the qigong master were highly correlated with a recoil motion in the distant opponent. There were fewer than 8 chances in 10,000 that the correlations could be explained by chance.

In the second experiment, the electroencephalogram (EEG) of the receiver was recorded while the qigong master performed *tohate*, again under randomized, sensory-shielded, blind conditions. The qigong master and receiver were in two rooms separated by a corridor, and the receiver sat quietly during the experiment to facilitate the recording. In fifty-seven trials, the receiver showed a significant difference in the alpha brain wave amplitudes from the right frontal part of the brain when the qigong master emitted qi and when he did not, suggesting that some type of nonenergetic information passed between the two.

In the third experiment, the sender and receiver were either located in the same room or shielded from sensory contact in separate rooms, while their EEGs were simultaneously measured just before, during, and after *tohate* was performed. EEG analysis showed that both were more relaxed during *tohate* than at rest, and that there was a correlation between their beta brain waves during *tohate*.

Is the threatening *tohate* motion of the qigong master, which is perceived by his faraway opponent, a type of distant negative intentionality? It appears to be so; the qigong master conveys a menacing intention, which results in the recoil of the distant person. These studies suggest, therefore, the existence of a type of nonsensory communication on which nonlocal negative prayers and curses depend.

BENEVOLENT VOODOO

Damn braces. Bless relaxes.

—William Blake, 1793

Effigies are used worldwide to convey harm or death to a distant victim. But as we've seen, scientists cannot study this effect directly in humans. To avoid this ethical dilemma, a research team at the University of Nevada, headed by Jannine M. Rebman and Dean I. Radin, asked, Can an effigy be used to convey *healing* influences to a distant person? Although it was not a study of distant negative intent, we will examine this experiment because it provides dramatic evidence that our thoughts can affect a distant individual through a magical ritual. This study implies that if we can use voodoo for good, we can also use it for harm.[38]

The researchers asked a "patient" to mold a doll in his or her likeness out of Play-doh and to place inside the figurine small personal belongings, messages, nail clippings, hair, or whatever else the participant felt to be a living part of himself or herself. The doll and personal information would then be used by the healer to form a distant, sympathetic connection to the patient—essentially a bridge for mental intentions.

Of the six members of the research team, three served as subjects in the experiment, switching roles as healer, patient, and experimenter in the various phases of the study. Outside subjects were not brought in, because the goal of the study was to directly influence another person's physiology; this required a high level of personal trust, which could be more easily achieved between professional colleagues who were used to working together and who liked each other.

The healer and the patient were placed in two adjacent buildings. The rooms were on different floors, separated by about 100 meters with several walls in between, and no telephones, cables, computer networks, or other connections between them. The healer's chamber was a quiet, acoustically and magnetically shielded room with black fabric walls and ceiling and a mirror on one wall. The purpose was to create an atmosphere that inhibited analytical, rational thought, that felt sacred, and that would stimulate the feeling of being sealed away from the outside, profane world. The ritual objects—the doll and personal items of the patient—were placed in the center of the room on a table covered with a black cloth, on which a golden candle burned. Instructions to the healer were provided via a laptop computer, which also rested on the table.

Healing rituals are claimed to influence a variety of physiological functions. The researchers elected to measure heart rate (HR), electrodermal activity, or the conduction of electrical impulses by the skin (EDA), and blood volume pulse (BVP) in the finger. These functions are affected by the changes in the body's autonomic nervous system and are indicators of psychological and physical stress.

After entering the healing chamber, the healer used the first five minutes to try to form a remote mental connection to the patient. This included reading the autobiography the patient had written. During the healing periods the healer used any strategy he or she felt would calm the patient's physiological state. This was done by directing calming thoughts toward the ritual doll and photographs, making passing gestures over the parts of the doll's body that were pointed out beforehand by the patient as being especially sensitive to stress, visualizing the patient in situations he or she felt to be calming, and making healing passes over the doll with the hands while visualizing the patient. Each healing session consisted of ten influence and control periods, according to a random scheme chosen by a computer, with each influence period lasting for one minute.

The patient's task was to sit quietly in his or her lighted room until the session ended. At the beginning of each session, the patient was asked to make a silent wish to connect to the healer. Throughout the entire session the patient simply gazed at a color screen saver on a computer monitor. This random display reminded him or her to maintain unstructured thoughts and to strive to be neither calm nor aroused—in other words, not to try to help or hinder the healer's influence.

The researchers' hypothesis was that the patient would be more relaxed during the influence periods than during the control periods, presumably due to the remote actions of the healer. The results indeed showed that the distant influence calmed the vascular system, as indicated by an increase in the BVP and a decrease in the HR, both changes indicating diminished physiological arousal or stress. A follow-up experiment replicated and confirmed these findings. The researchers concluded that the controlled use of a magical technique causes remote physiological changes, *"as though the healer and patient were actually next to each other."* [Emphasis in original.][39]

As of this writing, the University of Nevada team is conducting research in strategies for blocking remote mental influences, because the team is concerned about their potentially negative effects. We shall examine methods of protection in part V.

THE "TAINTED PRAYER" EXPERIMENT

> I prayed for humiliation so severe that she would come to her senses.
>
> —Daughter of an alcoholic woman

Dr. Scott Walker didn't set out to do an experiment that made people worse. A psychiatrist at the University of New Mexico School of Medicine in Albuquerque, he and his colleagues wished to examine the effects of distant, intercessory prayer on individuals suffering from substance abuse. They enlisted forty-two alcoholics who were being treated in an alcohol rehabilitation program. Walker's 1996 project was a pilot study, meaning it was a small experiment whose goal is to define appropriate questions for subsequent studies on the same subject. The study was well designed—a double-blind, prospective, randomized investigation in which neither the patients nor researchers knew who was and was not receiving prayer.

The alcoholics were told that if they volunteered for the study, they might or might not have people praying for them. All of them received full benefit of counseling and other treatments, but half of them were assigned to prayer volunteers who prayed on their behalf. The intercessors were drawn from the Albuquerque Faith Initiative, which represented a wide range of spiritual traditions. Each person prayed daily for six months for three clients each and recorded the nature and duration of each prayer.

Walker felt that it was important to know if the subjects might be receiving prayer from concerned individuals outside the study. At the outset, half the subjects reported that some family members were praying for them, and half said they weren't aware of anyone doing so. Six months into the study, those who had reported other family members praying for them (regardless of whether or not they received prayers from the study's prayer volunteers) were drinking significantly more heavily.

"[These findings] challenge simplistic beliefs about prayer," Walker says. "The notions that prayer is either harmless self-talk or a powerful, but always positive intervention, . . . need to be examined."

Why did those who were aware they were receiving prayer drink more? Were they defying those they knew were praying for them, as if to say, "You can't make me stop!"? Or could they actually have been harmed by the prayers of others? Although there is no evidence for this, Walker is open to this possibility. "We must consider that one's conscious and unconscious judgments, feelings and wishes may color prayer," he states.

Walker wonders about the interplay of prayer and human relationships, especially when hard-to-love habits like alcohol and drug addiction are involved. "Suppose . . . I'm an alcoholic, we're related, and I call you up drunk in the middle of the night, often. I cause scenes at family reunions. And you're praying for me. At some level, your prayers might be for me to die—to ease your misery and mine. I'd call that 'tainted prayer.' No one's ever looked at this before, yet according to a Gallup survey, five percent of our population admits to praying for harm for another."[40]

Walker is concerned that prayer may conceal the desire to harm others. If these wishes exist, they are likely unconscious. "The basic issue," Walker contends, "is that people haven't thought about what they do when they pray. People need to take responsibility for the power of their prayers."[41]

It is easier to pray for an infant with leukemia than for a chronic alcoholic or drug addict. The baby is blameless; the alcoholic or addict has wrecked his or her life and often the lives of others. When we pray for the alcoholic, it is not surprising that we might harbor unconscious, negative attitudes, in addition to whatever compassion we may feel. When we pray, which message gets through—our concern and compassion or our disapproving, hateful feelings?

If we harbor ambivalent feelings for another—and who doesn't?—our prayers for them may be tainted with negative wishes. This is one reason prayer should be considered a serious undertaking, not a casual enterprise. Before praying for another, we ought to ask, "How do I *really* feel about this person or situation? Am I praying with a divided mind?" If the answer is yes, perhaps our first prayer should be for ourselves—that our ambivalence and negativity be replaced by compassion and love.

TAKING THE EVIDENCE SERIOUSLY

What are we to make of these various experiments? There is no single study that makes an irrefutable case for distant negative intentionality such as negative prayers and curses. In this field, as in many areas of science, it is the linking together of many strands of evidence, not the results of any single study, that builds the case.

I feel this area of research should be taken seriously for several reasons. The evidence is abundant that our thoughts and intentions can inhibit or harm a variety of living, biological systems. Moreover, the evidence is not limited to a single type of organism; "targets" include a spectrum of entities such as bacteria, fungi, healthy and cancerous tissue in both humans and animals, and enzyme preparations. The variety of targets is immensely important. As we've seen, critics of this field claim that these effects are due only to psychological processes such as suggestion and expectation. However, the fact that nonhumans are used in these studies refutes this argument—unless skeptics wish to maintain that microbes, enzymes, and cells have an emotional life like human beings.

Skeptics also state that these studies have not been replicated, that they are not properly controlled, that they are done by rogue scientists operating outside the academic environment, and that the experiments are not published in peer-reviewed journals. They claim that significant results are found only in poorly designed studies and that these effects disappear when the quality of the studies is improved. The pettiest objections are the charge of fraud and the implication that researchers in this field suffer from a form of mental illness. I believe the critics are wrong on each of these points and that these objections have been soundly refuted.[42] One of the best attempts to debunk the debunkers is University of Nevada Las Vegas researcher Dean I. Radin's "A Field Guide to Skepticism" in his masterful book, *The Conscious Universe.*[43]

Researchers doing current work in the field of distant intentionality often hold faculty appointments at prestigious institutions, including major medical schools. Many of their studies embody the highest scientific standards, including proper randomization and control procedures, and a great many have been replicated. Moreover, the more precise these studies are, the more robust and significant their results tend to be, exactly opposite the charge of many skeptics.

This does not mean that all the studies we've looked at are perfect. The quality of experiments varies in any field of science, and this one is no exception. In assessing this or any other area, one should look at the very best studies that have been done and try to discover the general direction in which they point. This contrasts with the strategy of many skeptics, who often cite the very worst study they can find and generalize to condemn the entire field.

Several years ago, the favorite charge of critics was that evidence for distant mental effects did not exist. As the experimental evidence has increased and its quality has improved, critics now seem generally to be moving in a different direction—dismissing the evidence on the grounds that there is no scientific theory to support it. Since a generally accepted supporting theory does not exist, they suggest that all the studies should be disregarded. This is quite an odd point of view. Scientists are often challenged by facts that violate prevailing theories at the time they are discovered. When this happens, one does not toss out data; rather, one seeks to confirm or refute the new findings and, if necessary, to reshape the old theory to accommodate them. In medicine, we are often forced to dwell in a theoretical fog. For example, for the longest time we did not know how penicillin worked—or aspirin, quinine, colchicine, and many other therapies. We often know *that* something works before understanding *how* it works. So it is with the distant effects of mental intentions.

In a related charge, critics also claim that the field of distant intentionality is so out of step with the rest of science that its findings are untenable and should be dismissed. Again, this is a rather peculiar position. For decades physicists have recognized deep conflicts between special relativity and quantum mechanics, the two main pillars of modern physics. Rather than discarding one of them, they have sought to developed a comprehensive "theory of everything" that would bring them into harmony. Similarly, scientists currently have no idea how the brain produces consciousness or even if it does; yet no one favors ignoring either the brain or consciousness simply because we don't precisely know how they are related. Likewise, there is no reason to jettison the rich database of distant intentionality simply because we have not yet been able to integrate it with the rest of science.

EMERGING THEORIES

Many scientists do not believe that the events we've examined are in conflict with current scientific theory. For example, the eminent physicist Gerald Feinberg, speaking of nonlocal distant mental events, says, "[If] such phenomena indeed occur, no change in the fundamental equations of physics would be needed to describe them."[44]

The model of consciousness that is needed to accommodate distant mental intentions, whether positive or negative, is one that recognizes a nonlocal quality of the mind. *Nonlocal mind* is a term I introduced in 1989 in my book *Recovering the Soul*.[45] According to this concept, consciousness cannot be completely localized or confined to specific points in space, such as brains or bodies, or to discrete points in time, such as the present moment. A mind that is nonlocal might work *through* the brain and body, without being limited to them. Several models of consciousness have recently been proposed by eminent scientists that embody this quality of the mind. For example:

- Physicist Amit Goswami of the University of Oregon's Institute of Theoretical Science has proposed his Science Within Consciousness (SWC) theory, in which consciousness is recognized as a fundamental, causal factor in the universe, not confined to the brain, the body, or the present time.[46, 47]
- David J. Chalmers, a mathematician and cognitive scientist from University of California, Santa Cruz, also has suggested that consciousness is fundamental in the universe. It is not derived from anything else and cannot be reduced to anything more basic. Consciousness, Chalmers suggests, is perhaps on a par with matter and energy.[48] His view frees consciousness from its local confinement to the brain and opens the door for nonlocal, consciousness-mediated events such as we've discussed.
- Physicist Nick Herbert has long proposed a similar view. He suggests that consciousness abounds in the universe and that we have seriously underestimated the amount of it, just as early physicists drastically underestimated the size of the universe.[49]

- Nobel physicist Brian D. Josephson, of Cambridge University's Cavendish Laboratory, has proposed that consciousness makes possible "the biological utilization of quantum nonlocality." He believes that nonlocal events not only exist at the subatomic level, but also, through the actions of the mind, can be amplified and can emerge in our everyday experience as distant mental events of a broad variety.[50]

- Rupert Sheldrake, the British biologist, has proposed a nonlocal picture of consciousness in his widely known "hypothesis of formative causation."[51] Sheldrake sees great promise in his model for distant, mental events such as intercessory prayer and for negative mental intentions as well.

- Systems theorist Ervin Laszlo has proposed that nonlocal, consciousness-mediated events such as intercessory prayer, telepathy, precognition, and clairvoyance may be explainable through developments in physics concerning the quantum vacuum and zero-point field.[52]

- The late physicist David Bohm proposed that consciousness is present to some degree in everything. "Everything material is also mental and everything mental is also material," he stated. "The separation of the two—matter and spirit—is an abstraction. The ground is also one."[53] Bohm's views, like the above hypotheses, liberate consciousness from its confinement to the body and make possible, in principle, the distant, nonlocal phenomena we've examined.

- Robert G. Jahn, former dean of engineering at Princeton University, with his colleagues at the Princeton Engineering Anomalies Research lab, has proposed a model of the mind in which consciousness acts freely through space and time to create actual change in the physical world. Their hypothesis is based on their experimental evidence, which is the largest database ever assembled of the effects of distant intentionality.[54]

- Mathematician C. J. S. Clarke, of the University of Southampton's Faculty of Mathematical Studies, has proposed that "it is necessary to place mind first as the key aspect of the universe." Clarke's hypothesis is based in a quantum logic approach to physics and takes nonlocality as its starting point.[55]

Although these views are recent, they are part of a long tradition within modern science. Many of the greatest scientists of this century have been cordial to an extended, unitary model of the mind, which is a picture that permits the sort of distant mental intentions we've been examining.[56] This shows that a nonlocal view of consciousness is not a fringe or radical idea, as critics often claim. Examples include the following:

- Erwin Schrödinger, the Nobel physicist whose wave equations lie at the heart of modern quantum physics: "Mind by its very nature is a *singulare tantum*. I should say: the overall number of minds is just one."[57]
- Sir Arthur Eddington, the eminent astronomer-physicist: "The idea of a universal Mind or Logos would be, I think, a fairly plausible inference from the present state of scientific theory; at least it is in harmony with it."[58]
- Sir James Jeans, the British mathematician, astronomer, and physicist: "When we view ourselves in space and time, our consciousnesses are obviously the separate individuals of a particle-picture, but when we pass beyond space and time, they may perhaps form ingredients of a single continuous stream of life. As it is with light and electricity, so it may be with life; the phenomena may be individuals carrying on separate existences in space and time, while in the deeper reality beyond space and time we may all be members of one body."[59]

Nonlocal mind—mind beyond body, mind beyond time, which underlies both positive and negative prayers—is supported today by a four-letter word that makes all the difference: *data*.

PART 5

PROTECTION

Who ya gonna call?
        —*Title song from the film* Ghostbusters

PROTECTION

No ONE IS HELPLESS against the negative intentions of others. Methods of protection are real, powerful, and freely available.

But we can worry too much about these matters. Fretting over being victimized can become an obsession. Researcher Dean I. Radin of the University of Nevada, author of *The Conscious Universe*, remarks, "The[se negative mental] phenomena are largely unconscious, permeate everything and aren't getting any better or worse."[1] So, as we probe the question of how we can protect ourselves from the harmful intentions of others, we should put this problem in perspective. These events are not new. They probably have always been with us and likely always will be. They are a fact of life, to be accepted and dealt with as any other condition of existence. Taking a historical perspective may help calm our fears about the dark side of the mind. Parapsychology researcher John Palmer states,

> Any increase in human capacity, whether it be psychic powers or the benefits of education, can be used for either good or evil purposes. I tend to be an optimist in this regard. . . .Civilization has advanced in spite of its increased capacity for self-destruction."[2]

In dealing with the malevolent attitudes of others, we can be either grim or lighthearted. Consider, for example, the picture presented in Carlos Castaneda's books of Don Juan, the Yaqui shaman. Don Juan acknowledges the dark side of the mind and engages it fully. Although he becomes involved in titanic struggles with the negative intentions of other shamans, he does so naturally and gracefully and moves on to other things. He is not dominated by the evil forces; he does not dwell on them; he does not get hung up.

PROTECTION IS INHERENT IN NATURE

It is also reassuring to realize that we do not have to invent defenses against the negative thoughts of others. They exist naturally and come into play automatically when needed. It would be odd if this were not the case. Nature has provided us ways of resisting physical pathogens such as bacteria and viruses; why would we not have developed ways of resisting psychological pathogens as well?

How do we know natural defenses exist? We are continually bathed in the negative intentions of others—various "little curses," comments, and thoughts of an infinite variety. Most people are able to tune out this incessant barrage and live their lives without ever encountering, as far as they can tell, a curse, hex, or spell. If their psychospiritual immune system were not working adequately, this would not be possible. They would be like an infant born without a physical immune system, unable to survive because of lethal infections.

So let us be thankful for our innate forms of protection that come factory installed. They are our first line of defense and all that most people will ever need. Now let's examine how they can be supplemented.

BUNGLING

It is consoling that most people who try to harm others with their thoughts are bunglers. As the English psychic Dion Fortune (1890–1946) once said, "The great majority of dabblers in occultism are protected by their own ineptitude"[3]—which protects their potential victims as well.

PRAYER

In northern New Mexico, where I live, there is said to be a shaman behind every rock. When I began to investigate the negative powers of consciousness, this provided me the opportunity to inquire from healers whether they believed we can harm one another with our thoughts. When they all said yes, I decided to change the question. If these events are real, I began to ask, what can we do to protect ourselves? One native healer said, "Have you ever heard of the Lord's Prayer? Do you remember the words, 'Deliver us from evil'? You white people have one of the best forms of protection, and you don't even know it! Why, I even use it myself!" he said with a grin.

REVERSING MEDICAL CURSES THROUGH PRAYER

Modern medicine, as we have seen, contains the potential for harm through a variety of curses, spells, and hexes. Most of these are inadvertent; doctors don't spend their time concocting ways to intentionally do us in. Still, the harm is real, and we should consider how to avoid being victimized.

The week before his thirty-ninth birthday, Joseph Forgione experienced an episode of severe chest pain that radiated into his left arm. A cautious man, he sought medical advice, and an arteriogram revealed severely blocked arteries to his heart. It was like a nightmare coming true. His father had collapsed and died at the same age, when he lifted four-year-old Joseph and whirled him around. Two of his grandparents died of heart attacks also. Joseph was obsessed with the fear that he, too, would suffer the same fate.

In the hospital he was told that heart surgery might extend his life for a few years. A top Philadelphia cardiac surgeon was recommended. "The hospital staff was taken aback," Forgione recalls, "when I asked to talk with the surgeon before the operation." Suddenly, just before midnight, the drape by his bedside flew open and the surgeon appeared. When Forgione began to question him, the doctor became irritated. "I know what I'm doing," he announced imperiously. "But I didn't know what he was doing," Forgione thought, and he told the surgeon he didn't feel comfortable proceeding unless he gave him more information. Forgione's request apparently pushed the doctor over the edge. "It's your funeral," he said crisply, and wheeled and walked out.

Forgione followed his instincts. He signed himself out of the hospital, quickly read everything he could find about his condition, contacted other competent cardiac specialists, and proceeded with a successful surgical procedure. The surgeon he settled on, Dr. Lester Sauvage of the Hope Heart Institute in Seattle, was a strong believer in a spiritual component in life. After he had sent a copy of his medical records and his arteriogram to Dr. Sauvage, Forgione received a phone call from the physician. He wanted to know if Forgione believed in a higher power; why he wanted to live; what happiness meant to him; what he would do if his life were extended. "His questions cut through my despair," Forgione said. When he arrived in Seattle and met Dr. Sauvage for the first time, the physician said warmly, "Joe, I'm glad you're here. I'm confident you'll do fine." Later that evening Sauvage came by Forgione's hospital room after being in surgery all day. He handed his patient a card and said, "Let's repeat this prayer together." It was the prayer attributed to St. Francis of Assisi: "Where there is hatred, let me sow love. . . ." And the final words, ". . . we are born to eternal life." When it came time to leave, the surgeon said, "I am confident that God will bless our work."

When Dr. Sauvage left, Forgione read the prayer again and again. He felt confident, and when he was wheeled into the operating room at 6:30 the next morning he was prepared for whatever might happen. "To this day, my memories are almost indescribable," he relates, "yet they are as vivid as anything I have ever experienced. I felt no turmoil, no stress, just closeness to God and my loved ones—my wife and children, my deceased parents and grandparents. I had never been so happy."

Six days after surgery Forgione was ready to fly back home to Pennsylvania. Before he left, Dr. Sauvage came by. "You'll continue to have to cope with serious heart disease," he said. "But God wants you to live for a reason. Find that reason, and make a difference in the world."

He did. He joined the board of a homeless shelter organization, organized a workforce, and started a construction company to work on inner-city projects and help the unemployed learn a trade. He changed his diet, exercised, and practiced stress management. Nine years following surgery, he continues to follow a strict diet and runs six miles every morning.[4]

Researchers are discovering that Forgione's story isn't rare. In a study of coronary bypass patients by Dr. Thomas Oxman and his colleagues at Dartmouth Medical School, the factor that correlated most strongly with survival of surgery and a good post-op course was the degree of spiritual meaning in a patient's life.[5]

Medical curses such as "It's your funeral," "You're a walking time bomb," "You should have had surgery yesterday," "There's nothing more I can do," and so on, are not uncommon. Forgione's experience shows how a spiritual approach that includes prayer can annul their impact.

SELECTING A PRAYER OF PROTECTION

How should a prayer of protection be selected? To be most effective, it must ring true and come from the heart. The prayer of St. Francis of Assisi felt authentic and genuine to both Joseph Forgione and his physician. But other prayers, even prayers of silence, might be more meaningful to someone else.

Let us always recall that prayer is universal; it belongs to all of humankind, not to a specific religion. No spiritual tradition has a monopoly on prayer, which is why there probably will never be a universal prayer of protection that is linked to a particular creed.

For those who are interested, here is the prayer attributed to St. Francis (1181–1226), in which Forgione and Dr. Sauvage found comfort, protection, and assurance:

> *Lord, make me an instrument of your peace.*
> *Where there is hatred, let me sow love,*
> *Where there is injury, pardon;*
> *Where there is doubt, faith;*
> *Where there is despair, hope;*
> *Where there is darkness, light;*
> *Where there is sadness, joy.*
> *O divine Master, Grant that I may not so much seek*
> *To be consoled, as to console,*
> *To be understood, as to understand,*
> *To be loved, as to love,*
> *For it is in giving that we receive;*
> *It is in pardoning that we are pardoned;*
> *It is in dying that we are born to eternal life.*[6]

Certain prayers, through time, become recognized for their effectiveness. While doing research on folk medicine, Dr. Loudell F. Snow of Michigan State University's Department of Community Medicine was given a printed prayer by an informant to keep her safe.[7] The prayer carried a guarantee that the possessor would never burn or drown, poison would have no effect, eighty-two different kinds of accidents would be averted, childbirth would be eased, and epileptic seizures would be prevented. She discovered that the prayer had been making the rounds for a long time. It was identical to one sent to William Black over a century earlier, reported in his classic work on folk medicine.[8]

All spiritual traditions honor particular prayers for various purposes, including protection. Sources are widely available and are contained in my book *Prayer Is Good Medicine.*[9]

PROTECTIVE IMAGES

Drs. William G. Braud and Marilyn J. Schlitz performed a series of experiments at the Mind Science Foundation in San Antonio, Texas, in which persons were able mentally to influence the bodily systems of other individuals at a distance, outside their awareness.[10]

They chose to monitor electrodermal activity, the skin's ability to conduct an electrical impulse. The monitored person was stationed in one room and the influencer in a separate, distant room, unable to communicate with the other through the senses. The influencer attempted to change the distant person's electrodermal activity according to a random schedule. The experimental procedure, including all measurements, was computer controlled. Braud and Schlitz found that the autonomic activity of the distant person did indeed change, either increasing or decreasing, according to the intent or wishes of the influencer. Yet the target persons were not sitting ducks. They were able to block unwanted influences on their bodies by using their own mental imagery.

A variety of images was successful. In one experiment, when the monitored person visualized "a massive steel monolith—thick, solid, and impenetrable," the distant mental influence did not come through. In another study the recipient visualized "a bright, pulsating white oval of light," again with a significant blocking effect.

It is widely believed that healers can take on the illnesses of those they heal and therefore require protection. Folk medicine researcher Dr. Loudell F. Snow interviewed a woman who is a Pentecostal evangelist who spends much time at a local hospital praying for the sick. She realizes that many illnesses are caused by microorganisms that could conceivably harm her, but while making her rounds she believes God puts an invisible barrier around her that the germs cannot penetrate.[11] This image is virtually identical to those used in the above experiments.

The classic Braud-Schlitz "blocking experiments" show that we are not helpless victims of the thoughts and intentions of others. We can permit distant mental influences to get through if we choose, or we can block them. These studies show also that it is not necessary to resort to elaborate methods of protection such as complex rituals, exotic amulets, and so on. Effective protection can be as simple as a thought.

AROMAS

Olfactory stimuli are universally used to ward off evil influences. While garlic may be the best known, there are many others, such as aromatic oils, incense, candles, and even aerosol sprays.[12] One of the most unusual is asafetida, which I consider one of the vilest, most noxious substances ever discovered.

Asafetida—the word derived from a Persian word for gum and the Latin *foetida* or *fetid*—is a resin obtained from various Asiatic plants of the parsley family. In the deep South and in certain urban areas of the United States, asafetida bags are still worn around the neck to repel illnesses and hexes. Unlike other means of protection, such as mental images and prayers, the wearer has immediate evidence of its effectiveness. If humans won't come near the stench, presumably evil influences won't, either.

I shall always remember my initial encounter with asafetida. I obtained a degree in pharmacy as an undergraduate and worked during medical school as a registered pharmacist, often at a pharmacy in Dallas that was popular with ethnic minorities. Asafetida bags proved to be one of the most popular nonprescription items in the store. At first I had no idea what they were for. When I asked a woman who was purchasing one what purpose it served, she took the bag from its tightly wrapped container, shoved it under my nose, and said, "Smell this and you'll understand!" The odor stunned me. The woman had a good laugh, but I thought I would vomit on the spot. I saw the point of asafetida. If I were a demon or a curse, I'd come nowhere near anyone wearing an asafetida bag. Never have I understood how anyone can tolerate wearing asafetida or why this form of protection is not ruinous to interpersonal relations.

HUMILITY

Snow found that a popular folk method of preventing harm from the thoughts of others is to avoid exhibiting feelings of superiority and not to flaunt one's material possessions—to avoid "acting uppity," "putting on airs," or "thinking you are better than other people." Rising above one's station in society or boasting of one's good fortune invites divine displeasure or satanic intervention. It can also encourage envy, which is a common cause of the evil eye, as we have seen.

GET-WELL CARDS: A MODERN RITUAL OF PROTECTION?

Craig Shergold, a sixteen-year-old London lad, got into the *Guinness Book of Records* for receiving the most get-well cards ever—thirty-three million—following the diagnosis of a brain tumor that the doctor had declared incurable. "I feel great, fantastic," he told neurosurgeon Neal Kassell, four years after the doctor removed an egg-sized tumor from the boy's brain in March 1991.[13]

Although surgery may have saved Craig's life, we can also wonder what those thirty-three million cards were doing. Get-well cards always say, "You are not alone," and therefore promote a sense of connection with others. Many studies show that aloneness and isolation lead to illness and that social interaction promotes health and longevity. Get-well cards may therefore be a form of protection against hopelessness and fear, and thus a way of restoring health.

GUILT AND FORGIVENESS: LESSONS FROM THE KAHUNAS

"I was warned never to say, even in fun, 'He ought to be shot,' or 'I hope he chokes' . . . ," said Max Freedom Long, the American psychologist who explored the kahuna tradition of Polynesia and Hawaii, as we've seen (p. 98). The kahunas maintained that comments such as these could work as a curse, particularly if the person to whom they were directed felt guilty about something and had not made restitution or obtained forgiveness. The guilt, which could be for some real or imagined shortcoming, was believed to create a weak spot in one's psychological armor, making one susceptible to the offhand comments or deliberate curses of another. Long considered this a profound insight. "[This] has been the secret and greatly important thing known to the kahunas," he said, "but only faintly glimpsed and entirely misunderstood by religionists the world around."[14]

Several schools of psychology have begun to emphasize the value of seeking forgiveness from those we have hurt. Many twelve-step programs embody this principle as well. In them, forgiveness indeed seems to protect against curses—the curse of addiction to drugs and alcohol.

Getting rid of a sense of guilt involves doing solid psychological work. There is nothing exotic about this. This approach simply says, "If you want protection, clean up your act; take care of your stuff."

EXORCISM

> Noncooperation with evil is as much a duty as cooperation with good.
>
> —Mahatma Gandhi

Exorcism, strictly speaking, is not a form of protection but a therapy that is employed once protection has failed, when evil powers have gotten the upper hand and have possessed an individual. Nonetheless, because of its increasing popularity as an antidote to spells and curses, we will briefly examine exorcism. It isn't popular to do so. The words of psychologist William James around the turn of this century still apply.

> The refusal of modern "enlightenment" to treat "possession" as an hypothesis to be spoken of as even possible, in spite of the massive human tradition based on concrete experience in its favor, has always seemed to me a curious example of the power of fashion in things scientific. That the demon-theory will again have its innings is to my mind absolutely certain. One has to be

"scientific" indeed, to be blind and ignorant enough to suspect no such possibility.[15]

As the contemporary theologian Walter Wink puts it, "Angels, spirits, principalities, gods, Satan—these, along with all other spiritual realities, are the unmentionables of our culture."[16]

Canon David Goodacre fights devils. He is the convener of the Christian Deliverance team in the diocese of Newcastle in England, which provides services to people who believe they are possessed. "We treat them very seriously," Goodacre says.[17]

But not too seriously. "I think we can fairly claim that what in the past have been identified as 'demons,' are in reality inner objects based on parental figures and important others experienced in the past," he states. "Of course as therapists, as exorcists, we still want to help people to be rid of them."

Canon Goodacre may appear to fundamentalists to be a devil himself for not believing that devils are real entities bent on capturing human souls. He acknowledges that such beliefs once served a useful purpose. The writers of the New Testament believed in demons, and this gave them a handy explanation of human problems in the psychology of the day. The demon theories came largely from Persian psychology, Goodacre states, and other sources foreign to the Holy Land two centuries before Christ. Two dominant schools of thought arose about demons. One view was that they originated with the fall of the angels, were under the lordship of Satan, and caused general misfortune but not necessarily sickness. According to another perspective, although demons functioned as agents of Satan, they were somehow derived from human beings. As Josephus said in the first century, "The so-called demons are the spirits of evil men entering into the living."[18] By invading and taking possession of the mind and body, they could indeed cause sickness, particularly mental illness.

Demons have been invoked by our predecessors to explain all sorts of bizarre, unpredictable behavior. When someone had a sudden seizure, shouted out, made a scene, or seemed out of control, our predecessors saw Satan. Since there were no drugs to drive him out, words were used, and certain words quickly gained the reputation as magical formulae. "What [our forebears] missed," Canon Goodacre states, "as we do so often today, was that the healing factor was not so much the command or formula used, but the therapeutic presence of the healer." Goodacre sees in Jesus' action the power of what today is often called "therapeutic presence." "When Jesus met a sick soul, what healed was his person . . . a secure, harmonizing presence," says Goodacre. Jesus was able to "expel demons" because he "behaved naturally; he was not anxious, he was warm and spontaneous and above all he offered his real presence. It is these qualities which heal, as much today as then."

Goodacre relates the experience of a student who was found by church members on the streets of a major city. He was seriously depressed and "was blaspheming against God, especially against the Holy Spirit," which has long been considered evidence of possession. The church came to his aid, took him into its care, and performed an exorcism to drive out the evil spirits they judged were causing the problem. When it came time for him to leave the city, he did so confidently, believing he was cured. Years later, however, he was again in an appalling state. His obsessive thoughts had returned worse than ever. He could not hold a job, and his marriage was falling apart. At this point he met Canon Goodacre, anxious to have the bad spirits driven out of him again. This time, however, neither the exorcism nor the efforts of mental health professionals at the local hospital were very successful. What had happened? According to Goodacre, the church was spectacularly successful the first time because it took him in, accepted him in love, and restored the broken relationships in his life. This was far more important, Goodacre believes, than the deliverance from devils provided in the exorcism. But the church's efforts did not go far enough. They permitted him to repress the negative side of this psychological life. The devils merely receded into the shadows, ready to move center stage again at an opportune moment. The exorcism was a quick fix; deeper work was needed. Believing he was cured, he was unable to withstand the challenges of his life when he moved away from the sustaining influence of the church.

"We know where 'demons' come from and what they are," says Goodacre. "We do not need to depend on an out-of-date psychology and make the further mistake of divinizing and empowering them."[19] Psychoanalyst Harry Guntrip agrees. "Psychoanalysis," he says, "is exorcism, casting out the devils that haunt people in the unconscious world, devils who can be seen clearly enough in patients' dreams."[20]

M. Scott Peck, author of the celebrated book *The Road Less Traveled*, is also a psychiatrist who believes in the value of exorcism. In his book *People of the Lie*, he describes patients he has treated who seem to have been taken over by evil forces. Sometimes formal exorcism ceremonies were required before the power dominating their life could be eradicated. Peck does not believe, however, that Satan is physically real:

> [I]t is terribly important to understand that Satan is a spirit. I have said I have met Satan, and this is true. But it is not tangible in the way that matter is tangible. It no more has horns, hooves, and a forked tail than God has a long white beard. Even the name, Satan, is just a name we have given to something basically nameless. Like God, Satan can manifest itself in and through material beings, but it itself is not material.... In one case described it manifested itself through the patient's writhing serpentine body, biting teeth, scratching nails, and hooded reptilian eyes. But there were no fangs, no scales. It was, through the use of the patient's body, extraordinarily and dramatically and even supernaturally snakelike. But it is not itself a snake. It is spirit.... *Satan has no power except in a human body.* ... Satan's threats are always empty. They are all lies. In fact, *the only power that Satan has is through human belief in its lies.* [Emphasis in original.][21]

Perhaps no one has brought exorcism into public awareness more than Francis MacNutt, who may be the best-known practitioner of exorcism in the Western world. MacNutt's credentials are impressive. He is a graduate of Harvard University who earned his master's degree from Catholic University of America and a doctorate from the Aquinas Institute of Theology. For decades he and his wife, Judith, have run the Christian Healing Ministries out of Jacksonville, Florida, which is dedicated to healing in the Christian tradition. Anyone interested in the practice of exorcism and the rationale behind it should consult his fascinating book, *Deliverance from Evil Spirits: A Practical Manual.*[22] MacNutt not only describes actual cases of possession, he provides step-by-step methods of exorcism, including actual prayers that can be employed.

PROTECTION IN FOLKLORE AND FOLK MEDICINE

The methods humans have devised to protect themselves against the malevolent influences of others are wildly varied. On the surface many appear zany. But, like many of the ancient folk remedies used in healing, some of them may have a rational basis.

Consider the ancient belief that a witch can be thrown off the trail by crossing running water.[23] This may seem utterly irrational at first glance; but if we look closer we may find reasons why it might work.

When I first read about this means of protection, my thoughts turned to fly-fishing in a mountain stream, which one crosses many times in the course of a day. The water is crystal clear, the scenery majestic, the air bracing. My spirits are so elevated in this setting that I feel I can resist anything negative—including the influence of witches, if they exist.

More than rationalization may be involved. We know today that a positive attitude and physical exercise set in motion a host of mind-body events that can stimulate our immune function and increase our cardiovascular fitness. Perhaps we are drawn to certain activities such as hiking and crossing the running water of mountain streams because we have learned through generations that they are somehow good for us. Crossing mountain streams makes us healthier, stronger, more resistant—more "protected." Always looking for (yet another) reason to go fly-fishing, I have come to place great confidence in this method of protection and I employ it whenever I can.

BREAKING THE CURSE OF KARMA

> *And in the end the love you take*
> *Is equal to the love you make.*
> —The Beatles, "The End," *Abbey Road*

Karma—the idea that "as a man sows, so shall he reap"—is considered by millions of people to be a curse.* It is one of the most influential

---

* As with most ancient philosophical ideas, karma is not as simple as it seems. India's Jain religion enumerates 148 kinds of karma. Karma is classified into *prārabdha* (effects determining the unavoidable circumstances of human life), *saṁcita* (effects able to be expiated or neglected), and *āgāmi* (effects currently generated and determining the future). See Kurt F. Leidecker, "Karma," *Dictionary of Philosophy*, ed. Dagobert D. Runes (Totowa, NJ: Littlefield, Adams, 1962), 160.

religious ideas in human history. Huston Smith, the eminent scholar of world's religions, offers this description of karma:

> A summary of [the Buddha's] position [on karma] would run something like this: (1) There is a chain of causation threading each life to those that have led up to it, and to those that will follow. Each life is in its present condition because of the way the lives that led up to it were lived. (2) Throughout this causal sequence the will remains free. The lawfulness of things makes the present state the product of prior acts, but within the present the will is influenced but not controlled. People remain at liberty to shape their destinies.[24]

Karma suggests that all our current circumstances are due to our thoughts and behaviors in former lives. One is always either paying back or being rewarded for past actions. As Smith describes this process,

> The present condition of each interior life—how happy it is, how confused or serene, how much it sees—is an exact product of what it has wanted and done in the past. Equally, its present thoughts and decisions are determining its future states. Each act that is directed upon the world has its equal and opposite reaction on oneself. Each thought and deed delivers an unseen chisel blow that sculpts one's destiny.[25]

According to karma, everyone gets what she deserves; we make our beds and must lie in them, no exceptions. We are completely responsible for what is happening to us now, and we are now shaping what will happen to us in the future. "Most people are not willing to admit this," Smith observes. "They prefer, as the psychologists say, to project—to locate the source of their difficulties outside themselves. They want excuses, someone to blame so that they may be exonerated."[26]

Karma is harsh in its fairness. It is so fair that all appeals to chance, accident, or luck are ruled out. That means it is hopeless to drift through life waiting for the breaks to come our way. We are the breaks.

As some people look more deeply at karma, what originally seemed a splendid idea can begin to appear cruel. They may begin to develop a love-hate relationship with karma and may actually view it as a curse: My current situation is fixed because of what I've done in the past, and there is nothing I can do about it.

So why does the idea of karma seem to be making a comeback in our culture? This could be due to the popularity of the concept of past lives, with which the idea of karma is compatible. Karma is also a ringing endorsement for immortality, which almost everyone prefers to annihilation with death. Moreover, karma allows people who currently enjoy comfortable circumstances to feel good about themselves. They made wise choices in former lives and are now reaping the benefits; they can pat themselves on the back. Karma also appeals to those who wish to escape from self-responsibility. If my current status is already fixed because of what I've done in the past, why try to change it? Karma is also a handy rationalization for life's unfairness—why bad things happen to good people, and why reprobates often prosper.

It is the fatalism implied by karma that Westerners don't like. Smith suggests, however, that fatalism is never absolute. "A card player finds himself dealt a particular hand, but is left free to play that hand in a number of ways," he states. In other words, karma may not be the curse we take it to be.

Along these lines, novelist Arthur Koestler developed the concept of the code and the strategy. "The code defines the rules of the game, and the strategy defines the course of the game," he stated.[27] In human life, the code is the physical playing field on which we find ourselves—the body and the universe we inhabit, and the principles that govern them. The strategy is choices we make while we inhabit our body and our world.

Many spiritual teachers have been exquisitely mindful that the strategy operates within the code and not in opposition to it. The story is told of a Hindu sage who once took a wrong step and seriously sprained his knee. A disciple who was following him was perplexed. "Master, you can see into the future and therefore knew the mishap was coming. Why did you not avoid it?" The sage replied, "As long as I have a body, it will be subject to the laws that govern bodies." His comment brings to mind an anonymous saying, "That man is free who is conscious of being the author of the laws he must obey."

One of the criticisms often leveled at karma is that it implies a strictly linear form of existence—serial lives or incarnations stretching through time like beads on a string, held together by the glue of causality. This suggests that spiritual realization is a matter of growth and development through time—a matter of progress, of salvation, of becoming wiser and better in the future. This contrasts with the idea of an already-present, perfect, indwelling quality that is often expressed as the divine within. But some traditions, such as Zen Buddhism, do not believe that the ideas of progress-into-the-future and perfection-in-the-moment are mutually exclusive. "It is the seeking, the aspiring, the movement which is the thing," says R. H. Blyth, the Zen Buddhism scholar.

> Our [eternal] Buddha nature is our becoming Buddha. This "becoming" has two aspects: we are already there; our journey is already done; we have fought the good fight. But we shall never arrive there; we shall lose every battle with the stupidity and dullness of ourselves and others. We must teach the unteachable, do the impossible, make time eternal. . . . The truth is that we have not any specific thing that can be called the Buddha-nature, or shall we not rather say that we both have it and do not have it, at the same time. It is true that we have no immortality, but we have something far better, we have time, and we have timelessness.[28]

This sort of talk is infuriating to anyone who cannot tolerate paradox. But unless we learn to do so, karma will continue to appear a curse, a force that continually interferes with our free will.*

Even though many Westerners reject the concept of karma, it occurs in its most dramatic form not in Eastern religions but in Chris-

---

* It is unfair to attribute the paradoxes of karma to the inscrutability of the East. Christianity, too, is saturated with paradox. Consider, Blyth says, "the mediaeval idea, simple, profound, and humorous, that without Adam's sin there would be no salvation, and Christ would be still loitering in Heaven waiting for someone to die for" (Blyth, *Zen and Zen Classics,* 70). From this perspective, Adam, Eve, and the serpent deserve our gratitude. Or consider the Christian doctrine of eternal punishment for the damned, which is hopelessly paradoxical. Reason tells us that at some point the amount of punishment that is delivered will balance the seriousness of the crime, at which point the debt is repaid and the punishment will end. Against the stretches of time, even the worst crime would eventually be paid off. If God is just, how then could he create *eternal* punishment?

tianity in the form of original sin. According to this doctrine, everyone is cursed not because of his or her own actions but as a result of somebody else's—those of Adam and Eve. Their choices are sufficient to condemn all succeeding humans to eternal suffering in hell: karma with a vengeance. But occasionally Christian teachers let slip the idea that we humans may not be as vile as officially described. One such incident was reported to have taken place in the life of Mother Teresa, when a brash reporter asked curtly, "Are you a saint?" She immediately poked him in the chest with a gnarled finger and replied, "Yes, and so are you!"

All religions that believe in karma provide ways of breaking its hold. Among them are the following:

1. Eliminate the chain of cause and effect. The idea of cause and effect depends on a concept of linear, passing time. When one learns to experience time as an eternal present, flowing time is seen to be an illusion. This can be accomplished through various forms of contemplative prayer and meditation. As linear time yields to an abiding sense of eternity, causal chains break and karmic debts cancel.

2. Eliminate or transcend the ego. Karmic events happen to somebody. Who? When the "self" or ego is transcended, karmic chains fall away.

3. Overcome duality. Karmic forces act on an individual existing in a world "out there." If one is not separate from the world, to whom might these forces apply? When one learns to experience one's self nondually, as one with all there is, karma is overcome.

4. Learn the system. Visiting a foreign country can be agonizing if we do not know the language or customs; it can be a breeze if we are fluent and at ease in the culture. Similarly, karma can be a source of enslavement or liberation, depending on the extent to which we know and abide by the rules. Thus it is said, "The ignorant drown in the ocean in which the mystic swims." Learning to swim means gaining spiritual maturity—following a spiritual discipline and learning the ropes.

IS LOVE ENOUGH?

God is love, but get it in writing.

—Gypsy Rose Lee

The power of love in repelling the negative intentions of others is legendary, and many people believe that love is all you need to be protected. If we return hate with hate, it is said, we empower it; if we respond with love, the hatred is annulled. But this is only part of the picture.

If love is not balanced with action, the results can be disastrous. As Joseph Campbell, the great mythologist, put it, "Jesus said, 'Love your enemies.' He didn't say, 'Don't have any.'" Our enemies are real, and sometimes they try to destroy us. When they do, love needs a backup. To believe otherwise is to risk being broadsided emotionally, spiritually, and perhaps physically by the malevolent intentions of others.

Even though it is hazardous to rely on love alone for protection, love has a vital place in all the forms of protection we have considered. Those who are engaging in negative prayers and curses may seem unlovable, but they are not too different from ourselves. As Russian novelist Alexander Solzhenitsyn said,

> If only it were all so simple! If only there were evil people somewhere insidiously committing evil deeds, and it were necessary only to separate them from the rest of us and destroy them. But the line dividing good and evil cuts through the heart of every human being. And who is willing to destroy a piece of his own heart?[29]

If our methods of protection do not contain love, we risk becoming increasingly isolated from others through suspicion and fear. This can make us crazy, literally: *idiot* is derived from words meaning "solitary" and "alone."

Frank Zappa once observed, "Given that all religions preach brotherhood, love of your fellow man, and tolerance for all people without exception, why is it that all the world's different religions have never been able to achieve unity?"[30] Part of the reason is our fear of others and the need to be protected from them. This has led to the building of walls to exclude "evil" people, thus giving rise to deplorable divisions—God's people against Satan's, believers against heathens, us against them. It is not protection from evil people we need, but protection from their evil deeds—and there is a major difference. We are all evil—and when we make war on others we consider evil, we make war on ourselves. (See the Afterword, "Should We Clean Up Prayer?" p. 219.)

And perhaps also on the Absolute, however named, because the Absolute contains everything, or else it would not be absolute. Many great mystics have glimpsed that God's all-inclusive oneness knows no limits and takes in evil. A majestic example was Florence Nightingale (1820–1910), the founder of modern nursing. She observed, "Everybody tells us that the existence of evil is incomprehensible, whereas I believe it is much more difficult—it is impossible—to conceive the existence of God (or even of a good man) without evil."[31]

Love is required in protection—not because it can handle the job alone but because it is the best safeguard we have against foolishly seceding, in effect, from the rest of the human race.

If our methods of protection have not love, others need protection from us.

PROTECTION FROM THE PROTECTORS

We should always be cautious in asking others for advice about protection. We should ask ourselves whether they are motivated by love or by a need for power and control. If the latter, we need protection from them. If we do not sense love in their advice, we should reject it and move on. This point is made by psychiatrist M. Scott Peck, who is a Christian. "Were I to conduct an exorcism," he states,

> I would not exclude from the team any mature Hindu, Buddhist, Muslim, Jew, atheist, or agnostic who was a genuinely loving presence. But I would without hesitation exclude a nominal Christian or anyone else who was not such a presence. For the presence of one unloving person in the room is likely not only to cause the exorcism to fail but to subject the team members as well as the patient to the possibility of grave harm.[32]

Peck's observations about the central role of love apply to all methods of protection, not just exorcism. If love is not present, they will likely be ineffective or possibly harmful.

EXOTIC IS NOT BETTER

There are endless categories of protection we will not examine, such as chants and incantations, the use of affirmations and special phrases, the wearing of amulets and talismans, dietary programs, the visitation of sacred shrines, approaches based in numerology and astrology—the list is virtually endless. Books on these subjects abound and are readily available.

I have only a general comment about these methods. The more exotic a method of protection, the greater is the risk of being lured away from the basics. The most reliable forms of protection against the negative intentions of others involve psychological growth and maturity; honoring the presence of the Absolute in our life; and cultivating our capacity for love. Because these methods of protection are not easy, and because it may require a lifetime to cultivate them, it is tempting to focus instead on arcane, "fun" approaches—finding the most powerful gemstone; sleuthing a secret ritual; learning to use the "magic circle," and so on. There is no quick fix. Unless we follow a first-things-first approach, attending to the necessities of our psychological and spiritual life, it is unlikely that the more exotic forms of protection will work. If we rely on them exclusively, we may discover that we become more vulnerable, not less, to the malevolent intentions of others.

PROTECTION THROUGH PRAYING BETTER?

In chapter 2 we saw that our best-laid prayers can have unintended consequences. This means that we need protection from ourselves, including from our own prayers. C. S. Lewis summed up this situation by observing, "If God had granted all the silly prayers I've made in my life, where should I be now?"[33]

Can we find a way to pray that avoids the pitfalls of prayer? Can we avoid endangering ourselves and others by how we pray?

For many people, prayer is a form of thought. If we can learn to think better, they claim, we will know how to pray better.

Programs to help people think better are a virtual growth industry. What are their chances for success? In his book *The Logic of Failure,* German psychologist Dietrich Dörner describes the prospects for changing how we think:

> The probability that there is a secret mental trick that at one stroke will enable the human mind to solve complex problems better is practically zero. It is equally unlikely that our brains have some great cache of unused potential. If such things existed, we would be using them. Nowhere in nature does a creature run around on three legs and drag a fourth, perfectly functional but unused leg. Our brains function the way they function and not otherwise. We must make the best of that; there is no magic wand or hidden treasure that will instantly make us deep and powerful thinkers.[34]

Although we ought to use every ounce of intelligence and creativity we have, it seems to me that an intellectual approach will not overcome our limitations in thinking and that in all likelihood we will continue to pose a risk through our "silly prayers," as Lewis put it.

In this dilemma may lie our salvation. The best antidote for our folly may be, as we've seen, not in praying for anything at all, but in adopting an approach in prayer such as "Thy will be done" or "May the best outcome prevail." This approach might offer fabulous protection from the most serious threat we face: ourselves.

Willis W. Harman (1918–1997), the late futurist, scientist, author, and president of the Institute of Noetic Sciences, was a friend and mentor who taught me a lot about this point of view. Here's how Willis saw it:

> Let's suppose it is true that if I choose to pray for something, my prayer or intention can influence that something coming into being. The question is this: Who is doing the choosing? If I am intimately connected to the whole universe, then I am part of the whole. My ultimate being resides in the whole. In some real sense, then, I am the whole—I am a co-creator of the universe. If that's the case, when I intend something, do I really want what "I" think I want (that would just be the ego having its way)? Or,

rather, don't I really want exactly what the universe wants, since ultimately that is who I am? The prayer "Thy will be done" began to make a lot of sense for me.[35]

It also makes sense to the actor Albert Brooks, who said, in a lighter tone,

If I were gonna rewrite the Bible, I would say the main prayer to God should be: Dear God, I'm fine. I don't need anything. Amen. And then he might start answering. . . . But nothing comes to you when you're desperate; it just doesn't work that way. So if your going, "I need a hit, I need a hit," . . . you're never gonna get it.[36]

INNER BALANCE AND HARMONY

Richard Wilhelm, the sinologist who translated *The Secret of the Golden Flower: A Chinese Book of Life* and other works,[37] was once in a remote Chinese village that was suffering from an extended drought. Every kind of prayer had been offered to put an end to the drought, but nothing had worked and the people were desperate. The only remaining choice was to send to a remote area for a well-known rainmaker. This fascinated Wilhelm, and he was on hand when the rainmaker, a wizened old man, arrived in a covered cart. He alighted, sniffed the air in disdain, then asked for a cottage on the outskirts of the village. He insisted that he be totally undisturbed and that his food be left outside his door. Nobody heard from him for three days, then the village awoke to a downpour of rain mixed with snow, which was unheard of for that time of year.

Wilhelm, greatly impressed, approached the old man, who was now out of seclusion. "So you can make it rain?" he inquired. Of course he could not, the old man scoffed. "But there was the most persistent drought until you came," Wilhelm objected, "and then—within three days—it rains?" "Oh," responded the man, "that was something quite different. You see, I come from a region where everything is in order, it rains when it should and is fine when that is needed, and the people also are in order and in themselves. But that was not the case with the people here, they were all out of Tao and out of themselves. I was at once infected when I arrived, so I had to be quite alone until I was once more in Tao and then naturally it rained!"[38]

The villagers, the rainmaker saw, were trying to beat the climate into submission when they should have been looking inside. They were essentially cursing themselves.

If we try to fix things by praying for outward change when the source of the problem is inside, we are engaging in negative prayer, because the prayer forms a barrier to a solution. This is one of the most common forms of negative prayer and one from which we need to be protected. Protection comes in the form of understanding, of achieving inner harmony and balance, as the Chinese rainmaker described. This is, of course, an arduous task. It is much easier to hang an amulet around our neck or mutter an affirmation to a guardian angel than to do the hard work of self-analysis. But if we did so, this would eliminate most of the curses we encounter. We might not even need the amulet.

KEEPING IT SIMPLE

The methods of protection that have been devised throughout history to guard against the negative thoughts of others are often bewilderingly complex. In their search for protection, many people get sucked into this black hole and never emerge.

We need to be protected from methods of protection! Ninety-nine percent of these methods should be avoided. Protection need not be complex. Let us remember:

The Lord preserveth the simple. . . .

—Psalm 116:6

Afterword: Should We Clean Up Prayer?

ALTHOUGH IT'S NATURAL to want to put a respectable face on prayer and ignore its potential for harm, there are moments when we realize that prayer is a sword that can cut two ways. It can bless or curse, as the 5 percent of our population realizes who have prayed for harm for others. Can we tell the truth about prayer? Can we stop sanitizing it and allow it to be what it is? Can we acknowledge that prayer, like ourselves, contains dark, shadowy elements?

Jungian analyst Edward Whitmont describes why we *need* the shadow side of life:

> If everything continued "happily ever after" we would remain in an undisturbed and permanently dulled state. Nothing of interest could happen, no development would be possible, there would be no life play. A disturber of the peace, a spoiler, a serpent or corrupting agency is necessary to "get the play going." It must function as a "Lucifer," a bringer of light, of new information and awareness. Initially the disruptive element will tend to be perceived as evil, and the disturber who personifies it will be rejected and made a scapegoat. Although this element brings forth what needs to come into existence, the personifier will be blamed because it is felt to be painful or repellent. This is why the devil (the word is derived from the Greek *diabolos,* meaning "confuser") is also the angel of light, a Lucifer, and the scapegoat is a potential redeemer.[1]

The Almighty gave Lucifer an exalted place in heaven because he contributed something important to creation—what philosopher Alan Watts once called the "principle of irreducible rascality." This is the innate potential of all humans to behave shabbily. But it is just this element that is the key to psychological and spiritual transformation.

This is a way of saying that confrontation with the dark forces of life is also a confrontation with God, the ultimate transformer. As British writer T. F. Powys put it, " 'Tis a good loving act to be a sinner, for a sinner is the true savior of mankind."[2]

Since it is the business of consciousness to experience both pleasure and pain, both good and evil, the assault on the shadow side of life is an assault on consciousness itself. Honoring consciousness requires honoring all we arc, the light as well as the shadow. But that does not mean we should adopt a hands-off policy toward our nastier qualities. Our supreme challenge is to transform evil in all its forms into its counterpart. But transformation is not the same as destruction. We cannot annihilate the negative elements of our existence, including the negative aspects of prayer, no matter how hard we try. They are the salt in the stew, necessary to bring out the full flavor of life and consciousness.

Striving for a one-sided, light-filled version of life while ignoring the shadow leads invariably to short-term gains. This dilemma has been recognized throughout history. "Some people want to recognize God only in some pleasant enlightenment," Meister Eckhart said in thirteenth-century Germany, "—and then they get pleasure and enlightenment but not God."[3] Or as Jung put it centuries later, "One does not become enlightened by imagining figures of light, but by making the darkness conscious."[4]

THE REDEMPTION OF EVIL

> Prometheus and his Christian counterparts, Lucifer the bringer
> of light in the shape of the serpent of paradise, and Adam, the
> symbolic first man, all suffer for the sake of consciousness.
> —Edward Whitmont, *The Alchemy of Healing*

As we've seen, one of the most universal myths is the fall, the secession of humanity from a state of original purity and oneness with the divine. Prometheus, who stole fire from the gods and was punished, Adam and Eve, who ate the forbidden fruit and were banished, and Lucifer, the bringer of light who was exiled from heaven, symbolize this separation. Although our Western religions have lamented the fall, this event is an essential step in the transformation and evolution of consciousness. The fall is the *differentiation* of God and humanity—the arising of contrast and difference—without which consciousness has no meaning. The word *existence* comes from the Latin *ex sistere,* meaning "to stand apart." Therefore, if we fell into sin with the fall, we also fell into difference and into consciousness: into *existence.*

But we are not condemned to dwell forever in separation from the Source. The esoteric side of almost all religions maintains that a remnant of the divine remains in everyone—a spark or filament connecting us with the Absolute. Our task is to awaken to an awareness of the original connection and allow it to brighten. This process is expressed in various ways. Jung called it creating consciousness; Jesus called it being born again; the Buddha called it awakening. The meaning of these images is the same: the reclamation of our original union with the divine.

To see the connection between a prayer and a curse is to see the intrinsic unity of light and shadow. We require both. That is why our attempts to rid prayer completely of its negative qualities are misconceived. To clean up prayer totally is to dim the light of consciousness by retreating into the darkness of a one-sided, undifferentiated experience.

We cannot take the salt out of the stew once it's dissolved; neither can we remove the shadow from prayer. Can we learn to appreciate several flavors at once?

Notes

INTRODUCTION

1. Gallup poll reported in *Life* magazine, March 1994.

2. Karl Kerényi, *The Gods of the Greeks* (London: Thames and Hudson, 1951), 150. Thanks to John Roth for calling this quote to my attention.

3. Confidential communication to Larry Dossey, May 1994. Story has been confirmed by a second source.

4. Sir Edward Cook, *The Life of Florence Nightingale* (New York: The Macmillan Company, 1913), 469–70.

5. Michael Callen, quoted in Michael Onstott, "Beyond Belief," *POZ*, April 1997, 85.

6. Plato, quoted in Brian Inglis, *Natural and Supernatural: A History of the Paranormal* (Dorset, England: Bridport, 1992), 65.

7. "Faith and Medicine Curricula Funded," *Alternative Therapies* 2, no. 6 (1996): 29. Information regarding these developments may be obtained from the National Institute for Healthcare Research (NIHR), 6110 Executive Blvd., Suite 908, Rockville, MD 20852. The NIHR administers the grants, which are funded by the John Templeton Foundation.

8. Marilyn J. Schlitz, "Intentionality and Intuition and Their Clinical Implications: A Challenge for Science and Medicine," *Advances* 12, no. 2 (Spring 1996): 58–66.

9. Schlitz, "Intentionality and Intuition," 65.

10. Dion Fortune, *Psychic Self-Defense* (London: Rider, 1930; reprint, York Beach, ME: Samuel Weiser, 1994), 18–19.

11. Michael Murphy, *The Future of the Body* (Los Angeles: Jeremy P. Tarcher, 1992), 100.

PART ONE

1. Thanks to Rupert Sheldrake of London, England, for calling this information to my attention, and to the Reverend Ted Karpf, Washington, DC, Executive Director of the National Episcopal AIDS Coalition of the Episcopal Church of the United States of America, for his research and comments on the commination ritual.

2. A. N. Wilson, *Paul: The Mind of the Apostle* (New York: W.W. Norton, 1997), 105.

3. A. N. Wilson, *Paul: The Mind of the Apostle*, 106.

4. A. N. Wilson, *Paul: The Mind of the Apostle*, 106.

5. Richard Cavendish, *A History of Magic* (New York: Penguin, 1987), 51.

6. Cavendish, *History of Magic,* 51.

7. Cavendish, *History of Magic,* 44.

8. Cavendish, *History of Magic,* 50.

9. Cavendish, *History of Magic,* 51.

10. Cavendish, *History of Magic,* 51.

11. Cavendish, *History of Magic,* 51.

12. Rupert Sheldrake, *Seven Experiments That Could Change the World* (New York: Riverhead, 1995).

13. Written communication from Rupert Sheldrake, December 1996.

14. Confidential communication to Larry Dossey, July 1996. Used with permission.

15. Confidential communication to Larry Dossey, November 1995. Used with permission.

16. Francis Huxley, *The Way of the Sacred* (Garden City, NY: Doubleday, 1974), 56.

17. Personal communication from Dennis Gersten, M.D., July 13, 1996.

18. Lyall Watson, *Dark Nature: A Natural History of Evil* (New York: HarperCollins, 1996), 186.

19. Confidential communication to Larry Dossey, May 1997. Used with permission.

20. Gallup poll, published in *Life* magazine, March 1994.

21. Rick Reilly, "Man of Steel," *Sports Illustrated,* January 13, 1997, 28–31.

22. Michael Murphy, *The Future of the Body* (Los Angeles: Jeremy P. Tarcher, 1992), 123.

23. R. H. Blyth, *Zen and Zen Classics,* comp. with drawings by Frederick Franck (New York: Random House, 1978), 40.

24. Henry Dreher, *The Immune Power Personality* (New York: Dutton, 1995), 168–210; G. F. Solomon, L. Temoshok, A. O'Leary, and J. Zich, "An Intensive Psychoimmunologic Study of Long-Surviving Persons with AIDS," *Annals of the New York Academy of Sciences* 496 (1987): 647–55.

25. Dreher, *Immune Power Personality,* 171–72.

26. Confidential communication to Larry Dossey, June 1995. Used with permission.

27. Confidential communication to Larry Dossey, June 1995. Used with permission.

28. Mary Eddy Baker, "Obtrusive Mental Healing," *Miscellaneous Writings.* Published by the trustees under the will of Mary Baker G. Eddy (Boston, MA, 1986), 282.

29. Eddy, "Obtrusive Mental Healing," 282.

30. Loudell F. Snow, "Folk Medical Beliefs and Their Implications for Care of Patients," *Annals of Internal Medicine* 81 (1974): 82–96.

31. Written communication from Alice Thompson, July 15, 1996. Used with permission.

32. Alex Ayres, ed., *The Wit and Wisdom of Abraham Lincoln* (New York: Meridian, 1992), 86.

33. Joseph Pereira, "The Healing Power of Prayer Is Tested by Science," *Wall Street Journal,* Dec. 20, 1995, B1.

34. Annie L. Gaylor, quoted by Steve Brewer, "UNM [University of New Mexico] Study on Prayer Raises Ire," *Albuquerque Journal*, May 3, 1995.

35. Larry Dossey, "Healing and the Mind: Is There a Dark Side?" *Journal of Scientific Exploration* 8, no. 1 (1994): 73–90.

36. The role of belief and meaning in health is the subject of my book *Meaning & Medicine*.

37. J. W. L. Fielding, "An Interim Report of a Prospective, Randomized, Controlled Study of Adjuvant Chemotherapy in Operable Gastric Cancer: British Stomach Cancer Group," *World Journal of Surgery* 7 (1983): 390–99.

38. S. Wolf and R. H. Pinsky, "Effects of Placebo Administration and Occurrence of Toxic Reactions," *Journal of the American Medical Association* 155, no. 4 (1954): 339–41.

39. R. W. Rhein, Jr., "Placebo: Deception or Potent Therapy?" *Medical World News* (February 4, 1980), 39–47.

40. Wolf and Pinsky, "Effects of Placebo Administration," 339–41.

41. Beryl Statham, "Miracles: Divine Intervention, Natural Events, or Illusory Experiences?" *Journal of Religion and Psychical Research* 19, no. 4 (October 1996): 205–19.

42. David G. Myers and Ed Diener, "The Pursuit of Happiness," *Scientific American* 274, no. 5 (1996): 71.

43. David B. Larson and Mary A. Greenwold Milano, "Are Religion and Spirituality Clinically Relevant in Health Care?" *Mind/Body Medicine* 1, no. 3 (1995): 147–57.

44. Myers and Diener, "Pursuit of Happiness," 72.

45. Source unknown. Quoted in Sy Syfransky, ed., *Sunbeams: A Book of Quotations* (Berkeley: North Atlantic, 1990), 43.

46. M. Csikszentmihalyi, *The Evolving Self* (New York: Harper-Collins, 1993), 35–37.

47. Csikszentmihalyi, *Evolving Self*, 7.

48. Dietrich Dörner, *The Logic of Failure* (New York: Metropolitan/Henry Holt, 1996), 8.

49. Charles Perrow, *Normal Accidents: Living with High-Risk Technologies* (New York: Basic Books, 1984).

50. Edward Tenner, *Why Things Bite Back: Technology and the Revenge of Unintended Consequences* (New York: Knopf, 1996), 15–16.

51. Reuters News Service, December 15, 1995.

52. Dörner, *Logic of Failure*, 2–3.

53. Dörner, *Logic of Failure*, 4.

54. T. Kleyn and J. Jozefowicz, "Wasteland Created by Human Hands," reviewed in *Hamburg Evening News*, December 28–29, 1985, cited in Dörner, *Logic of Failure*, 5.

55. Bruce Bower, "Depressing News for Low-Cholesterol Men," *Science News* 143 (January 16, 1993): 37; Richard Monastersky, "Kidney Stones: Don't Curb the Calcium," *Science News* 143 (March 17, 1993): 196.

56. John Robbins, *Reclaiming Our Health* (New York: H. J. Kramer, 1996), 348–50. Robbins cites as sources the following: W. McNeill, Appendix, "Epidemics in China," in *Plagues and People* (New York: Doubleday, 1976); Laurie Garrett, *The Coming Plague* (New York: Penguin, 1994); and Nick Chiles, "In Rat's Realm," *New York Newsday,* May 9, 1994.

57. The Dalai Lama, quoted in Keith Thompson, "The Imaginal Realm," *Noetic Sciences Review,* no. 39 (Autumn 1996): 32–33.

58. Morris L. West, *The Shoes of the Fisherman* (Thorndike, ME: Thorndike Press, a division of MacMillan Press, 1991).

59. Rumi, quoted in "Sunbeams," *The Sun,* issue 245 (May 1996): 40. George Bernard Shaw, cited by Nicholas Mosley, "Human Beings Desire Happiness," in *The Encyclopedia of Delusions*, ed. Ronald Duncan and Miranda Weston-Smith (New York: Simon & Schuster, 1979), 212. Dostoyevsky, quoted in "Sunbeams," *The Sun,* issue 242 (February 1996): 40. John Keats, quoted in "Sunbeams," *The Sun,* issue 249 (September 1996): 40. William Blake, quoted by M. Woodman, "Chaos or Creativity?" (Lecture delivered in 1990, recorded by Oral Tradition Archives, San Francisco, 1990). Friedrich Nietzsche, *Thus Spake Zarathustra,* quoted in Holger Kalweit, *Shamans, Healers, and Medicine Men* (Boston: Shambhala, 1992), 175. The Dalai Lama, quoted in "Sunbeams," *The Sun,* issue 249 (September 1996): 40.

60. R. H. Blyth, *Zen and Zen Classics* (New York: Random House, 1978), 68–69.

61. Blyth, *Zen and Zen Classics,* 69.

62. One account says that Rocky Mountain crickets, not grasshoppers, were involved. See "Mormons," *The World Book Encyclopedia,* vol. 17 (Chicago: Field Enterprises, 1954), 8401.

63. *World Book Encyclopedia,* 14:6949.

64. *Victoria (British Columbia) Times-Colonist,* November 24, 1996.

PART TWO

1. Confidential communication to Larry Dossey, July 1996.

2. David B. Larson and Mary A. Greenwold Milano, "Are Religion and Spirituality Relevant in Health Care?" *Mind/Body Medicine* 1, no. 3 (1995): 145–57.

3. F. D. Whitwell and M. G. Barker, "Possession in Psychiatric Patients in Britain," *British Journal of Medical Psychology* 53 (1980): 287–95.

4. *Fortean Times* 90 (September 1996): 9.

5. A. S. Hale and N. R. Pinninti, "Exorcism-resistant Ghost Possession Treated with Clopenthixol," *British Journal of Psychology* 165 (1994): 386–88. See also Ian Stevenson, "Possession and Exorcism: An Essay Review," *Journal of Parapsychology* 59 (March 1995): 69–76.

6. Richard Cavendish, *The Black Arts* (New York: Perigee Books, 1967), 19.

7. J. K. Boitnott, "Clinicopathological Conference: Case Presentation," *Bulletin of Johns Hopkins Hospital,* no. 120 (1967): 186–87. This case is reported in a classic paper by anthropologist Joan Halifax-Grof, "Hex Death," in *Parapsychology and Anthropology: Proceedings of an International Conference Held in London, August 29–31, 1973,* ed. Allan Angoff and Diana Barth (New York: Parapsychology Foundation, 1974), 59–79.

8. The following quotations are from J. A. Carrese and Lorna A. Rhodes, "Western Bioethics on the Navajo Reservation," *Journal of the American Medical Association* 274, no. 10 (1995): 826–29. The following discussion relies heavily on this source.

9. G. Witherspoon, *Language and Art in the Navajo Universe* (Ann Arbor: Univ. of Michigan Press, 1977), 34.

10. Loudell F. Snow, "Folk Medical Beliefs and Their Implications for Care of Patients," *Annals of Internal Medicine* 81 (1974): 84.

11. Snow, "Folk Medical Beliefs," 85.

12. Snow, "Folk Medical Beliefs," 85.

13. Elizabeth M. Meek in the *Arkansas Historical Quarterly,* cited in Dee Brown, *Wondrous Times on the Frontier* (New York: HarperCollins, 1992), 187.

14. Clifton K. Meador, "Hex Death: Voodoo Magic or Persuasion?" *Southern Medical Journal* 85, no. 3 (1992): 244–47.

15. Walter B. Cannon, "'Voodoo' Death," *Psychosomatic Medicine* 19 (1957): 182–90, reprinted from *American Anthropologist* 44 (1942): 169–81.

16. For the complete story, see Larry Dossey, "Hexes and Molecules," *Space, Time & Medicine* (Boston: Shambhala, 1982), 3–6.

17. Richard Cavendish, *A History of Magic* (New York: Penguin, 1987), 138.

18. Snow, "Folk Medical Beliefs," 82–96.

19. Andrew Weil, *Spontaneous Healing* (New York: Alfred A. Knopf, 1995), 61.

20. Adapted from Jon Kabat-Zinn, *Full Catastrophe Living: A Practical Guide to Mindfulness, Meditation, and Healing* (New York: Delacorte, 1990). See Larry Dossey, "The Patient Patient: The Hazards of the Medical Experience," *Meaning & Medicine* (New York: Bantam, 1991), 74–79.

21. Quoted in Weil, *Spontaneous Healing,* 63–64.

22. Bernard Lown, *The Lost Art of Healing* (New York: Houghton Mifflin, 1996), 65.

23. Bruno Klopfer, "Psychological Variables in Human Cancer," *Journal of Projective Techniques* 21 (1957): 331–40.

24. Howard Hall, "Suggestion and Illness," *International Journal of Psychosomatics* 33, no. 2 (1986): 24–27.

25. Anthony E. Lalli, "Contrast Media Reactions: Data Analysis and Hypothesis," *Radiology* 134 (1980): 1–12. Thanks to Howard J. Barnhard, M.D., Department of Radiology, University of Arkansas Medical School at Little Rock, for calling my attention to Lalli's work. Retold from Dossey, *Meaning & Medicine,* 78–79.

26. Retold from Larry Dossey, "Your Doctor's Beliefs and Why They Matter," *Healing Words* (San Francisco: HarperSanFrancisco, 1993), 140–41.

27. Rachel Naomi Remen, "All Emotions Are Potentially Life Affirming," *Advances* 12, no. 2 (1996): 23–28.

28. Rebecca Voelker, "Nocebos Contribute to Host of Ills," *Journal of the American Medical Association* 275, no. 5 (1996): 345.

29. Adapted from William Mainord, Barry Rath, and Frank Barnett, "Anesthesia and Suggestion" (paper presented at the annual meeting of the American Psychological Association, August 1983), reported in Daniel Goleman, *Vital Lies, Simple Truths: The Psychology of Self-Deception* (New York: Simon & Schuster, 1985), 89–90.

30. Linda Rodgers, "Music for Surgery," *Advances: The Journal of Mind-Body Health* 2, no. 3 (Summer 1995): 49–57.

31. Rodgers, "Music for Surgery," 49–50.

32. Rodgers, "Music for Surgery," 50.

33. Rodgers, "Music for Surgery," 50.

34. An excellent musical resource is Healing Healthcare Systems, Inc., P.O.B. 8010, Reno, NV, 89593, operated by professional musicians Susan Mazer and Dallas Smith. Their music videos and cassette tapes are used in many hospitals throughout the U.S. For additional sources, see Linda Rodgers, "Reduce Surgical Anxiety Simply by Listening: How Perioperative Audiotapes Inform, Reassure and Offer Suggestions to Patients Throughout the Stages of Surgery," in *New Directions in Healing: A Practitioner's Source for Mind/Body Medicine* (Mansfield Center, CT.: National Institute for the Clinical Application of Behavioral Medicine, 1993). For information on music in surgery, an excellent entry into this field is Cathie E. Guzzetta, "Music Therapy: Hearing the Melody of the Soul," in *Holistic Nursing: A Handbook for Practice,* 2d ed., ed. Barbara M. Dossey, Lynn Keegan, Cathie E. Guzzetta, and Leslie G. Kolkmeier (Rockville, MD: Aspen, 1995), 669–98.

35. Bruce Bower, "Anxiety Before Surgery May Prove Healthful," *Science News* 141 (June 20, 1992): 407.

36. Weil, *Spontaneous Healing,* 64.

37. Sandra Ingerman, *Welcome Home: Life After Healing* (San Francisco: HarperSanFrancisco, 1993). Ingerman has pioneered a form of psychotherapy called shamanic journeying, which is elaborated in her remarkable book *Soul*

Retrieval (San Francisco: HarperSan-Francisco, 1991).

38. Says Andrew Weil, "I note some confusion between emotions as predisposing causes of diseases and emotions in the process of healing established disease," "Response to Dafter," *Advances* 12, no. 2 (1996): 41–42; see also Weil, *Spontaneous Healing.*

39. The following discussion is adapted with permission from Larry Dossey, "Running Scared: How We Hide from Who We Are," *Alternative Therapies* 3, no. 2 (1997): 8–15.

40. Jule Eisenbud, *Parapsychology and the Unconscious* (Berkeley: North Atlantic Books, 1992), 101–2.

41. Eisenbud, *Parapsychology and the Unconscious,* 139.

42. Eisenbud, *Parapsychology and the Unconscious,* 102.

43. Jan Ehrenwald, "A Neurophysiological Model of Psi Phenomena," *Journal of Nervous and Mental Diseases* 154, no. 6 (1972): 406–18.

44. Ehrenwald, "Neurophysiological Model," 141.

45. Berthold E. Schwarz, "Possible Telesomatic Reactions," *Journal of the Medical Society of New Jersey* 64, no. 11 (1967): 600–603.

46. J. H. Rush, "New Directions in Parapsychology Research," *Parapsychological Monographs,* no. 4 (New York: Parapsychology Foundation, 1964), 18–19.

47. Ian Stevenson, *Telepathic Impressions. A Review and Report of 35 New Cases* (Charlottesville: Univ. Press of Virginia, 1970), 144.

48. Brian Inglis, *Natural and Supernatural: A History of the Paranormal* (Bridport, Dorset, England: Prism/Unity, 1992), 113.

49. Inglis, *Natural and Supernatural,* 113–14.

50. Inglis, *Natural and Supernatural,* 113–14.

51. Iris M. Owen with Margaret Sparrow, *Conjuring Up Philip* (New York: Harper & Row, 1976).

52. Richard S. Broughton, *Parapsychology: The Controversial Science* (New York: Ballantine, 1991), 152.

53. Broughton, *Parapsychology,* 151–55. See also Rosemary Ellen Guiley, "Philip," *Harper's Encyclopedia of Mystical & Paranormal Experience* (San Francisco: HarperSan Francisco, 1991), 443–44.

54. The following account of the work of Batcheldor, Brookes-Smith, and Hunt relies on Broughton, *Parapsychology,* 153–55.

55. Broughton, *Parapsychology,* 153.

56. The original report is K. J. Batcheldor, "Report on a Case of Table Levitation and Associated Phenomena," *Journal of the Society for Psychical Research* 43 (1966): 339–56.

57. The description is from Broughton. The original reports are: C. Brookes-Smith and D. W. Hunt, "Some Experiments in Psychokinesis," *Journal of the Society for Psychical Research* 45 (1970): 265–81; and C. Brookes-Smith, "Data-type Recorded Experimental PK Phenomena," *Journal of the Society for Psychical Research* 47 (1973): 69–89.

58. Broughton, *Parapsychology,* 155.

59. Broughton, *Parapsychology*, 155.

60. Serge Kahili King, *Kahuna Healing* (Wheaton, IL: Theosophical Publishing House, 1983), 34–35.

61. The following story is taken from Max Freedom Long, *The Secret Science Behind Miracles* (Marina del Rey, CA: DeVorss, 1948), 89–96.

62. Michael Harner, *The Way of the Shaman* (New York: Bantam, 1982).

63. For the complete story, see Larry Dossey, *Healing Words*, 150–51.

64. King, *Kahuna Healing*, 34–35. Researchers Pukui, Haertig, and Lee, in their extensive analysis of kahuna practices, agree. They describe many types of kahunas, one of which infuses harmful power into objects, and another of which sends spirits on destructive missions. See Mary Kawena Pukui, E. W. Haertig, and Catherine A. Lee, *Look to the Source*, vol. 2 (Honolulu: Hui Hanai/Queen Lili'uokalani Children's Center, 1972), 161.

65. Snow, "Folk Medical Beliefs," 82–96.

66. Snow, "Folk Medical Beliefs," 84.

67. Long, *Secret Science*, 87–89.

68. Marc Simmons, *Witchcraft in the Southwest* (Lincoln: Univ. of Nebraska Press, 1974), 157.

69. The following account is taken from Simmons, *Witchcraft in the Southwest*, 154–57. Simmons cites Ruth Laughlin Barker, "New Mexico Witch Tales," in *Tone the Bell Easy*, ed. J. Frank Dobie (Austin: Univ. of Texas Press, 1932), 66.

70. Jenny Randles and Peter Hough, *Spontaneous Human Combustion* (New York: Dorset Press, 1992), 20–25.

71. Alex Ayres, ed., *The Wit and Wisdom of Abraham Lincoln* (New York: Meridian, 1992), 62–64.

72. Stephen E. Braude, *The Limits of Influence: Psychokinesis and the Philosophy of Science* (London and New York: Routledge & Kegan Paul, 1986); and Stephen E. Braude, *ESP and Psychokinesis: A Philosophical Examination* (Philadelphia: Temple Univ. Press, 1979).

73. Stephen E. Braude, "Psi and Our Picture of the World," *Inquiry* 30 (1987): 277–94.

74. Confidential communication, December 1995; the disease has been changed to preserve anonymity.

75. Confidential communication, June 1996. Used with permission.

76. Personal communication from Georg Feuerstein, Ph.D., Yoga Research Center, Lower Lake, CA, April 1997.

77. Francis Huxley, *The Way of the Sacred* (Garden City, NY: Doubleday, 1974), 54.

78. Rupert Sheldrake, *Seven Experiments That Could Change the World* (New York: Riverhead Books, 1995), 112–13.

79. The above information comes chiefly from Rosemary Ellen Guiley, *Harper's Encyclopedia of Mystical & Paranormal Experience* (San Francisco: HarperSanFrancisco, 1991), 187–88 and Alan Dundes, ed., *The Evil Eye* (Madison, WI: The Univ. of

Wisconsin Press, 1981), 150–67.

80. Angelos Tanagras, *Psychological Elements in Parapsychological Traditions* (New York: Parapsychology Foundation, 1967), 64.

81. Lyall Watson, *Beyond Supernature* (New York: Bantam, 1988), 58–60.

82. Watson, *Beyond Supernature,* 59.

83. Watson, *Beyond Supernature,* 60.

84. Huxley, *Way of the Sacred,* 55.

85. Huxley, *Way of the Sacred,* 55.

86. Dee Brown, *Wondrous Times on the Frontier* (New York: Harper-Collins, 1991), 110. Original source: *Chloride* (New Mexico) *Black Range,* Dec. 2, 1887, reprinted in Peter Hertzog, *Frontier Humor* (Santa Fe, NM: The Press of the Territorian, 1966)), 31–32.

87. Norman Cousins, "It All Began with Mesmer" (address to the 10th International Congress of Hypnosis and Psychosomatic Medicine, Toronto, August 1985), cited in Howard Hall, "Suggestion and Illness," *International Journal of Psychosomatics* 33, no. 2 (1986): 24–27.

88. Rebecca Voelker, "Nocebos Contribute to Host of Ills," *Journal of the American Medical Association* 75, no. 5 (February 7, 1996): 345–47.

89. Voelker, "Nocebos Contribute to Host of Ills," 345–47.

90. Voelker, "Nocebos Contribute to Host of Ills," 345.

91. Voelker, "Nocebos Contribute to Host of Ills," 345.

92. Randall C. Mason, Jr., Graham Clark, Robert B. Reeves, Jr., and S. Bruce Wagner, "Acceptance and Healing," *Journal of Religion & Health* 8, no. 2 (April 1969): 123–43.

93. Mason et al., "Acceptance and Healing," 123ff.

94. Edgar Mitchell, *The Way of the Explorer* (New York: G. P. Putnam's Sons, 1996), 85–87.

PART THREE

1. Gallup poll, reported in *Life* magazine, March 1994.

2. Robert Wright, cited in Lyall Watson, *Dark Nature: A Natural History of Evil* (New York: Harper-Collins, 1995), 277.

3. Watson, *Dark Nature,* 277.

4. Watson, *Dark Nature,* 282–83.

5. Brian Goodwin, *How the Leopard Changed Its Spots* (New York: Charles Scribner's Sons, 1994), 30–31.

6. Goodwin, *Leopard,* 31, 182.

7. John Horgan, "Doubts about Doubts about Science," *The Sciences* 36, no. 3 (May/June 1996): 43–48.

8. Richard C. Duke, David M. Ojcius, and John Ding-E Young, "Cell Suicide in Health and Disease," *Scientific American* (December 1996), 80–87.

9. Duke et al., "Cell Suicide," 82.

10. Martin C. Raff, "Death Wish," *The Sciences* 36, no. 4 (July/August 1996): 36–40.

11. Leonard Laskow, *Healing with Love* (San Francisco: HarperSan-Francisco, 1992).

12. Glen Rein, "The Scientific Basis for Healing with Subtle Energies," Appendix A in Leonard

Laskow, *Healing with Love,*
279–319.

13. Larry Dossey, "'Let It Be' or
'Make It Happen' : The Spindrift
Studies," *Healing Words* (San Francisco: HarperSanFrancisco, 1993),
97–100.

14. Angelos Tanagras, *Psychological
Elements in Parapsychological Tradi-
tions* (New York: Parapsychology
Foundation, 1967), 65–66
(abridged). Thanks to Emilie
Stowell.

15. Tanagras, *Psychological Elements,* 66.

16. Tanagras, *Psychological Elements,* 65.

17. Personal communication from
Stanley Krippner, Ph.D., Director of
Research, Saybook Institute, San
Francisco, CA, June 1994.

18. Howard Bloom, *The Lucifer
Principle* (New York: Atlantic
Monthly Press, 1995).

19. Spindrift Research and Development, Inc., P.O. Box 550011, Fort
Lauderdale, FL 33355–0011.

20. Richard S. Broughton,
"Glimpsing the Future," *Parapsychology: The Controversial Science*
(New York: Ballantine, 1991),
341–66.

21. Larry Niven, *Ringworld* (New
York: Del Rey, 1970).

22. Broughton, *Parapsychology,* 348.

23. Broughton, *Parapsychology,* 350.

24. Broughton, *Parapsychology,* 350.

25. Dean I. Radin and Roger D.
Nelson, "Consciousness-related
Effects in Random Physical Sys-
tems," *Foundations of Physics* 19

(1989): 1499–1514; Dean I. Radin,
"On Complexity and Pragmatism,"
Journal of Scientific Exploration 8, no.
4 (1994): 523–33.

26. Broughton, *Parapsychology,* 351.

27. George C. Williams, cited in
Watson, *Dark Nature,* 252–53.

PART FOUR

1. Joan Halifax-Grof, "Hex
Death," in *Parapsychology and
Anthropology,* ed. Allan Angoff and
Diana Barth, proceedings of an
international conference held in
London, England, August 29–31,
1973 (New York: Parapsychology
Foundation, 1974), 59–79.

2. William G. Braud, "On the
Use of Living Target Systems in
Distant Mental Influence Research,"
Research in Parapsychology 1984, ed.
Rhea A. White and Jerry Solfvin
(Metuchen, NJ: Scarecrow Press,
1985), 149–88.

3. Andrew N. Rowan, "The
Benefits and Ethics of Animal
Research," *Scientific American* (Feb-
ruary 1997), 79. In the same issue,
see Madhusree Mukerjee, "Trends in
Animal Research," 86–93; Neal D.
Barnard and Stephen R. Kaufman,
"Animal Research Is Wasteful and
Misleading," 80–82; Jack H. Botting
and Adrian R. Morrison, "Animal
Research Is Vital to Medicine,"
83–85.

4. For a similar view, see Henryk
Skolimowski, "The Participatory
Universe and Its New Methodology,"
Frontier Perspectives 5, no. 2 (1996).

5. Jean Barry, "General and Com-

parative Study of the Psychokinetic Effect on a Fungus Culture," *Journal of Parapsychology* 32, no. 4 (1968): 237–43.

6. Daniel J. Benor, *Healing Research*, vol. 1 (Munich: Helix Verlag, 1993), 145.

7. William H. Tedder and Melissa L. Monty, "Exploration of Long-distance PK: A Conceptual Replication of the Influence on a Biological System," In *Research in Parapsychology 1980*, ed. W. G. Roll et al. (Metuchen, NJ: Scarecrow Press, 1981), 90–93. See also Benor, *Healing Research*, 1:145–46.

8. Carroll B. Nash, "Psychokinetic Control of Bacterial Growth," *Journal of the Society for Psychical Research* 51 (1982): 217–21.

9. Benor, *Healing Research*, 1:153.

10. Carroll B. Nash, "Test of Psychokinetic Control of Bacterial Mutation," *Journal of the American Society for Psychical Research* 78, no. 2 (1984): 145–52.

11. Benor, *Healing Research*, 1:156–58.

12. Keith Stewart Thomson, "The Revival of Experiments on Prayer," *American Scientist* 84 (1996): 532–34.

13. E. Haraldsson and T. Thorsteinsson, "Psychokinetic Effects on Yeast: An Exploratory Experiment," in *Research in Parapsychology 1972*, ed. W. C. Roll et al. (Metuchen, NJ: Scarecrow Press, 1973), 20–21.

14. For a glimpse into the life of this remarkable woman and her talented husband, see Ambrose A. and Olga N. Worrall, *Explore Your Psychic World* (New York: Harper & Row, 1970; reprint Columbus, OH: Ariel Press, 1989).

15. Beverly Rubik and Elizabeth Rauscher, "Effects on Motility Behavior and Growth Rate of *Salmonella typhimurium* in the Presence of Olga Worrall," in *Research in Parapsychology 1979*, ed. W. G. Roll (Metuchen, NJ: Scarecrow Press, 1980), 140–42. See also E. Rauscher, "Human Volitional Effects on a Model Bacterial System," *Subtle Energies* 1, no. 1 (1990): 21–41.

16. Benor, *Healing Research*, 1:135–36.

17. Glen Rein, *Quantum Biology: Healing with Subtle Energy* (Palo Alto: Quantum Biology Research Labs, 1992). Quantum Biology Research Labs is located at P.O. Box 60653, Palo Alto, CA 94306. See Benor, *Healing Research*, 1:138–42. See also Glen Rein, "The Scientific Basis for Healing with Subtle Energies," Appendix A in *Healing with Love*, Leonard Laskow (San Francisco: HarperSanFrancisco, 1992), 279–319.

18. Kenneth S. Cohen, *The Way of Qigong* (New York: Ballantine, 1997), 3.

19. Kenneth M. Sancier, "Medical Applications of Qigong and Emitted Qi on Humans, Animals, Cell Cultures, and Plants: Review of Selected Scientific Research," *American Journal of Acupuncture* 19, no. 4 (1991): 367–77.

20. Wang Yao-Lan and Lu Zu-Yin,

"A Method of Detecting Qi Field," in *Yeng Xing's Scientific Qigong* (Hong Kong: China Books Press, 1988); Liu Yanang, Zhao Xinhus, Cao Kie, Hu Yulan, and Zhao Yungsheng, "The Effects of Taoist Qigong on the Photon Emission from the Body Surface and Cells," *Proceedings of the First World Conference for Academic Exchange of Medical Qigong* (Beijing, China, October 1988).

21. Du Luoyi, "The Effect of Mind-Control in Qigong Exercise Investigated by an Infrared Thermo-vision Imager," *Proceedings of the First World Conference for Academic Exchange of Medical Qigong* (Beijing, China, October 1988).

22. W. Benji, W. Xiubi, W. Zijon, and L. Jianben, "The Study of Magnetic Signals Under the Qigong State by Superconducting Biomagnetometer," *Proceedings of the Second World Conference for Academic Exchange of Medical Qigong* (Beijing, China, September 1993).

23. Gui Yongian, Chen Qi, Li Yinfa, and Jiang Shen, "Physical Characteristics of the Emitted Qi," *Proceedings of the First World Conference for Academic Exchange of Medical Qigong* (Beijing, China, October 1988).

24. Peng Xueyan and Liu Guolong, "The Effect of the Emitted Qi and Infrasonic Sound on Somatosensory Evoked Potential and Slow Vertex Response," *Proceedings of the First World Conference for Academic Exchange of Medical Qigong* (Beijing, China, October 1988).

25. David Eisenberg, with Thomas Lee Wright, *Encounters with Qi* (New York: W. W. Norton, 1995), 213.

26. For information about the Qigong Database™, contact the Qigong Institute, 561 Berkeley Avenue, Menlo Park, CA 94025, e-mail matsu@nanospace.com.

27. Lawrence LeShan, *The Medium, the Mystic, and the Physicist* (New York: Viking, 1974), 106.

28. David J. Muehsam, M. S. Markov, Patrician A. Muehsam, Arthur A. Pilla, Ronger Shen, and Yi Wu, "Effect of Qigong on Cell-free Myosin Phosphorylation: Preliminary Experiments," *Subtle Energies* 5, no. 1 (1994): 93–108.

29. Bernard R. Grad, "Some Biological Effects of Laying-On of Hands: A Review of Experiments with Animals and Plants," *Journal of the American Society for Psychical Research* 59 (1965)(vol. a): 95–127.

30. Benor, *Healing Research.* 1:172–74.

31. Larry Dossey, "Healing, Energy, and Consciousness: Into the Future or a Retreat to the Past?" *Subtle Energies* 5, no. 1 (1994): 1–34; Larry Dossey, "But Is It Energy? Reflections on Consciousness, Healing, and the New Paradigm," *Subtle Energies* 3, no. 3 (1992): 69–82.

32. Jacobo Grinberg-Zylberbaum and Julieta Ramos, "Patterns of Interhemispheric Correlation during Human Communication," *International Journal of Neurosciences* 36, nos. 1/2 (1987): 41–55. For a review of

the relevance of these studies to medicine, see Larry Dossey, "Healing at a Distance," *Meaning & Medicine* (New York: Bantam, 1991), 178–93.

33. A. Einstein, B. Podolsky, and N. Rosen, "Can Quantum-mechanical Description of Physical Reality Be Considered Complete?" *Physics Review* 47 (1935): 777.

34. A. Aspect, J. Dalibard, and G. Roger, "Experimental Test of Bell's Inequalities Using Time-Varying Analyzers," *Physics Review Letters* 49 (1982): 1804.

35. J. Grinberg-Zylberbaum, M. Delaflor, L. Attie, and A. Goswami, "The Einstein Podolsky-Rosen Paradox in the Brain: The Transferred Potential," *Physics Essays* 7, no. 4 (1994): 422–28.

36. M. Yamamoto, M. Hirasawa, K. Kawano, H. Kokubo, T. Kokado, T. Hirata, N. Yasuda, A. Furukawa, and N. Fukuda, "An Experiment on Remote Action against Man in Sensory-Shielding Condition, Part 2," *Journal of the International Society of Life Information Sciences* 14, no. 2 (1996): 228–39.

37. M. Yamamoto, M. Hirasawa, K. Kawano, N. Yasuda, and A. Furukawa, "An Experiment on Remote Action against Man in Sense Shielding Condition," *Journal of the International Society of Life Information Sciences* 14, no. 1 (1996): 97–99.

38. Jannine M. Rebman, Rens Wezelman, Dean I. Radin, Paul Stevens, Russell A. Hapke, and Kelly Z. Gaughan, "Remote Influence of Human Physiology by a Ritual Healing Technique," *Subtle Energies* 6, no. 2 (1997).

39. Rebman, "Remote Influence of Human Physiology," 131.

40. Gallup poll, reported in *Life* magazine, March 1994.

41. Katie Singer, "Scott Walker's Research on the Complexity of Prayer," *Medicine and Prayer*, Newsletter of the Santa Fe Institute for Medicine and Prayer (September/October 1996), 1.

42. Charles Honorton, "Rhetoric Over Substance: The Impoverished State of Skepticism," *Journal of Parapsychology* 57, no. 2 (1993): 191–214.

43. Dean I. Radin, "A Field Guide to Skepticism," *The Conscious Universe* (San Francisco: HarperEdge, 1997), 205–27.

44. Gerald Feinberg, "Precognition—A Memory of Things Future," in *Quantum Physics and Parapsychology*, ed. L. Oteri (New York: Parapsychology Foundation, 1975), 54–73.

45. Larry Dossey, *Recovering the Soul* (New York: Bantam, 1989).

46. Amit Goswami, *The Self-Aware Universe: How Consciousness Creates the Material World* (New York: Tarcher/Putnam, 1993).

47. Amit Goswami, "Science Within Consciousness: A Progress Report." Talked delivered at a seminar on consciousness, University of Lisbon, Lisbon, Portugal, 1996.

48. David J. Chalmers, "The Puzzle of Conscious Experience,"

Scientific American 273, no. 6 (1995): 80–86; Chalmers, *The Conscious Mind* (New York: Oxford Univ. Press, 1996).

49. Nick Herbert, *Quantum Reality* (New York: Dutton, 1986); Herbert, *Elemental Mind* (New York: Dutton, 1993).

50. Brian D. Josephson and F. Pallikara-Viras, "Biological Utilization of Quantum Nonlocality," *Foundations of Physics* 21 (1991): 197–207.

51. Rupert Sheldrake, *A New Science of Life* (Los Angeles: Jeremy P. Tarcher, 1981); Sheldrake, *The Presence of the Past* (New York: Times Books, 1988).

52. Ervin Laszlo, *The Interconnected Universe: Conceptual Foundations of Transdisciplinary Unified Theory* (River Edge, NJ: World Scientific Publishing, 1995).

53. David Bohm, quoted in Renée Weber, *Dialogue with Scientists and Sages: The Search for Unity* (London: Arkana, 1990), 101, 151.

54. Robert G. Jahn and Brenda J. Dunne, *Margins of Reality: The Role of Consciousness in the Physical World* (New York: Harcourt Brace Jovanovich, 1987).

55. C. J. S. Clarke, "The Nonlocality of Mind," *Journal of Consciousness Studies* 2, no. 3 (1995): 231–40.

56. Ken Wilber, ed., *Quantum Questions: The Mystical Writings of the World's Great Physicists* (Boston: Shambhala, 1984).

57. Erwin Schrödinger, *What Is Life? and Mind and Matter* (London: Cambridge Univ. Press, 1969), 145.

58. Arthur Eddington, "Defense of Mysticism," in *Quantum Questions: The Mystical Writings of the World's Great Physicists,* ed. Ken Wilber (Boston: Shambhala, 1984), 206.

59. James Jeans, *Physics and Philosophy* (New York: Dover, 1981), 204.

PART FIVE

1. Interview with Dean Radin, *Magical Blend* no. 53 (1996): 36. See Dean Radin, *The Conscious Universe* (San Francisco: HarperEdge, 1997).

2. John Palmer, "From Survival to Transcendence: Reflections of Psi as Anomalous," *Journal of Parapsychology* 56 (1992): 249.

3. Dion Fortune, *Psychic Self-Defense* (London: Rider, 1930; reprint, York Beach, ME: Samuel Weiser, 1994), 97.

4. Joseph Forgione, "Life Is a Rosebud," *Guideposts,* September 1996, 43–46.

5. T. E. Oxman, D. H. Freeman, and E. D. Manheimer, "Lack of Social Participation or Religious Strength or Comfort as Risk Factors for Death after Cardiac Surgery in the Elderly," *Psychosomatic Medicine* 57 (1995): 5–15.

6. From George Appleton, ed., *The Oxford Book of Prayer* (New York: Oxford Univ. Press, 1987), 75.

7. Loudell F. Snow, "Folk Medical Beliefs and Their Implications for Care of Patients," *Annals of Internal Medicine* 81 (1974): 82–96.

8. William G. Black, *Folk-Medicine: A Chapter in the History of*

Culture (London: Elliot Stock, 1883), 76–85, 136–38, 162.

9. Larry Dossey, "Further Readings: Prayer and Meditation," *Prayer Is Good Medicine* (San Francisco: HarperSanFrancisco, 1996).

10. William Braud and Marilyn Schlitz, "A Method for the Objective Study of Transpersonal Imagery," *Journal of Scientific Exploration* 3, no. 1 (1989): 43–63.

11. Loudell F. Snow, "Folk Medical Beliefs and Their Implications for Care of Patients," *Annals of Internal Medicine* 81 (1974): 82–96.

12. Snow, "Folk Medical Beliefs," 82–96.

13. *Orange County Register,* November 30, 1995. Thanks to Michael Villaire.

14. Max Freedom Long, *The Secret Science Behind Miracles* (Marina del Rey, CA: DeVorss, 1948), 279.

15. *William James on Psychical Research,* comp. and ed. Gardner Murphy and Robert O. Ballou (London: Chatto and Windus, 1961), 207.

16. Walter Wink, *Unmasking the Powers* (Philadelphia: Fortress, 1986), 1.

17. David Goodacre, "Possession and Exorcism," *The Christian Parapsychologist* 11, no. 4 (1995): 126–31. The following quotations by Goodacre refer to this article.

18. C. F. Evans, *St. Luke* (London: SCM Press, 1990), 378–79. See also Elaine Pagels (New York: Vintage, 1995).

19. Goodacre, "Possession and Exorcism," 130.

20. Harry Guntrip, *The Psychotherapist and Exorcist* (Leeds: Leeds Department of Psychiatry, 1952), 72, cited in Goodacre, "Possession and Exorcism," 130.

21. M. Scott Peck, *People of the Lie* (New York: Touchstone, 1983), 206.

22. Francis MacNutt, *Deliverance from Evil Spirits: A Practical Manual* (Grand Rapids, MI: Chosen Books, 1995).

23. Dion Fortune, *Psychic Self-Defense* (London: Rider, 1930), 177.

24. Huston Smith, *The World's Religions* (San Francisco: HarperSanFrancisco, 1991), 115–16.

25. Smith, *The World's Religions,* 64.

26. Smith, *The World's Religions,* 64.

27. Arthur Koestler, *Janus: A Summing Up* (New York: Random House, 1978), 44–45.

28. R. H. Blyth, *Zen and Zen Classics* (New York: Vintage/Random House, 1978), 55–56.

29. Alexander Solzhenitsyn, quoted in *Meeting the Shadow,* ed. Connie Zweig and Jeremiah Abrams (Los Angeles: Jeremy P. Tarcher, 1991), v.

30. Frank Zappa, quoted in "Sunbeams," *The Sun,* issue 226 (October 1994): 40.

31. Sir Edward Cook, *The Life of Florence Nightingale,* vol. 1 (London: Macmillan, 1913), 21. See also Florence Nightingale, "On Sin and Evil," *Suggestions for Thought: Selections and Commentaries,* ed. Michael

D. Calabria and Janet D. Macrae (Philadelphia: Univ. of Pennsylvania Press, 1994), 77–96; and Barbara Montgomery Dossey, *Florence Nightingale: Mystic, Visionary, Reformer. An Illustrated Biography* (forthcoming, 1998).

32. Peck, *People of the Lie*, 201.

33. C. S. Lewis, *Letters to Malcolm: Chiefly on Prayer* (New York: Harcourt Brace Jovanovich, 1964), 28.

34. Dietrich Dörner, *The Logic of Failure* (New York: Metropolitan/Henry Holt, 1996), 7.

35. Willis W. Harman, "Biology Revisited," *Noetic Sciences Review*, no. 41 (Spring 1997): 14ff. Excerpt from Willis W. Harman and Elisabet Sahtouris, *Biology Revisioned* (forthcoming, 1997).

36. Interview with Albert Brooks, "Albert Brooks Backs into the Spotlight," *Psychology Today* 30, no. 1 (January/February 1997): 26–30.

37. Richard Wilhelm, *The Secret of the Golden Flower: A Chinese Book of Life*, trans. Cary F. Baynes, rev. ed. (New York: Harvest/HBJ, 1962). Story told in Barbara Hannah, *Jung: His Life and Work* (Boston: Shambhala, 1991), 128.

38. Tao is the Chinese idea of "the way," the natural expression of all things.

AFTERWORD

1. Edward Whitmont, *The Alchemy of Healing* (Berkeley: North Atlantic Books, 1993), 90–91. Whitmont cites Sylvia Perera, *The Scapegoat Complex* (Toronto: Inner City Books, 1986), 73ff.

2. T. F. Powys, quoted by Francis Huxley, *The Way of the Sacred* (Garden City, NY: Doubleday, 1974), 19.

3. Meister Eckhart, quoted in Raymond B. Blakney, *Meister Eckhart* (New York: Harper & Row, 1941), 249–50.

4. C. G. Jung, quoted in Gerhard Wehr, *An Illustrated Biography of C. G. Jung*, trans. Michael H. Kohn (Boston: Shambhala, 1989), 55.

Bibliography

Achterberg, Jeanne. *Imagery in Healing.* Boston: Shambhala, 1985.

———. *Woman as Healer.* Boston: Shambhala, 1990.

Appleton, George, ed. "The Prayer of St. Francis" and "Prayers of Protection." *The Oxford Book of Prayer.* New York: Oxford Univ. Press, 1987.

Aspect, A., J. Dalibard, and G. Roger. "Experimental Test of Bell's Inequalities Using Time-Varying Analyzers." *Physics Review Letters* 49 (1982): 1804.

Ayres, Alex, ed. *The Wit and Wisdom of Abraham Lincoln.* New York: Meridian, 1992.

Barnard, Neal D., and Stephen R. Kaufman. "Animal Research Is Wasteful and Misleading." *Scientific American,* vol. 276, no. 2 (1997): 80–82.

Barry, Jean. "General and Comparative Study of the Psychokinetic Effect on a Fungus Culture." *Journal of Parapsychology* 32, no. 4 (1968): 237–43.

Batcheldor, K. J. "Report on a Case of Table Levitation and Associated Phenomena." *Journal of the Society for Psychical Research* 43 (1966): 339–56.

Baumeister, Roy F. *Evil: Inside Human Violence and Cruelty.* New York: W. H. Freeman, 1997.

Bennett, H., H. Davis, and J. Giannini. "Posthypnotic Suggestions During General Anesthesia and Subsequent Dissociated Behavior." Paper presented to the Society for Clinical and Experimental Hypnosis, October 1981. Cited in Goleman, Daniel, *Vital Lies, Simple Truths.* New York: Simon & Schuster, 1985: 89–90.

Benor, Daniel J. *Healing Research.* Volume 1. Munich: Helix Verlag, 1993.

Black, William G. *Folk-Medicine: A Chapter in the History of Culture.* London: Elliot Stock, 1883.

Blakney, Raymond B., trans. *Meister Eckhart.* New York: Harper & Row, 1941.

Bloom, Howard. *The Lucifer Principle.* New York: Atlantic Monthly Press, 1995.

Blyth, R. H. *Zen and Zen Classics,* compiled with drawings by Frederick Franck. New York: Vintage/Random House, 1978.

Boitnott, J. K. "Clinicopathological Conference: Case Presentation." *Bulletin of Johns Hopkins Hospital,* no. 120 (1967): 186–87.

Borysenko, Joan. *Fire in the Soul.* New York: Warner, 1993.

————. *Guilt Is the Teacher, Love Is the Lesson.* New York: Warner, 1990.

Botting, Jack H., and Adrian R. Morrison. "Animal Research Is Vital to Medicine." *Scientific American,* vol. 276, no. 2 (1997): 83–85.

Bower, Bruce. "Anxiety Before Surgery May Prove Healthful." *Science News* 141 (June 20, 1992): 407.

Braud, William G. "On the Use of Living Target Systems in Distant Mental Influence Research." *Research in Parapsychology 1984* , edited by Rhea A. White and Jerry Solfvin. Metuchen, NJ: Scarecrow Press, 1985.

Braud, William, and Marilyn Schlitz. "A Method for the Objective Study of Transpersonal Imagery." *Journal of Scientific Exploration* 3, no. 1 (1989): 43–63.

Braude, Stephen E. *ESP and Psychokinesis: A Philosophical Examination.* Philadelphia: Temple Univ. Press, 1979.

————. *The Limits of Influence: Psychokinesis and the Philosophy of Science.* London and New York: Routledge & Kegan Paul, 1986.

Brav, Aaron, "The Evil Eye Among the Hebrews," in Alan Dundes, *The Evil Eye.* Madison, Wisconsin: Univ. of Wisconsin Press, 1981, 44–54.

Brewer, Steve. "UNM [Univ. of New Mexico] Study on Prayer Raises Ire." *Albuquerque Journal,* May 3, 1995.

Brookes-Smith, C. "Data-type Recorded Experimental PK Phenomena." *Journal of the Society for Psychical Research* 47 (1973): 69–89.

Brookes-Smith, C., and D. W. Hunt. "Some Experiments in Psychokinesis." *Journal of the Society for Psychical Research* 45 (1970): 265–81.

Brooks, Albert. "Albert Brooks Backs into the Spotlight." *Psychology Today* 30, no. 1 (January/February 1997): 26–30.

Broughton, Richard S. *Parapsychology: The Controversial Science.* New York: Ballantine, 1991.

Brown, Dee. *Wondrous Times on the Frontier.* New York: HarperCollins, 1992.

Budge, Sir E. A. Wallis. *Amulets and Superstitions.* New York: Dover, 1978.

Campbell, Don. *The Mozart Effect.* New York: Avon, 1997.

Cannon, W. B. " 'Voodoo' Death." *American Anthropologist* 44 (1942): 169–81.

Carrese, J. A., and L. A. Rhodes. "Western Bioethics on the Navajo Reservation." *Journal of the American Medical Association* 274, no. 10 (1995): 826–29.

Cavendish, Richard. *The Black Arts.* New York: Putnam, 1967.

————. *A History of Magic.* New York: Penguin, 1987.

Chalmers, David J. *The Conscious Mind.* New York: Oxford Univ. Press, 1996.

————. "The Puzzle of Conscious Experience." *Scientific American* 273, no. 6 (1995): 80–86.

Clarke, C. J. S. "The Nonlocality of Mind." *Journal of Consciousness Studies* 2, no. 3 (1995): 231–40.

Cohen, Kenneth S. *The Way of Qigong.* New York: Ballantine, 1997.

Cook, Sir Edward. *The Life of Florence Nightingale,* vol. 1. London: Macmillan, 1913.

Csikszentmihalyi, M. *The Evolving Self.* New York: HarperCollins, 1993.

David-Neel, Alexandra. *Magic and Mystery in Tibet.* New York: Dover, 1971.

Delbanco, Andrew. *The Death of Satan: How Americans Have Lost the Sense of Evil.* New York: Farrar, Straus & Giroux, 1995.

Dörner, Dietrich. *The Logic of Failure.* New York: Metropolitan/Henry Holt, 1996.

Dossey, Barbara Montgomery. *Florence Nightingale: Mystic, Visionary, Reformer. An Illustrated Biography.* Forthcoming, 1998.

———. "Florence Nightingale: A Nineteenth-Century Mystic." Forthcoming, 1998.

Dossey, Larry. "But Is It Energy? Reflections on Consciousness, Healing, and the New Paradigm." *Subtle Energies* 3, no. 3 (1992): 69–82.

———. "Healing and the Mind: Is There a Dark Side?" *Journal of Scientific Exploration* 8, no. 1 (1994): 73–90.

———. "Healing, Energy, and Consciousness: Into the Future or a Retreat to the Past?" *Subtle Energies* 5, no. 1 (1994): 1–34.

———. *Healing Words.* San Francisco: HarperSanFrancisco, 1993.

———. "Hexes and Molecules." *Space, Time & Medicine.* Boston: Shambhala, 1982.

———. "In Praise of Unhappiness." *Alternative Therapies* 2, no. 1 (1996): 7–10.

———. *Meaning & Medicine.* New York: Bantam, 1991.

———. *Prayer Is Good Medicine.* San Francisco: HarperSanFrancisco, 1996.

———. *Recovering the Soul.* New York: Bantam, 1989.

———. "Running Scared: How We Hide from Who We Are." *Alternative Therapies* 3, no. 2 (1997): 8–15.

Dreher, Henry. *The Immune Power Personality.* New York: Dutton, 1995.

Duke, R. C., D. M. Ojcius, and J. D.-E. Young. "Cell Suicide in Health and Disease." *Scientific American,* vol. 275, no. 6 (1996): 80–87.

Duncalf, Frederic. "The First Crusade: Clermont to Constantinople." In *A History of the Crusades: The First Hundred Years,* edited by Marshall W. Baldwin, 263–82. Philadelphia: Univ. of Pennsylvania Press, 1955.

Dundes, Alan, ed. *The Evil Eye.* Madison: Univ. of Wisconsin Press, 1981.

Eddington, Sir Arthur. "Defense of Mysticism," in *Quantum Questions: The Mystical Writings of the World's Great Physicists,* edited by Ken Wilber. Boston: Shambhala, 1984.

Eddy, Mary Baker. "Obtrusive Mental Healing." *Miscellaneous Writings.* Boston: Christian Science Church, published by the trustees under the will of Mary Baker G. Eddy, 1896.

Ehrenwald, Jan. "A Neurophysiological Model of Psi Phenomena." *Journal of Nervous and Mental Diseases* 154, no. 6 (1972): 406–18.

Einstein, A., B. Podolsky, and N. Rosen. "Can Quantum-mechanical Description of Physical Reality Be Considered Complete?" *Physics Review* 47 (1935): 777.

Eisenberg, David, with Thomas Lee Wright. *Encounters with Qi.* New York: W. W. Norton, 1995.

Eisenbud, Jule. *Parapsychology and the Unconscious.* Berkeley: North Atlantic Books, 1992.

Engel, G. L. "Sudden and Rapid Death During Psychological Stress: Folklore or Folk Wisdom?" *Annals of Internal Medicine* 74 (1971): 771–82.

Feinberg, Gerald. "Precognition—A Memory of Things Future." In *Quantum Physics and Parapsychology,* edited by L. Oteri. New York: Parapsychology Foundation, 1975.

Fielding, J. W. L. "An Interim Report of a Prospective, Randomized, Controlled Study of Adjuvant Chemotherapy in Operable Gastric Cancer: British Stomach Cancer Group." *World Journal of Surgery* 7 (1983): 390–99.

Fischer, Louis, ed. *The Essential Gandhi.* New York: Vintage, 1962.

Fortune, Dion. *Psychic Self-Defense.* London: Rider, 1930; reprint, York Beach, ME: Samuel Weister, 1994.

Girard, René. *Violence and the Sacred.* Translated by Patrick Gregory. Baltimore: The Johns Hopkins Univ. Press, 1977.

Goldberg, Natalie. *Wild Mind: Living the Writer's Life.* New York: Bantam, 1990.

Goleman, Daniel. *Vital Lies, Simple Truths: The Psychology of Self-Deception.* New York: Simon & Schuster, 1985.

Goodacre, David. "Possession and Exorcism." *The Christian Parapsychologist* 11, no. 4 (1995): 126–31.

Goodwin, Brian. *How the Leopard Changed Its Spots.* New York: Charles Scribner's Sons, 1994.

Gordon, Stuart. *The Book of Spells, Hexes, and Curses.* New York: Citadel, 1995.

Goswami, Amit. "Science Within Consciousness: A Progress Report." Paper presented at a seminar on consciousness, Univ. of Lisbon, Lisbon, Portugal, 1996.

———. *The Self-Aware Universe: How Consciousness Creates the Material World.* New York: Tarcher, 1993.

Grad, Bernard R. "Some Biological Effects of Laying-On of Hands: A Review of Experiments with Animals and Plants." *Journal of the American Society for Psychical Research* 59, issue a (1965): 95–127.

Grinberg-Zylberbaum, J., M. Delaflor, L. Attie, and A. Goswami. "The Einstein-Podolsky-Rosen Paradox in the Brain: The Transferred Potential." *Physics Essays* 7, no. 4 (1994): 422–28.

Grinberg-Zylberbaum, J., and J. Ramos. "Patterns of Interhemispheric Correlation during Human Communication." *International Journal of Neurosciences* 36, nos. 1/2 (1987): 41–55.

Guiley, Rosemary Ellen. *Harper's Encyclopedia of Mystical and Paranormal Experience.* San Francisco: HarperSanFrancisco, 1991.

Guzzetta, Cathie E. "Music Therapy: Hearing the Melody of the Soul." In *Holistic Nursing: A Handbook for Practice,* edited by Barbara M. Dossey, Lynn Keegan, Cathie E. Guzzetta, and Leslie G. Kolkmeier, 2d ed., 669–98. Rockville, MD: Aspen, 1995.

Hale, A. S., and N. R. Pinninti. "Exorcism-resistant Ghost Possession Treated with Clopenthixol." *British Journal of Psychology* 165 (1994): 386–88.

Halifax-Grof, Joan. "Hex Death." In *Parapsychology and Anthropology: Proceedings of an International Conference Held in London, August 29–31, 1973,* edited by Allan Angoff and Diana Barth, 59–79. New York: Parapsychology Foundation, 1974.

Hall, Howard. "Suggestion and Illness." *International Journal of Psychosomatics* 33, no. 2 (1986): 24–27.

Hannah, Barbara. *Jung: His Life and Work.* Boston: Shambhala, 1991.

Haraldsson, E., and T. Thorsteinsson. "Psychokinetic Effects on Yeast: An Exploratory Experiment." In *Research in Parapsychology 1972,* edited by W. C. Roll, R. L. Morris, and J. D. Morris, 20–21. Metuchen, NJ: Scarecrow Press, 1973.

Harman, Willis W. "Biology Revisited." *Noetic Sciences Review,* no. 41 (Spring 1997): 14ff.

Harman, Willis W., and Elisabet Sahtouris. *Biology Revisioned.* Forthcoming, 1997.

Harner, Michael. *The Way of the Shaman.* New York: Bantam, 1982.

Herbert, Nick. *Elemental Mind.* New York: Dutton, 1993.

———. *Quantum Reality.* New York: Dutton, 1986.

Honorton, Charles. "Rhetoric over Substance: The Impoverished State of Skepticism." *Journal of Parapsychology* 57, no. 2 (1993): 191–214.

Horgan, John. "Doubts about Doubts about Science." *The Sciences* 36, no. 3 (1996): 43–48.

Huxley, Francis. "The Evil Eye." *The Eye: The Seer and the Seen.* New York: Thames and Hudson, 1990.

————. *The Way of the Sacred.* Garden City, NY: Doubleday, 1974.

Ingerman, Sandra. *Soul Retrieval.* San Francisco: HarperSanFrancisco, 1991.

————. *Welcome Home: Life After Healing.* San Francisco: HarperSanFrancisco, 1993.

Inglis, Brian. *Natural and Supernatural: A History of the Paranormal.* Bridport, Dorset, England: Prism Press, 1992.

Jahn, Robert G., and Brenda J. Dunne. *Margins of Reality: The Role of Consciousness in the Physical World.* New York: Harcourt Brace Jovanovich, 1987.

Jeans, Sir James. *Physics and Philosophy.* New York: Dover, 1981.

Jones, Louis C., "Evil Eye Among European-Americans," in Alan Dundes, *The Evil Eye.* Madison, Wisconsin: Univ. of Wisconsin Press, 1981, 150–67.

Josephson, Brian D., and F. Pallikara-Viras. "Biological Utilization of Quantum Nonlocality." *Foundations of Physics* 21 (1991): 197–207.

Kabat-Zinn, Jon, *Full Catastrophe Living: A Practical Guide to Mindfulness, Meditation, and Healing.* New York: Delacorte, 1990.

Kee, Howard Clark. *Medicine, Miracle & Magic in New Testament Times.* New York: Cambridge Univ. Press, 1986.

King, Serge Kahili. *Kahuna Healing.* Wheaton, IL: Theosophical Publishing House, 1983.

Klopfer, Bruno. "Psychological Variables in Human Cancer." *Journal of Projective Techniques* 21 (1957): 331–40.

Koestler, Arthur. *Janus: A Summing Up.* New York: Random House, 1978.

Kropf, Richard W. *Evil and Evolution: A Theodicy.* Cranbury, NJ: Associated Univ. Presses, 1984.

Lalli, Anthony E. "Contrast Media Reactions: Data Analysis and Hypothesis." *Radiology* 134 (1980): 1–12.

Lanier, Jean. "From Having a Mystical Experience to Becoming a Mystic." *ReVision* 12, no. 1 (1989): 41–44.

Larson, David B., and Mary A. Greenwold Milano. "Are Religion and Spirituality Clinically Relevant in Health Care?" *Mind/Body Medicine* 1, no. 3 (1995): 147–57.

Laskow, Leonard. *Healing with Love.* San Francisco: HarperSan Francisco, 1992.

Laszlo, Ervin. *The Interconnected Universe: Conceptual Foundations of Transdisciplinary Unified Theory.* River Edge, NJ: World Scientific Publishing, 1995.

Lawlis, Frank. *Transpersonal Medicine.* Boston: Shambhala, 1996.

Leidecker, Kurt F. "Karma." *Dictionary of Philosophy,* edited by Dagobert D. Runes. Totowa, NJ: Littlefield, Adams, 1962.

LeShan, Lawrence. *An Ethic for the Age of Space.* York Beach, ME: Samuel Weiser, 1996.

————. *The Medium, the Mystic, and the Physicist.* New York: Viking, 1974.

Lewis, C. S. *Letters to Malcolm: Chiefly on Prayer.* New York: Harcourt Brace Jovanovich, 1964.

Long, Max Freedom. *The Secret Science Behind Miracles.* Marina del Rey, CA: DeVorss, 1948.

Lowe, Walter. *Evil and the Unconscious.* American Academy of Religion Studies in Religion, edited by James O. Duke. Chico, CA: Scholars Press, 1983.

Lown, Bernard. *The Lost Art of Healing.* New York: Houghton Mifflin, 1996.

Luks, Allan. "Helpler's High." *Psychology Today* (October 1988), 39–42.

MacNutt, Francis. *Deliverance from Evil Spirits: A Practical Manual.* Grand Rapids, MI: Chosen Books, 1995.

Mannix, Daniel. *The History of Torture.* New York: Dell, 1964.

Marwick, Max, ed. *Witchcraft and Sorcery.* New York: Penguin, 1982.

Mason, R., Jr., G. Clark, R. B. Reeves, Jr., and S. B. Wagner. "Acceptance and Healing." *Journal of Religion and Health* 8, no. 2 (1969): 123–43.

Meador, C. K. "Hex Death: Voodoo Magic or Persuasion?" *Southern Medical Journal* 85, no. 3 (1992): 244–47.

Meek, E. M. "Two Pioneer Doctors of Southeast Arkansas." *Arkansas Historical Quarterly* 5 (1946): 121.

Mitchell, Edgar. *The Way of the Explorer.* New York: G. P. Putnam's Sons, 1996.

Muehsam, D. J., M. S. Markov, P. A. Muehsam, A. A. Pilla, R. Shen, and Y. Wu. "Effect of Qigong on Cell-free Myosin Phosphorylation: Preliminary Experiments." *Subtle Energies* 5, no. 1 (1994): 93–108.

Mukerjee, M. "Trends in Animal Research." *Scientific American,* vol. 276, no. 2 (1997): 86–93.

Murphy, Gardner, and Robert O. Ballou, comps. and eds. *William James on Psychical Research.* London: Chatto and Windus, 1961.

Murphy, Michael. *The Future of the Body.* Los Angeles: Jeremy P. Tarcher, 1992.

Myers, D. G. *The Pursuit of Happiness: Who Is Happy and Why.* New York: William Morrow, 1992.

Myers, D. G., and E. Diener. "The Pursuit of Happiness." *Scientific American,* vol. 274, no. 5 (1996): 70–72.

Nash, Carroll B. "Psychokinetic Control of Bacterial Growth." *Journal of the Society for Psychical Research* 51 (1982): 217–21.

————. "Test of Psychokinetic Control of Bacterial Mutation." *Journal of the American Society for Psychical Research* 78, no. 2 (1984): 145–52.

Nightingale, Florence. "On Sin and Evil." In *Suggestions for Thought: Selections and Commentaries,* edited by Michael D. Calabria and Janet D. Macrae, 77–96. Philadelphia: Univ. of Pennsylvania Press, 1994.

Niven, Larry. *Ringworld.* New York: Del Rey, 1970.

Oppenheimer, Paul. *Evil and the Demonic: A New Theory of Monstrous Behavior.* Washington Square, NY: New York Univ. Press, 1996.

Owen, Iris M., with Margaret Sparrow. *Conjuring Up Philip.* New York: Harper & Row, 1976.

Oxman, T. E., D. H. Freeman, and E. D. Manheimer. "Lack of Social Participation or Religious Strength or Comfort as Risk Factors for Death after Cardiac Surgery in the Elderly." *Psychosomatic Medicine* 57 (1995): 5–15.

Pagels, Elaine. *The Origin of Satan.* New York: Random House, 1996.

Palmer, John. "From Survival to Transcendence: Reflections of Psi as Anomalous." *Journal of Parapsychology* 56 (1992): 249.

Peck, M. Scott. *People of the Lie.* New York: Touchstone, 1983.

Pereira, Joseph. "The Healing Power of Prayer Is Tested by Science." *Wall Street Journal,* Dec. 20, 1995, B1.

Perrow, Charles. *Normal Accidents: Living with High-Risk Technologies.* New York: Basic Books, 1984.

Pukui, Mary Kawena, E. W. Haertig, and Catherine A. Lee. *Look to the Source.* Volume 2. Honolulu: Hui Hanai/Queen Lili'uokalani Children's Center, 1972.

Radin, Dean I. *The Conscious Universe.* San Francisco: HarperEdge, 1997.

———. "Interview with Dean Radin." *Magical Blend* 53 (1996): 36.

———. "On Complexity and Pragmatism." *Journal of Scientific Exploration* 8, no. 4 (1994): 523–33.

Radin, Dean I., and Roger D. Nelson. "Consciousness-related Effects in Random Physical Systems." *Foundations of Physics* 19 (1989): 1499–1514.

Raff, Martin C. "Death Wish." *The Sciences* 36, no. 4 (July/August 1996): 36–40.

Randles, Jenny, and Peter Hough. *Spontaneous Human Combustion.* New York: Dorset Press, 1992.

Rauscher, Elizabeth. "Human Volitional Effects on a Model Bacterial System." *Subtle Energies* 1, no. 1 (1990): 21–41.

Rebman, J. M., R. Wezelman, D. I. Radin, P. Stevens, R. A. Hapke, and K. Z. Gaughan. "Remote Influence of Human Physiology by a Ritual Healing Technique." *Subtle Energies* 6, no. 2 (1997): 111–34.

Reilly, Rick. "Man of Steel." *Sports Illustrated,* January 13, 1997, 28–31.

Rein, Glen. *Quantum Biology: Healing with Subtle Energy.* Palo Alto: Quantum Biology Research Labs, 1992.

———. "The Scientific Basis for Healing with Subtle Energies." Appendix A in Leonard Laskow, *Healing with Love,* 279–319. New York: Harper-Collins, 1992.

Remen, Rachel Naomi. "All Emotions Are Potentially Life Affirming." *Advances* 12, no. 2 (1996): 23–28.

Rhein, R. W., Jr. "Placebo: Deception or Potent Therapy?" *Medical World News* (February 4, 1980), 39–47.

Rodgers, Linda. "Music for Surgery." *Advances* 11, no. 3 (1995): 49–57.

———. "Reduce Surgical Anxiety Simply by Listening: How Perioperative Audiotapes Inform, Reassure and Offer Suggestions to Patients Throughout the Stages of Surgery." In *New Directions in Healing: A Practitioner's Source for Mind/Body Medicine.* Mansfield Center, CT.: National Institute for the Clinical Application of Behavioral Medicine, 1993.

Rowan, Andrew N. "The Benefits and Ethics of Animal Research." *Scientific American,* vol. 276, no. 2 (1997): 79.

Rubik, Beverly, and Elizabeth Rauscher. "Effects on Motility Behavior and Growth Rate of *Salmonella typhimurium* in the Presence of Olga Worrall." In *Research in Parapsychology 1979,* edited by W. G. Roll, 140–42. Metuchen, NJ: Scarecrow Press, 1980.

Rush, J. H. "New Directions in Parapsychology Research." *Parapsychological Monographs,* no. 4. New York: Parapsychology Foundation, 1964.

Russell, Jeffrey Burton. *The Devil: Perceptions of Evil from Antiquity to Primitive Christianity.* Ithaca: Cornell Univ. Press, 1977.

Sancier, Kenneth M. "Medical Applications of Qigong and Emitted Qi on Humans, Animals, Cell Cultures, and Plants: Review of Selected Scientific Research." *American Journal of Acupuncture* 19, no. 4 (1991): 367–77.

Sanford, John A. *Evil: The Shadow Side of Reality.* New York: Crossroad, 1996.

Schlitz, Marilyn J. "Intentionality and Intuition and Their Clinical Implications: A Challenge for Science and Medicine." *Advances* 12, no. 2 (1996): 58–66.

Schrödinger, Erwin. *What Is Life? and Mind and Matter.* London: Cambridge Univ. Press, 1969.

Schwarz, B. E. "Possible Telesomatic Reactions." *Journal of the Medical Society of New Jersey* 64, no. 1 (1967): 600–603.

Sheldrake, Rupert. *A New Science of Life: The Hypothesis of Formative Causation.* Los Angeles: Jeremy P. Tarcher, 1981.

———. *The Presence of the Past.* New York: Times Books, 1988.

———. *Seven Experiments That Could Change the World.* New York: Riverhead, 1995.

Sheldrake, Rupert, and Matthew Fox. "Prayer." In *Natural Grace,* 90–113. London: Bloomsbury, 1996.

Simmons, Marc. *Witchcraft in the Southwest.* Lincoln: Univ. of Nebraska Press, 1974.

Singer, Katie. "Scott Walker's Research on the Complexity of Prayer." *Medicine & Prayer,* Newsletter of the Santa Fe Institute for Medicine and Prayer (September/October 1996), 1.

Skolimowski, Henryk. "The Participatory Universe and Its New Methodology." *Frontier Perspectives* 5, no. 2 (1996).

Smith, Huston. *The World's Religions.* (San Francisco: HarperSanFrancisco, 1991).

Smith, Morton. *Jesus the Magician.* New York: Harper & Row, 1978.

Snow, Loudell F. "Folk Medical Beliefs and Their Implications for Care of Patients." *Annals of Internal Medicine* 81 (1974): 82–96.

Solomon, G. F., L. Temoshok, L. A. O'Leary, and J. Zich. "An Intensive Psychoimmunologic Study of Long-Surviving Persons with AIDS." *Annals of the New York Academy of Sciences* 496 (1987): 647–55.

Statham, Beryl. "Miracles: Divine Intervention, Natural Events, or Illusory Experiences?" *Journal of Religion and Psychical Research* 19, no. 4 (1996): 205–19.

Stevenson, Ian. "Possession and Exorcism: An Essay Review." *Journal of Parapsychology* 59, no. 1 (March 1995): 69–76.

———. *Telepathic Impressions. A Review and Report of 35 New Cases.* Charlottesville: Univ. Press of Virginia, 1970.

Stoeber, Michael, and Hugo Meynell, eds. *Critical Reflections on the Paranormal.* Albany: State Univ. of New York Press, 1996.

Swain, John. *The Pleasures of the Torture Chamber.* New York: Dorset, 1995.

Syfransky, Sy, ed. *Sunbeams: A Book of Quotations.* Berkeley: North Atlantic Press, 1990.

Tanagras, Angelos. *Psychological Elements in Parapsychological Traditions.* New York: Parapsychology Foundation, 1967.

Tedder, William H., and Melissa L. Monty. "Exploration of Long-distance PK: A Conceptual Replication of the Influence on a Biological System." In *Research in Parapsychology 1980,* edited by W. G. Roll et al., 90–93. Metuchen, NJ: Scarecrow Press, 1981.

Tenner, Edward. *Why Things Bite Back: Technology and the Revenge of Unintended Consequences.* New York: Knopf, 1996.

Thomson, Keith Stewart. "The Revival of Experiments on Prayer." *American Scientist* 84 (1996): 532–34.

Voelker, Rebecca. "Nocebos Contribute to Host of Ills." *Journal of the American Medical Association* 275 no. 5 (1996): 345–47.

Watson, Lyall. *Beyond Supernature.* New York: Bantam, 1988.

———. *Dark Nature: A Natural History of Evil.* New York: HarperCollins, 1996.

———. *Lifetide.* New York: Simon & Schuster, 1979.

Watts, Alan. "Odyssey of Aldous Huxley." Audiocassette tape. San Anselmo, CA: Electronic Univ., 1995.

Weber, Renée. *Dialogue with Scientists and Sages: The Search for Unity.* London: Arkana, 1990.

Wehr, Gerhard. *An Illustrated Biography of C. G. Jung.* Trans. Michael H. Kohn. Boston: Shambhala, 1989.

Weil, Andrew. *Spontaneous Healing.* New York: Knopf, 1995.

———. "Response to Dafter." *Advances* 12, no. 2 (1996): 41–42.

Whitmont, Edward. *The Alchemy of Healing.* Berkeley: North Atlantic Books, 1993.

Whitwell, F. D., and M. G. Barker. "Possession in Psychiatric Patients in Britain." *British Journal of Medical Psychology* 53 (1980): 287–95.

Wilber, Ken, ed. *Quantum Questions: The Mystical Writings of the World's Great Physicists.* Boston: Shambhala, 1984.

Wilhelm, Richard. *The Secret of the Golden Flower: A Chinese Book of Life.* Translated by Cary F. Baynes. Rev. ed. New York: Harvest/HBJ, 1962.

Williams, George C. "Mother Nature Is a Wicked Old Witch." In *Evolutionary Ethics,* edited by M. H. Nitecki and D. V. Nitecki. New York: State Univ. of New York Press, 1993.

Wilson, Colin. *The Occult.* New York: Barnes & Noble, 1971.

Wilson, E. O. *On Human Nature.* Harvard: Harvard Univ. Press, 1978.

Wink, Walter. *Unmasking the Powers.* Philadelphia: Fortress Press, 1986.

Witherspoon, G. *Language and Art in the Navajo Universe.* Ann Arbor: Univ. of Michigan Press, 1977.

Wolf, S., and R. H. Pinsky. "Effects of Placebo Administration and Occurrence of Toxic Reactions." *Journal of the American Medical Association* 155, no. 4 (1954): 339–41.

Woodruff, Paul, and Harry A. Wilmer, eds. *Facing Evil.* LaSalle, IL: Open Court Press, 1988.

Wright, Robert. *The Moral Animal.* New York: Pantheon, 1994.

Xueyan, P., and L. Guolong. "The Effect of the Emitted Qi and Infrasonic Sound on Somatosensory Evoked Potential and Slow Vertex Response." *Proceedings of the First World Conference for Academic Exchange of Medical Qigong.* Beijing, China, October 1988.

Yamamoto, M., M. Hirasawa, K. Kawano, N. Yasuda, and A. Furukawa. "An Experiment on Remote Action against Man in Sense Shielding Condition." *Journal of the International Society of Life Information Sciences* 14, no. 1 (1996): 97–99.

Yamamoto, M., M. Hirasawa, K. Kawano, H. Kokubo, T. Kokado, T. Hirata, N. Yasuda, A. Furukawa, and N. Fukuda. "An Experiment on Remote Action against Man in Sensory-Shielding Condition (Part 2)." *Journal of the International Society of Life Information Sciences* 14, no. 2 (1996): 228–39.

Yanang, L., Z. Xinhus, C. Kie, H. Yulan, and Z. Yungsheng. "The Effects of Taoist Qigong on the Photon Emission from the Body Surface and Cells." *Proceedings of the First World Conference for Academic Exchange of Medical Qigong.* Beijing, China, October 1988.

Yao-Lan, W., and L. Zu-Yin. "A Method of Detecting Qi Field." In *Yeng Xing's Scientific Qigong.* Hong Kong: China Books Press, 1988.

Yongian, G., C. Qi, L. Yinfa, and J. Shen. "Physical Characteristics of the Emitted Qi." *Proceedings of the First World Conference for Academic Exchange of Medical Qigong.* Beijing, China, October 1988.

Zweig, Connie, and Jeremiah Abrams, eds. *Meeting the Shadow.* Los Angeles: Tarcher, 1991.

Index